PROPOSALS THAT WORK

PROPOSALS THAT WORK

Third Edition

A Guide for Planning
Dissertations and
Grant Proposals

Lawrence F. Locke
Waneen Wyrick Spirduso
Stephen J. Silverman

SAGE Publications
International Educational and Professional Publisher
Newbury Park   London   New Delhi

For information address:

 SAGE publications, Inc.
2455 Teller Road
Newbury Park, California 91320
E-mail: order@sagepub.com

SAGE publications Ltd.
6 Bonhill Street
London EC2A 4PU
United Kingdom

SAGE Publications India Pvt. Ltd.
M-32 Market
Greater Kailash I
New Delhi 110 048 India

Printed in the United States of America

Library of Congress Cataloging-in-Publication Data

Locke, Lawrence F.
    Proposals that work: a guide for planning dissertations and grant proposals / Lawrence F. Locke, Waneen Wyrick Spirduso, Stephen J. Silverman.— 3rd ed.
        p. cm.
    Includes bibliographical references and index.
    ISBN 0-8039-5066-7. —ISBN 0-8039-5067-5 (pbk.)
        1. Proposal writing in research—Handbooks, manuals, etc.
    2. Dissertations, Academic—Handbooks, manuals, etc. 3. Research grants—Handbooks, manuals, etc. 4. Fund raising—Handbooks, manuals, etc. I. Spirduso, Waneen Wyrick. II. Silverman, Stephen J. III. Title.
    Q180.55.P7L63   1993
    001.4.4—dc20   93-5256

96 97 98 99 00 01 12 11 10 9 8 7 6

Sage Production Editor: Diane S. Foster

Contents

APPENDICES

Preface to the Third Edition

This guide contains no direct instruction concerning how to do research. Rather, the material herein deals with the problem of how to write a research proposal. Although the two capacities—skill in conducting research and skill in writing about plans for that research—have a close relationship, they are far from coterminous. Individuals who have acquired considerable information about the mysteries of research methods and data analysis do not necessarily know how to undertake the task of planning and effectively proposing their own investigations.

The importance and, therefore, the perceived difficulty of the proposal task will seem greater under some conditions than under others. Even the novice in research is likely to appreciate fully the significance of the research proposal in preparing a grant application. It is obvious that the probability of funding will rest mostly on the selection of a target for inquiry and the competence displayed in designing and justifying the study. A deceptively large contribution toward funding, however, is made by the clarity and style of writing in the proposal. Many excellent ideas are lost among the multitude of proposals submitted for funding because they were poorly presented and the proposal was difficult to decipher. Conversely, and unhappily, some mediocre research ideas are funded because they are spectacularly presented.

In contrast, few graduate students initially recognize that preparation of the proposal will represent a major hurdle in gaining approval for their thesis or dissertation. No magic formula can make writing such an important document an easy task. When money, academic career, or both are in the balance, a great deal is at stake. Our intention in preparing this guide, however, is to reduce both the perceived and real dimensions of the hurdle.

In the context of graduate education the research proposal plays a role that reaches beyond its simple significance as a plan of action. In most instances the decision to permit the student to embark on a thesis or dissertation is made solely on the basis of that first formal document. The quality of writing in the proposal is likely to be used by advisors as a basis for judging the clarity of thought that has preceded the document, the degree of facility with which the study will be implemented if approved, and the adequacy of expository skills the student will bring to reporting the results. In sum, the proposal is the instrument through which faculty must judge whether there is a reasonable hope that the student can conduct any research project at all.

Some readers may feel that the explanatory material contained in this guide places disproportionate emphasis on experimental and quasi-experimental forms of investigation. To the degree that this is true, such a bias reflects generic demands the authors have found likely to be encountered in the requirements for any proposal. Quite simply, our experience has been that writing about the problems of proposing an experimental study represents the most economical method for assisting readers who have a wide variety of research interests.

Proposals for historical or philosophical study must reflect canons unique to those areas of inquiry, and plans for qualitative/ethnographic research will begin with some assumptions (that we present in Chapter 5) that are foreign to the natural science model for research. Nevertheless, all must begin with questions, must define data sources, must present plans for analysis, and must persuade readers of the author's competence. For this guide, then, the value of the experiment rests not in its unique virtues, but in how much it shares in common with all models for inquiry.

Finally, a word of caution for readers who are graduate students. From time to time, it may appear that we have attempted to enter into a kind of "collusion" with the student for the purpose of outwitting the research advisor. The realities of university life, with which both students and their advisors are painfully familiar, make such a position difficult to avoid. Nothing, however, could be further from the authors' actual intention. If the student-advisor relationship resembles a contest, there is small chance that reference to a guide for proposal writing will be of any real assistance.

Our purpose from start to finish has been to assist in achieving one end—a fair and useful hearing for your proposed research. If the proposal is rejected, it should be because the investigation lacks sufficient merit or feasibility, not because the document has been inadequately prepared.

Suggestions for Using the Guide

This guide has been divided into two major parts: Part I, Writing the Proposal, and Part II, Specimen Proposals. The chapters that constitute Part I represent the core of the guide, serving both to present generic information that applies to all research proposals and to discuss some of the problems peculiar to the use of proposals in graduate education and funding agencies. In Chapter 1 we present an introduction to generic elements found in nearly all proposals. In Chapter 2 we discuss the ethical issues that may be a part of the research process and graduate education. In Chapter 3 we address the needs of graduate students facing the task of preparing their first research proposal. Chapters 4 and 6 contain information appropriate to both the graduate student preparing a thesis or dissertation proposal and the novice preparing a first grant proposal. Chapter 7 has information for doing oral presentations of proposals and research. The unique demands of proposing studies using the qualitative paradigm for research are addressed in Chapter 5. The last two chapters, 8 and 9, are directed specifically to those interested in preparing submissions to funding agencies.

In Part II, four sample proposals are presented. The sections of the first proposal relate directly to each of the tasks presented in Chapter 1. We have provided a short commentary with each section of this proposal to highlight the key elements. The final three proposals are presented with critical evaluations that illuminate their individual strengths and weaknesses. These proposals represent a wide variety of strategies. The specimens include both successful graduate student proposals and a funded grant proposal. In addition to the two major parts of this guide, two appendices are included. In Appendix A supplemental texts are reviewed, and in Appendix B examples and guidelines are provided for developing informed consent materials.

Readers with different backgrounds will find it useful to employ different methods in using this guide. Those who are completely inexperienced in writing proposals should begin with Chapter 1, which deals with the basic functions of the proposal. Each task is illustrated by a corresponding section in the first proposal in Part II. Some readers may wish to continue in Part II, which then presents three other examples with different research designs. They then can select an additional proposal to skim quickly, noting how the basic functions are performed. This will make it possible to return to the remaining discussion of content and format with an appreciation of the proposal task based on a concrete illustration.

Readers with some previous experience in research may wish to turn directly to Chapter 3, that deals with specific problems in identifying research topics and initiating the proposal process. Alternately, experienced students or faculty interested in the particular demands and problems presented by the grant proposal should begin with Chapter 8, subsequently turning to other sections of the guide as needed. Readers interested in preparing proposals for qualitative research should read Chapter 5, examine the specimen proposal using a qualitative research design in Part II, and then go to other parts of the text as needed.

If particular points of content or style in the specimen proposals present difficulty, it may be helpful to consult the accompanying critique or the corresponding section of general discussion in Chapter 6. In some instances, the reader may wish to refer to a more extensive or specialized text selected from Appendix A.

Before embarking on the construction of a proposal, we urge all readers to review Chapter 4, which deals with special problems in developing proposals. Familiarity with the items in this group of commonly encountered difficulties can both forewarn and forearm the novice researcher, saving time by directing attention to problems that must be confronted in all plans for scientific inquiry.

Finally, in preparing this new edition we give special attention to the issue of ethics in research and graduate education. In Chapter 2 we have given prominence to ethical concerns that have become increasingly troublesome for researchers everywhere. While we believe that all scholars, novice and veteran, should be concerned about what is right and wrong to do in research, it clearly is the unwary novice who is most at risk. Inquiry can present serious ethical pitfalls, and the proposal is the place to begin avoiding them. A close reading of Chapter 2 is not all that you will need to navigate through all the ethical problems you may encounter—but it is a reliable guide with which to begin the journey.

Acknowledgments

As in most complex writing endeavors, this guide is the product of many persons whose names do not appear on the cover. First, we would like to thank the students in our classes at the University of Massachusetts at Amherst, The University of Texas at Austin, and the University of Illinois at Urbana-Champaign who used earlier versions of this text and provided helpful advice for revision. Nell H. Gottlieb, John MacDonald, Lance Osborne, and Mary Bray Schatzkammer wrote the excellent specimen proposals used in this edition of the guide. We particularly appreciate their willingness to allow us to reprint and critique their work. Special appreciation goes to Jenny Parker and Lorraine Goyette at the University of Massachusetts and to Kim C. Graber at the University of Arizona, whose careful attention to the editing of manuscript drafts trapped many of our blunders before they could become public embarrassments, and to Patricia Moran of the University of Illinois Foundation for her insight into the inner workings of foundations. We would like to express our appreciation to Mitch Allen, our editor at Sage Publications, who got us started again and kept us on track. Finally, our deepest thanks to Lorraine, Craig, and Pat for their patience and understanding as we completed this task.

PART I

Writing the Proposal

1

The Function of the Proposal

A proposal sets forth both the exact nature of the matter to be investigated and a detailed account of the methods to be employed. In addition, the proposal usually contains material supporting the importance of the topic selected and the appropriateness of the research methods to be employed.

FUNCTION

A proposal may function in at least three ways: as a means of communication, as a plan, and as a contract.

Communication

The proposal serves to communicate the investigator's research plans to those who provide consultation, give consent, or disburse funds. The document is the primary resource on which the graduate student's thesis or dissertation committee must base the functions of review, consultation, and, more important, approval for implementation of the research project. It also serves a similar function for persons holding the purse strings of foundations or governmental funding agencies. The quality of assistance, the economy of consultation, and the probability of financial support will all depend directly on the clarity and thoroughness of the proposal.

Plan

The proposal serves as a plan for action. All empirical research consists of careful, systematic, and pre-planned observations of some restricted set of phenomena. The acceptability of results is judged exclusively in terms of the adequacy of the methods employed in making, recording, and interpreting the planned observations. Accordingly, the plan for observation, with its supporting arguments and explications, is the basis on which the thesis, dissertation or research report will be judged.

The research report can be no better than the plan of investigation. Hence, an adequate proposal sets forth the plan in step-by-step detail. The existence of a detailed plan that incorporates the most careful anticipation of problems to be confronted and contingent courses of action is the most powerful insurance against oversight or ill-considered choices during the execution phase of the investigation. The hallmark of a good proposal is a level of thoroughness and detail sufficient to permit another investigator to replicate the study, that is, to perform the same planned observations with results not substantially different from those the author might obtain.

Contract

A completed proposal, approved for execution and signed by all members of the sponsoring committee, constitutes a bond of agreement between the student and the advisors. An approved grant proposal results in a contract between the investigator (and often the university) and a funding source. The approved proposal describes a study that, if conducted competently and completely, should provide the basis for a report that would meet all standards for acceptability. Accordingly, once the contract has been made, all but minor changes should occur only when arguments can be made for absolute necessity or compelling desirability.

With the exception of plans for qualitative research (see Chapter 5), proposals for theses and dissertations should be in final form prior to the collection of data. Under most circumstances, substantial revisions should be made only with the explicit consent of the full committee. Once the document is approved in final form, neither the student nor the sponsoring faculty members should be free to alter the fundamental terms of the contract by unilateral decision.

REGULATIONS GOVERNING PROPOSALS

All funding agencies have their own guidelines for submissions and these should be followed exactly. In the university, however, no set of universal rules or guidelines presently exists to govern the form or content of the research proposal. There may be, however, several sources of regulation governing the form and content of the final research report. The proposal sets forth a plan of action that must eventuate in a report conforming to these latter regulations; therefore it is important to consider them in writing the proposal.

Although it is evident that particular traditions have evolved within individual university departments, any formal limitation on the selection of either topic or method of investigation is rarely imposed. Normally, the planning and execution of student research are circumscribed by existing departmental policy on format for the final report, university regulations concerning theses and dissertation reports, and informal standards exercised by individual advisors or study committees.

Usually departmental and university regulations regarding graduate student proposals are either so explicit as to be perfectly clear (e.g., "The proposal may not exceed 25 typewritten pages" or "The proposal will conform to the style established in the *Publication Manual of the American Psychological Association*") or so general as to impose no specific or useful standard (e.g., "The research topic must be of suitable proportions" or "The proposal must reflect a thorough knowledge of the problem area"). The student, therefore, should find no serious difficulty in developing a proposal that conforms to departmental and university regulations.

Some universities now allow students to elect alternative dissertation or thesis formats—such as a research paper (or series of papers) with an expanded literature review and supporting materials in the appendix. You might consider such an option because the more compact research paper format can save considerable time in turning the completed dissertation into a publication. Alternative formats for the final report, however, do not alter the need for a complete proposal. A good study requires a sound plan, irrespective of the format used for reporting the results.

Another potential source of regulation, the individual thesis or dissertation committee, constitutes an important variable in the development of the thesis or dissertation proposal. Sponsoring committee members may have strong personal commitments concerning particular working procedures, writing styles, or proposal format. The student must confront these as a unique constellation of demands that will influence the form of the proposal. It always is wise to anticipate conflicting demands and to attempt their resolution before the collection of data and the preparation of a final report.

Committees are unlikely to make style and format demands that differ substantially from commonly accepted modes of research writing. As a general rule, most advisors subscribe to the broad guidelines outlined in this document. Where differences occur, they are likely to be matters of emphasis or largely mechanical items (e.g., inclusion of particular subheadings within the document).

GENERAL CONSIDERATIONS

Most problems in proposal preparation are straightforward and relatively obvious. The common difficulties do not involve the subtle and complex problems of design and data management. They arise instead from the most basic elements of the research process: What is the proper question to ask? Where is the best place to look for the answer? What is the best way to standardize, quantify, and record observations? Determining the answers to these questions remains the most common obstacle to the development of adequate proposals.

Simplicity, clarity, and parsimony are the standards of writing that reflect adequate thinking about the research problem. Complicated matters are best communicated when they are the objects of simple, well-edited prose. In the early stage of development, the only way to obtain prompt and helpful assistance is to provide advisors with a document that is easily and correctly understood. At the final stage, approval of the study will hinge not only on how carefully the plan has been designed, but also on how well that design has been communicated. In the mass of detail that goes into the planning of a research study, the writer must not forget that the proposal's most immediate function is to inform readers quickly and accurately.

The problem in writing a proposal is essentially the same as in writing the final report. When the task of preparing a proposal is well executed, the task of preparing the final report is more than half done (an important consideration for the graduate student with an eye on university deadlines). Under ideal conditions, such minor changes as altering the tense of verbs will convert the proposal into the opening chapters of the thesis or dissertation, or into initial sections of a research report.

Many proposals evolve through a series of steps. Preliminary discussion with colleagues and faculty members may lead to a series of drafts that evolve toward a final document presented at a formal meeting of the full dissertation or thesis committee, or to a proposal submitted through the university hierarchy to a funding source. This process of progressive revision can be accelerated and made more productive by following these simple rules:

1. Prepare clean, updated copies of the evolving proposal and submit them to advisors or colleagues in advance of scheduled consultations.
2. Prepare an agenda of questions and problems to be discussed and submit them in advance of scheduled consultations.
3. Keep a carefully written and dated record of all discussions and decisions that occur with regard to each item on the consultation agenda.

GENERAL FORMAT

Guidelines for the format of proposals, even when intended only as general suggestions, often have an unfortunate influence on the writing process. Once committed to paper, such guidelines quickly tend to acquire the status of mandatory prescription. In an attempt to conform to what they perceive as an invariant format, students produce proposal documents that are awkward and illogical as plans for action—as well as stilted and tasteless as prose.

Some universities and many funding agencies make very specific demands for the format of proposals. Others provide general guidelines for form and content. Whatever the particular situation confronting the writer, it is vital to remember that *no universally applicable and correct format exists for the research proposal.* Each research plan requires that certain communication tasks be accomplished, some that are common to all proposals and others that are unique to the specific form of inquiry. Taken together, however, the tasks encompassed by all proposals demand that what is written fits the real topic at hand, not some preconceived ideal. It is flexibility, not rigidity, that makes strong proposal documents.

SPECIFIC TASKS

The following paragraphs specify communication tasks that are present in nearly all proposals for empirical research. Each proposal, however, will demand its own unique arrangement of these functions. Within a given proposal the tasks may or may not be identified by such traditional section designations as "Background," "Importance of the Study," "Review of Literature," "Methodology," "Definitions," or "Limitations." Individual proposals are sure to demand changes in the order of presentation, or attention to other tasks not specified below. This particularly will be the case with some of the tasks that are specific to grant proposals (see Chapter 9). Finally, it is important to note that some of the adjacent tasks, shown as headings in the following paragraphs, often may be merged into single sections.

As you read each of the tasks below, an illustration can be found by turning to the first proposal in Part II of this guide. In that particular specimen, we have edited the proposal so the sections correspond to the discussion of each task. We have provided a critique preceding each section of the specimen proposal to summarize the suggestions presented in this chapter.

Introducing the Study

Proposals, like other forms of written communication, are best introduced by a short, meticulously devised statement that establishes the overall area of concern, arouses interest, and communicates information essential to the reader's comprehension of what follows. The standard here is "gentle introduction," which avoids both tedious length and the shock of technical detail or abstruse argument. A careful introduction is the precursor of the next three tasks (statement, rationale, and background). In many cases, it may be written simply as the first paragraph(s) of an opening proposal section that includes all three.

For most proposals, the easiest and most effective way to introduce the study is to identify and define the central construct(s) involved. In the sense that constructs are concepts that provide an abstract symbolization of some observable attribute or phenomenon, all studies employ constructs. Constructs such as "intelligence" or "teacher enthusiasm" are utilized in research by defining them in terms of some observable event, that is, "intelligence" as defined by a test score, or "teacher enthusiasm" as defined by a set of classroom behaviors. When the reader asks, "What is this study about?" the best answer is to present the key constructs and explain how they will be represented in the investigation. The trick in these opening paragraphs of introduction is to sketch the study in the bold strokes of major constructs without usurping the function of more detailed sections that will follow.

Relationships among constructs that will be of particular interest or about which explicit hypotheses will be developed should be briefly noted. Constructs with which the reader probably is familiar may be ignored in the introduction for they are of less interest than the relationships proposed by the author.

The most common error in introducing research is failure to get to the point—usually a consequence of engaging in grand generalizations. For instance, in a proposed study of attributes contributing to balance ability the opening paragraph might contain a sentence such as "The child's capacity to maintain balance is a factor of fundamental importance in the design of elementary school curriculum." The significance of the construct "balance" in accomplishing motor tasks may make it an attribute of some importance in elementary education, but that point may be far from the heart of a study involving balance. If, for example, the proposed study deals with the relationship of muscle strength to balance, observations about balance as a factor in the design of school curriculum belong, if anywhere, in a later discussion. What belongs up front is a statement that gets to the point: "The task of maintaining static balance requires muscular action to hold the pelvis in a horizontal position. When muscle strength is inadequate to accomplish this, performance is impaired."

Some indication of the importance of the study to theory or practice may be used to help capture the reader's interest, but in the introduction it is not necessary to explain completely all of the study's significance. Present the basic facts first and leave the detail of thorough discussion until a more appropriate point. Use of unnecessary technical language is another impediment to the reader's ability to grasp the main idea. Similarly, the use of quotations and extensive references are intrusions into what should be a clear, simple preliminary statement. As a general rule, the first paragraph of the introduction should be free of citations. Documentation of important points can wait until a full discussion of the problem is launched.

Stating the Question

Early in the proposal, often in the introductory paragraph(s), it is wise to set forth an explicit statement of the question to which the investigation will be directed. The statement need not include all subtopics, nor need it be written in the language of formal research questions or hypotheses. It should, however, provide a specific and accurate synopsis of the primary target for the study. An early and specific announcement of this kind satisfies the reader's most pressing need. Such information allows the reader to attend to the author's subsequent exposition and topic development without the nagging sense that the main object of the study has yet to be discovered. Consequently, it is useful to give high visibility to an opening statement of the question.

Providing a Rationale

Once the reader understands the topic of investigation, the next logical points to be confronted are "Why bother with that question?" and "Is the basic formulation of the question correct?" In explaining why the study is a worthwhile endeavor, the author can point to potential utility of results in either or both of two domains: what might be contributed to the evolving structure of knowledge, or what application might be made in a practical setting. The formulation of the research question is supported by explanation of why the major elements in the study were set forth in a particular way: for example, why particular relationships are proposed, or why particular events or attributes are singled out for observation and description.

Persuasive logic and documentation with factual evidence are what convince readers, but no rationale can be effective until it is clear. To this end it often is helpful to diagram the factors and relationships that support your formulation of the problem. Suppose the proposed hypothesis for an experimental study was that older adults who had oxygen therapy for six months would have greater cognitive function than a control group. The implication of this

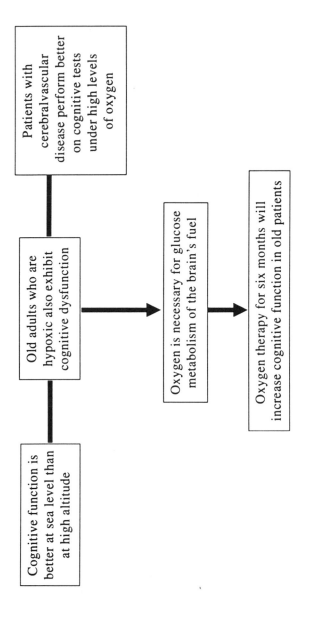

Figure 1.1. Example of Diagram of Logic for Rationale

11

complex statement is that there may be a relationship between oxygen to the brain and cognitive capacity in older adults. The reasons for such a supposition can be diagrammed in a simple form like the one shown in Figure 1.1. Assuming that the constructs have been defined, the rationale now can be developed simply by explaining and documenting the information in the boxes.

In most cases, this early attention to rationale should be limited to the larger issues of clarifying and justifying major assumptions. The detail of rationale for particular choices in methodology or analysis can be deferred until such matters are discussed in subsequent parts of the proposal.

Formulating Questions or Hypotheses

All proposals must arrive at a formal statement of questions or hypotheses. These statements should be written in carefully constructed language that specifies each variable in explicit terms. A statement such as "Studying each day should result in improved learning" is better written as "Sixty minutes of studying each day will result in significantly increased scores on a standardized test of achievement." These statements of questions or hypotheses may be set aside as a separate section or simply included in the course of other discussion. Such statements differ from what was contained in the statement of the question in that (a) they are normally stated in formal terms appropriate to the design and analysis of data to be employed, and (b) they display, in logical order, all subsections of the research topic.

The question form is most appropriate when the research is exploratory. The researcher should indicate by the specificity of questions, however, that the problem has been subject to thorough analysis. By careful formulation of questions, the proposed study should be directed toward outcomes that are foreshadowed by the literature or pilot work, rather than toward a scanning of potentially interesting findings.

The hypothesis form is employed when the state of existing knowledge and theory permits formulation of reasonable predictions about the relationship of variables. Hypotheses ordinarily have their origin in theoretical propositions already established in the review of literature. Because the proposal must ensure that the reader grasps how the relationships expressed in theory have been translated into the form of testable hypotheses, it often is useful to provide a succinct restatement of the theoretical framework at a point contiguous to the presentation of formal research hypotheses.

The most common difficulty in formulating a research question is the problem of clarity. Students who have read and studied in the area of their topic for weeks or months often are distressed to discover how difficult it is to reduce all they want to discover to a single, unambiguous question.

The clarity of a research question hinges on adequate specificity and the correct degree of inclusiveness. The major elements of the investigation must be identified in a way that permits no confusion with other elements. At the same time the statement must maintain simplicity by including nothing beyond what is essential to identify the main variables and any relationships that may be proposed among them. Questions for quantitative studies, for example, must meet three tests of clarity and inclusiveness:

1. Is the question free of ambiguity?
2. Is a relationship among variables expressed?
3. Does the question imply an empirical test?

By applying these standards to the question "Does a relationship exist between self-esteem and reading achievement in children?" the study's main elements apparently are identified in reasonably clear fashion. Self-esteem and reading achievement are variables and children are the subject population. A relationship is suggested and correlation of self esteem and reading scores clearly is implied as an appropriate empirical test of the relationship. The constructs of self-esteem and reading achievement, however, are quite broad and might be taken by some readers to indicate variables different from those intended. These potential sources of ambiguity might be resolved without destroying the simplicity of the question by altering it to ask, "Does a relationship exist between scores on the Children's Test of Self-Esteem and scores on the reading portion of the Tri-State Achievement Test?" Whether it also might be important to provide more specifically for the generic word "children" would depend on whether the intent was to examine self-esteem and reading in a particular type of child. If not, the generic word would be adequate. If so, the importance of that variable calls for more careful specification in the question.

In the case of qualitative research (discussed at length in Chapter 5), because pre-established hypotheses are seldom used, questions are the tool most commonly employed to provide focus for thesis and dissertation studies. Although there is disagreement among scholars about the use of formal questions in qualitative research, there is no escape from the need to have a question (whether explicit or implicit) that will serve to direct what is observed, or who is interviewed—at least at the outset of the study.

The question(s) frequently are phrased in ways that make them appear very different from those used in the natural science model (and, thereby, discrepant with some aspects of the advice given in this chapter). Some, for example, will sound highly generalized, as in the following examples paraphrased from qualitative proposals.

1. What is going on in this urban school classroom?
2. How do professional wrestlers understand their work?
3. What does residence in a hospice mean to a patient?

Other question statements reflect the intention to use a particular theoretical framework in the study.

1. What perspective do medical students adopt to make sense of their experience in medical school?
2. How do gay and lesbian soldiers manage the presentation of their sexual preference within the social setting of their workplace?
3. How do social roles influence the interaction between teachers and students as they attempt to realize personal goals in the classroom?

In contrast with experimental research, questions in a qualitative proposal often are treated as more tentative and contingent on the unfolding of the study. Nevertheless, their careful formulation is no less important. They must give initial direction to planning, bring the power of theoretical constructs to the process of analysis, and reflect the degree of sophisticated thought employed in determining the focus of inquiry.

Experienced qualitative researchers sometimes do, in fact, elect not to package their curiosity, interests, concerns, and foreshadowings into the form of explicit research questions. Graduate students, however, embarked on their first attempt within the qualitative paradigm, often find that their advisors are greatly reassured when the proposal contains a careful accounting of what the data are expected to reveal that is not already known. In other words, it is a good idea for the novice to explicate the questions that motivate their interest, thereby firmly grounding the study in the conventions of scholarly inquiry. How a qualitative investigator's assumptions about the world, and about research, serve to shape those questions will be addressed in Chapter 5.

Research *hypotheses* differ from research *questions* in that hypotheses both indicate the question in testable form and predict the nature of the answer. A clear question is readily transformed into a hypothesis by casting it in the form of a declarative statement that can be tested so as to show it to be either true or false. Getting precisely the hypothesis that is wanted, however, often is more exacting than it appears.

Unlike a question, the hypothesis exerts a direct influence on each subsequent step of the study, from design to preparation of the final report. By specifying a prediction about outcome, the hypothesis creates a bridge between the theoretical considerations that underlie the question and the ensuing research process designed to produce the answer. The investigator is limited to procedures that will test the truth of the proposed relationship, and any implications to be deduced from the results will rest entirely on the particular test selected. Because it exerts such powerful a priori influence, a hypothesis demands considerable attention at the start of a study but makes it easier to preserve objectivity in the later stages of design and execution.

Aside from specific impact on design of the study, the general advantage of the hypothesis over the question is that it permits more powerful and persuasive conclusions. At the end of a study, a research question never permits the investigator to say more than "Here is how the world looked when I observed it." In contrast, hypotheses permit the investigator to say, "Based on my particular explanation of how the world works, this is what I expected to observe, and behold—that is exactly how it looked! For that reason my explanation of how the world works must be given credibility." When a hypothesis is confirmed, the investigator is empowered to make arguments about knowledge that go far beyond what is available when a question has been asked and answered.

A hypothesis can be written either as a null statement (conveniently called a null hypothesis), "There is no difference between . . . ," or as a directional statement indicating the kind of relationship anticipated (called a research or directional hypothesis): "When this, also that" (positive) or "When this, not that" (negative). Some clear technical advantages are gained by using the null format, particularly when inferential statistics will be used to analyze the data. Research specialists, however, are not in complete agreement on the wisdom of writing hypotheses in directional form.

Many arguments favor the use of directionality because it permits more persuasive logic and more statistical power. If a pilot study has been completed or the literature review provides strong reasoning for a directional result, then directional hypotheses are clearly appropriate. In some instances, particularly evaluation studies, practical matters may dictate use of a directional hypothesis. For instance, if a therapy program is being evaluated and the only practical consequence would be finding that therapy provides greater gains in stress reduction than the program in current use, a directional hypothesis would permit a direct test of this singular outcome.

Some of the technical debate about the form of hypotheses is beyond the scope of this guide, but a good rule of thumb for the novice is to employ directional hypotheses when pilot data are available that clearly indicate a direction, or when the theory from which the hypotheses were drawn is sufficiently robust to include some persuasive evidence for directionality. If the investigation is a preliminary exploration in an area for which there is no well established theory, and if it has been impossible to gather enough pilot data to provide modest confidence in a directional prediction, the format of the null hypothesis is the better choice. Ultimately, as a researcher pursues a line of questioning through several investigations, directional hypotheses become more obvious and the null format less attractive.

Hypotheses can be evaluated by the same criteria used to examine research questions (lack of ambiguity, expression of relationship, and implication of appropriate test). In addition, the statement must be formulated so that the entire prediction can be dealt with in a single test. If the hypothesis is so complex that one portion could be rejected without also rejecting the remainder, it requires rewriting.

Several small, perfectly testable hypotheses always are preferable to one that is larger and amorphous. For example, in the following hypothesis the word "but" signals trouble. "Males are significantly more anxious than females, but male nurses are not significantly more anxious than female teachers." The F test for the main effect of sex in the implied analysis of variance (ANOVA) will handily deal with males and females, but a separate test as a part of a factorial ANOVA would be required for professional status. Should the tests yield opposite results, the hypothesis would point in two directions at once.

Similarly, the presence of two discrete dependent variables foreshadows difficulty in the following example: "Blood pressures on each of five days will be significantly lower than the preceding day, whereas heart rate will not decrease significantly after day 3." The implied multiple analysis of variance (MANOVA) could not rescue the hypothesis by indicating whether we could accept or reject it. The required follow-up test might reject the blood pressure prediction while accepting it for heart rate. In all cases division into smaller, unitary hypotheses is the obvious cure.

When a number of hypotheses are necessary, as a result of interest in interaction effects or as a consequence of employing more than one dependent variable, the primary hypotheses should be stated first. These primary statements may even be separated from hypotheses that are secondary or confirmatory, as a means of giving prominence to the main intent of the study.

Finally, hypotheses should be formulated with an eye to the qualitative characteristics of available measurement tools. If, for example, the hypothesis specifies the magnitude of relationship between two variables, it is essential that this be supportable by the reliability of the proposed instrumentation. Returning to the earlier example of self-esteem and reading, the fact should be considered that the correlation between scores from two tests cannot exceed the square root of the product for reliability in each test. Accordingly, if reliability of the self-esteem test is .68 and the reading test is .76, then a hypothesis of a positive correlation greater than .80 is doomed to failure ($\sqrt{.76 \times .68} = .72$).

Delimitations and Limitations

Often a listing of delimitations and limitations is required to clarify the proposed study. Delimitations describe the populations to which generalizations may be safely made. The generalizability of the study will be a function of the subject sample and the analysis employed. *Delimit* literally means to define the limits inherent in the use of a particular construct or population.

Limitations, as used in the context of a research proposal, refer to limiting conditions or restrictive weaknesses. They occur when all factors cannot be controlled as a part of study design, or sometimes the optimal number of observations simply cannot be made because of problems involving ethics or feasibility. If the investigator has given careful thought to these problems, and has determined that the information to be gained from the compromised aspect of the study is nevertheless valid and useful, then the investigator proceeds, but duly notes the limitation.

All studies have inherent delimitations and limitations. Whether these are listed in a separate section or simply discussed as they arise is an individual decision. If they are few in number and perfectly obvious, the latter is desirable. Whatever format is used, however, it is the investigator's responsibility to understand these constraints and to assure the reader that they have been considered during the formulation of the study.

Providing Definitions

All proposals for research use systematic language that may be specific to that field of research or to that proposal. We discuss the use of definitions in greater detail in the section of Chapter 6 titled "Clarity and Precision: Speaking in System Language."

Discussing the Background of the Problem

Any research problem must show its lineage from the background of existing knowledge, previous investigations, or, in the case of applied research, from contemporary practice. The author must answer three questions:

1. What do we already know or do? (The purpose here, in one or two sentences, is to support the legitimacy and importance of the question. Major discussions of the importance and significance of the study will come under the "significance of the study" section.)
2. How does this particular question relate to what we already know or do? (The purpose here is to explain and support the exact form of questions or hypotheses that serve as the focus for the study.)
3. Why select this particular method of investigation? (The purpose here is to explain and support the selections made from among alternative methods of investigation.)

In reviewing the research literature that often forms the background for the study, the author's task is to indicate the main directions taken by workers in the area and the main issues of methodology and interpretation that have arisen. Particular attention must be given to a critical analysis of previous methodology and the exposition of the advantages and limitations inherent in various alternatives. Close attention must be given to conceptual and theoretical formulations that are explicit or implicit within the selected studies.

By devising, when appropriate, a theoretical basis for the study that emerges from the structure of existing knowledge, by making the questions or hypotheses emerge from the total matrix of answered and unanswered questions, and by making the selection of method contingent upon previous results, the author inserts the proposed study into a line of inquiry and a developing body of knowledge. Such careful attention to background is the first step in entering the continuing conversation that is science.

The author should select only those studies that provide a foundation for the proposed investigation, discuss these studies in sufficient detail to make their relevance entirely clear, note explicitly the ways in which they contribute to the proposed research, and give some indication of how the proposal is designed to move beyond earlier work. The second section of Chapter 4 provides guidelines for preparing the literature review.

It is important for students and novice proposal writers to resist the impulse to display both the extent of their personal labors in achieving what they know and the volume of interesting, but presently irrelevant information accumulated in the process. The rule in selecting studies for review is exactly the same as that used throughout the proposal—limit discussion to what is essential to the main topic. A complete list of all references used in developing the proposal (properly called a bibliography as distinct from the list of references) may be placed in an appendix, thereby providing both a service to the interested reader and some psychological relief to the writer.

Whenever possible, the author should be conceptually or theoretically clear by creating organizing frameworks that encompass both the reviewed studies and the proposed research. This may take the form of something as obvious and practical as grouping studies according to certain methodological features (often for the purpose of examining divergent results), or something as esoteric as identifying and grouping the implicit assumptions made by various researchers in formulating their statement of the problem (often for the purpose of clarifying the problem elected in the present proposal).

In many proposals, creating an organized conceptual framework represents the most important single opportunity for the application of original thought. In one sense, the organizing task is an extension of the need to achieve clarity in communication. A category system that allows division of diverse ideas or recondite events into easily perceived and remembered subsets is an organizational convenience for the author, as well as for the reader. Beyond convenience, however, organizing frameworks identify distinctive threads of thought. The task is to isolate the parallel ways by which researchers, working at different times and in varying degrees of intellectual isolation, have conceived of reality. In creating a schema that deals meaningfully with similarities and dissimilarities in the work of others, the author not only contributes to the body of knowledge, but also deals with the immediate needs of communicating this research to others.

Even relatively simple organizing or integrating systems demand the development of underlying conceptual plans and, often, new ways of interpreting old results and presumed relationships. The sequence of variables in the study may provide a simple and generally adequate place to begin arranging the review. Such questions as "What is the relationship between social class and school achievement when ability is held constant?" consist of concepts placed within a convenient sequential diagram. In turn, such conceptual schemata often contain useful assumptions about causal relationships and thus can serve as effective precursors to explanatory theory. The most elegant kind of research proposals achieve exactly that sort of linkage, using the framework for organizing the review of literature as a bridge connecting existing knowledge, a proposed theory, and the specific, theory-based hypotheses to be empirically tested.

Explaining Procedures

All proposals for empirical research must embody a plan for the careful and systematic observation of events. The methods selected for such observations determine the quality of data obtained. For this reason, the portion of the proposal dealing with procedures the researcher intends to employ will be subject to the closest critical scrutiny. Correspondingly, the presentation of methodology requires great attention to detail. The discussion of method must include sources of data, the collection of data, and the analysis of data. In addition, the discussion must show that the specific techniques selected will not fall short of the claims established in previous sections of the proposal.

The section(s) dealing with methodology must be freely adapted to the purpose of the study. Whatever the format, however, the proposal must provide a step-by-step set of instructions for conducting the investigation. For example, most studies demand explication of the following items:

1. Identification and description of the target population and sampling methods to be used
2. Presentation of instruments and techniques for measurement
3. Presentation of a design for the collection of data
4. Presentation of procedures for collecting and recording data
5. Explanation of data analysis procedures to be used
6. Development of plans for contingencies such as subject mortality.

Many justifications for particular method selections will emerge in the development of background for the problem. The rationale for some choices, however, will most conveniently be presented when the method is introduced as part of the investigation plan.

In describing such elements, proposals can include pages of description that fatigue and frustrate the reader without yielding a clear picture of the overall pattern. In many cases this problem can be avoided by the use of diagrams. Although Figure 1.2 displays a counterbalanced treatment design of moderate complexity, it would require no more than a brief paragraph of accompanying text to provide a clear account of the procedure.

When data are to be gathered from multiple subject groups the proposal can consume pages of explanatory text without providing the reader with an adequate sense of how subject variables are related. Figure 1.3, however, shows a complex design in which a subject population is divided into 16 subgroups using the four variables of gender, role, education level, and affective state, with immediate transparent clarity. Diagrams also are helpful when presenting statistical models that will be tested later once the data are collected. Note how clearly the interrelations of a hypothetical statistical model

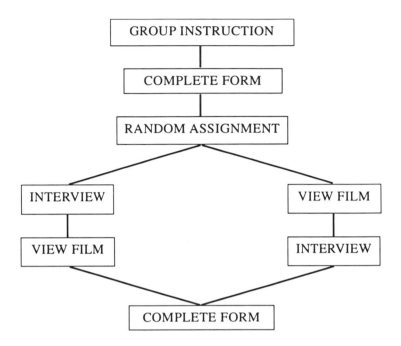

Figure 1.2. Example of Method Flow Chart

appear in Figure 1.4. In the figure, the ovals (designated with Greek letters) represent clusters of variables, the boxes show the variables in each cluster, and the various arrows represent interrelationships. Imagine how many words it would take to describe these relationships! Given a brief exposure to these figures, however, most readers would find further explanation unnecessary.

Providing Supplementary Material

For the purpose of clarity and economical presentation, many items may be placed in appendices keyed to appropriate references in the main text. So placed, such materials become options available to the reader as needed, rather than distractions or impediments to understanding the main themes of the proposal. Included in the appendices may be such items as the following:

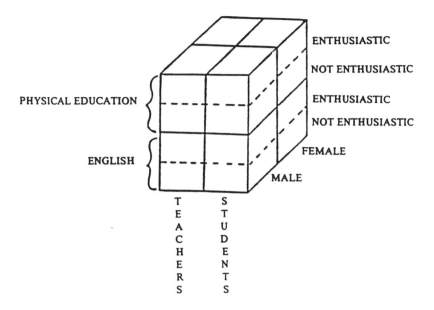

PHYSICAL EDUCATION

ENGLISH

ENTHUSIASTIC

NOT ENTHUSIASTIC

ENTHUSIASTIC

NOT ENTHUSIASTIC

FEMALE

MALE

TEACHERS   STUDENTS

Figure 1.3. Example of Sample With Multiple Subgroups

1. Specifications for equipment
2. Instructions to subjects
3. Subject consent forms
5. Raw data or tabular material from pilot studies
6. Tabular materials from related research
7. Copies of paper and pencil instruments
8. Questions for structured interviews
9. Credentials of experts, judges, or other special personnel to be employed in the study
10. Diagrammatic models of the research design
11. Diagrammatic models of the statistical analysis
12. Schematics for constructed equipment
13. Chapter outline for the final report
14. Proposed time schedule for executing the study
15. Supplementary bibliographies

24

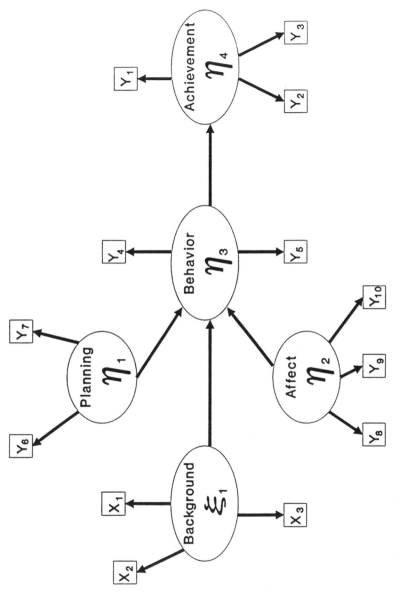

Figure 1.4. Example of Statistical Model

2

Doing the Right Thing
"The Habit of Truth"

The foundation of scholarship as a collective human enterprise is neither intellect nor technical skill. It is simple honesty. If scholars did not have what Jacob Brownowski (1965) called "the habit of truth," there could be no accumulation of reliable knowledge, and thus no science. The rules for this habit of conscience are absolute: no compromises, no evasions, no shortcuts, no excuses, and no saving face. Planning, conducting, and reporting research make sense only so long as the social contract among scholars is honored— *everyone tells the truth as well as he or she can know it.*

Certainly, there is no reason to believe that researchers are paragons of virtue. Nor should we expect that by some magic of nature or nurture they have been exempted from the human frailties of temptation. Pride, selfishness, greed, sloth, and vindictiveness are possibilities for them as much as for anyone else. And the opportunities to succumb are fully as plentiful in the course of inquiry as they are in any other human undertaking.

Why the habit of truth is sustained in any individual scholar is a complex, personal matter. Intellectual integrity, like love, may defy complete analysis. Of this much we can be certain. Researchers understand that there is no way to cheat "just a little." Any dishonesty, large or small, corrodes and contaminates both the process and the products of inquiry—doing harm to guilty and innocent alike by denying truth to all. To which we add another fact that should be noted by anyone proposing to do research: To be discovered, to be caught at cheating in scholarship, brings swift and awful consequences. In this game, the spoilsport is never forgiven.

There may once have been a time when science, as the avocation of people with the leisure to pursue their curiosity, did not invite unethical conduct. But our world has changed, and so has research as a social process. In business, the defense industry, medicine, and the university, research often is a deadly serious contest, played for big stakes and fraught with the tension of competition.

In commercial laboratories with astonishing budgets, large staffs of investigators race around the clock to beat other research teams to lucrative patents and new contracts. In university departments, professors struggle to attract external funding, keep the favor of the institution's managers, and court the possibility of academic honors. Meanwhile, young assistant professors grind out publications in a sometimes desperate pursuit of tenure and promotion. And everywhere, graduate students hurry to complete dissertations so they can win a faculty appointment and rise at last above the enforced penury of teaching assistantships. Anyone who does not see fertile ground for unethical conduct in all of that, simply does not understand human nature.

As with any social statistic, it is difficult to know whether the incidence of scientific cheating has undergone an increase that is truly out of proportion to the growth of the research industry itself. What is certain, however, is that we now hear and read regularly about senior investigators, assistants, and graduate students who have been caught doctoring the data, plagiarizing information, or otherwise violating the canons of good scholarship by failing to tell the truth about their work (Adler, 1991; Safrit, 1993). In their haste to complete the project and reap the rewards, they have broken the fragile habit of truth.

In some cases, of course, that habit never was adequately established. In the preparation of researchers, many universities fail to socialize students into the ethical norms of honest scholarship with the same thoroughness and rigor employed to induct them into the mysteries of sound data analysis. Courses in the philosophy of science and seminars on ethical issues in scholarship have been crowded out of the curriculum. Professors, busy in the frantic pace of their own studies, fail to give time to mentoring students in the complexities of what is acceptable and unacceptable behavior among scholars. We believe that the academic community will be living with the consequences of that neglect for many years to come.

This chapter is no substitute for thorough, on-the-job indoctrination into the ethical standards of inquiry in your field. What we can accomplish here is only to flag with warnings those areas in which the proposal writer is likely to encounter problems related to the ethics of scholarship. One set of those issues attends the process itself (acquiring the cooperation of subjects, gaining access to research sites, gathering data, writing reports, and publishing results). A second category contains ethical problems encountered in relationships, personal and professional, with mentors (notably in the case of professors and graduate students) and colleagues.

Throughout the chapter we will note sources for learning more about the topic of ethics in research. We urge, however, that you use every opportunity to initiate informal discussions about ethics with active researchers, that you seek out courses and seminars dealing with the moral dimensions of scholarship, and that you attend symposia and workshops on ethical issues whenever they are offered at research conferences in your own field. In scholarship, as elsewhere, proper behavior is shaped less by good intentions and far more by healthy doses of forewarning and forearming.

Ethics and the Research Process

THE PROTECTION OF HUMAN SUBJECTS

All universities that receive funding from a federal agency must have in place a system of mandatory review of all research proposals that involve the use of human subjects. The purpose of the review is to ensure protection of the participants' health and welfare. The process may operate at one or several levels, in some cases functioning through a department or college committee and in others by means of a university board (in some institutions, both are employed). Whatever the structure of review procedures, most institutions have published guidelines that lay out the process for obtaining approval and specify the ethical issues to be addressed in the proposal. We strongly recommend that you obtain that document and digest its contents *before* beginning to prepare your proposal. The humane treatment of human beings is far easier to build in, than it is to add on!

In addition to the institutional review of protection given human participants, some research journals now have ethical guidelines that must be met if a manuscript is to be considered for review. Professional and scholarly organizations have published standards that should govern research conducted by members. In all of these, attention is given as to how the researcher must think and act concerning the people who make themselves available for scrutiny. We believe this body of writing reflects a vital dialogue in which every novice researcher should become a witness—and then a participant.

The proposal for a thesis or a dissertation is not intended just to prepare graduate students to undertake and finish a study. For all, it is basic instruction about what science must be if it is to serve us well and wisely, and for some it is the first rite of initiation into a career of scholarship. Accordingly, all students should invest time in learning and thinking about human rights and the ways in which they become entangled with research. If you have no convenient vehicle for that exercise, a valuable first step can be achieved by reading *Ethical Standards of the American Educational Research Association* (American Educational Research Association, 1992), *Ethical Principles of Psychologists* (American Psychological Association, 1990), *Ethical Principles in the Conduct of Research with Human Participants*, published by the American Psychological Association (1982), and *On Being A Scientist* (1989), prepared by the Committee on the Conduct of Science of the National Academy of Science for students about to begin their first research study. Also available are a number of books on the topic of ethics in research (for example: Burgess, 1989; Kimmel, 1988; Reece & Siegal, 1986; and Sieber, 1982, 1992). Finally, for vivid examples of the complex tensions between our desire to protect participants against unethical use in research investigations and our need to preserve the integrity of research designs, we suggest a recent review of the problem by Kroll (1993).

It is easy for the novice to feel overwhelmed by all the responsibilities that seem to come with the direct study of other human beings. It is true that in recent years the domain of concerns about the health and welfare of participants has expanded. In large part, this reflects the fact that a greater volume and diversity of research activity has necessitated a wider definition of what constitutes ethical behavior for the investigator and reasonable protection for the subjects of investigation. Indeed, even at a great distance from the physical intrusions required to study human physiology, there is much to consider in writing that required proposal section on "Protection of Human Subjects."

An Ethical Benchmark

In the thickets of ethical complexity faced by the novice researcher, it sometimes is difficult to keep one's moral bearings. Our suggestion is to keep sight of something basic in your value system and use it as a benchmark to test each decision. For us, the starting place is simpler and far more encompassing than any of the now traditional concerns about the physical and psychological safety of participants. We believe that the right to protection begins with the right of free and informed choice.

Every human has the right not to be used by other people. That means the investigator's need for a human source of data is always subordinate to the other person's right to decide whether to provide it or not. The right not to be used applies with equal force to fifth-graders, college sophomores, trash collectors, professional athletes, and residents in retirement communities. People who are asked to participate in a study have a right to know what they are getting into and the right to give or withhold their cooperation on the basis of that information.

The Self-Interest of Respect

The fact that an investigator uses volunteers responding to a newspaper advertisement, or paid subjects from a prison population, does not alter the participant's right not to be used as chattel. Research workers have both a responsibility and a special interest here. That the rule of informed consent has so often been ignored or compromised in the past accounts in large measure for the difficulties, both obvious and subtle, in obtaining cooperation from prospective participants. Subjects do not always miss (or choose to ignore) the fact that they have suffered the disrespect of having been used by a researcher. They may remember such violation of their person for a long time and on the next occasion may protect themselves by not cooperating. Worse still, they may take a measure of revenge by finding a way to make mischief in the study.

The Danger of Seeming Innocent

What constitutes an unethical use of people is not always clearly established. Social scientists, for example, disagree on the degree to which the use of psychometric instruments, questionnaires, and survey interviews should be circumscribed by procedures to protect respondents' right to informed consent. At the least, this is an issue to be discussed with advisors during development of a proposal that involves such methods.

Our own position on such questions is unequivocal. Concern for the rights of participants should accompany the use of research tools such as questionnaires and interviews, just as it does any other form of data collection. The procedures used to protect the participant's rights may be much less elaborate than those used in an experiment involving physical discomfort or some degree of risk, but they should nonetheless be designed with care and applied with scrupulous uniformity.

It is the ubiquity of questionnaires, the conversational friendliness of interviews, the seeming innocuousness of a Likert Scale, and the innocence of jotting field notes in social settings that present the greatest danger. Where hazards may be obvious, as for example in medical studies, careful attention to subject protection is the norm. Where risks are less obvious, and where they attach to intangibles such as "the right to full disclosure," the need for protection may be brushed aside as a mere formality, and abuse itself then becomes the insidious norm.

Each time people are treated as though they have no right to the privacy of their bodies, their thoughts, or their actions, the implication is that such treatment is right and acceptable. It is not. In contrast, when an investigator treats entry into the private world of a participant as a special privilege, granted by a fellow being as an act of informed cooperation, the opposite instruction is given—and it will be learned. From that lesson, we all profit.

A Protocol for Informed Consent

At minimum, you should consider the following standards for any proposed study that involves the use of human subjects.

1. Participants should be informed of the general nature of the investigation and, within reasonable limits, of their role in terms of time and effort. A script may be used when such information is transmitted orally. (However it is accomplished, a complete, word-for-word account of the information provided should be placed in the appendix of the proposal.)

2. Participants should be informed of procedures used to protect their anonymity. It should be made clear that anonymity cannot be guaranteed. All that should be promised is the use of rigorous procedures for protection.

3. Participants should, after reasonable consideration (including the right to ask questions), sign a document affirming that they have been informed of the nature of the investigation and have consented to give their cooperation. (A copy of this should be included in the proposal.) Specimens of such documents and a checklist for preparing informed consent forms are included here in Appendix B.

4. In experimental studies, participants should receive an explanation of all treatment procedures to be used and any discomforts or risks involved. If risks, physical or psychological, are more than minimal, procedures that will be taken to protect the well-being of the subject should be fully explained.

5. Participants should be told what benefits they will receive by participating in the study and what alternative benefits are being made available to other subjects in the study.

6. Participants should be explicitly instructed that they are free to withdraw their consent and to discontinue participation in the study at any time. In some circumstances it is essential that they also be assured that no reprisal will attend such a decision. (Complicated issues, such as setting a time limit on this right or establishing the right to withdraw data already provided if cooperation is withdrawn, require careful attention in the proposal.)

7. Participants should be provided with the name of the person responsible for the study, to whom they can direct questions related to their role or any consequence of their participation. In the case of research conducted by graduate students, this should include the name, address, and telephone number of both the student and the supervising professor.

8. Participants should be offered the opportunity to receive feedback about the results of the study. This should be in a form that is appropriate to the needs and interests of the participant.

The Reactive Effects of Honesty

Arguments to the effect that procedures for informed consent introduce unknown bias effects are, for the most part, spurious. All contacts between investigators and participants hold the potential for generating unknown effects. The procedures for ensuring the rights of subject do no more to produce response biases than any other interaction. On the other hand, respectful observance of these protections, quite aside from their ethical import, can exercise a measure of steadying influence over the most fundamental (and sometimes the most capricious) of all subject-related variables—the participant's cooperation.

Omission of Information

If it seems essential to withhold some specific item of information from participants, then the omission may be considered. This can be done, however, only after a careful search for any harm or substantial disadvantage that might occur. The use of placebo treatments and control groups sometimes involve exactly this form of limitation on full disclosure. The fact that such procedures are commonplace, however, does not make them less ethically problematic.

The seriousness of any decision to limit what the participant knows is underscored by the fact that deception in the form of giving false information about the nature of the study or the risks of participation (actual deception) is absolutely prohibited in every field of inquiry. As everyone knows, the boundary between sins of omission and commission is dangerously thin!

When participants are not given complete disclosure, they should know, in virtually every instance, that this is the case before making a decision about joining the study. When any information is withheld from the participants, the proposal must present explicit detail about how and when they will be debriefed and how any disadvantage created by the omission will be rectified.

Cooperation by Coercion

There is a spirit as well as a letter to be observed in rules about informed consent. When individuals are under the supervision or control of another individual, it may be difficult for them to refuse an invitation to participate in a study. In a sense, it may truly be impossible for them to freely give their cooperation. Thus a graduate student may be loath to refuse an advisor's request to serve as a subject, or an undergraduate may feel reluctant to decline a teaching assistant's suggestion that he or she become a participant in a dissertation study. Secretaries and classified staff may be too intimidated to refuse a chairperson's invitation. Any of these individuals may sign the consent form and participate but inwardly feel resentful. People's rights are violated just as much by coercion that is unintended as by that which is so designed.

Many researchers feel that it is good ethical practice not to use students who are in their classes or under their supervision. Some institutions now have regulations that forbid such practice. It may be wise to use the media to solicit volunteers or, in the case of students, to invite only those from other departments or from places outside the purview of your authority.

Reciprocity

If participants give cooperation, time, effort, and access to what is by right theirs to control (not least of all their privacy), what does the researcher give in return? Once that question is allowed legitimacy, satisfying answers may prove more scarce than the novice might expect. It is difficult to establish what is proper compensation for serving as a study participant. In any case, few researchers could afford the purchase price for what their subjects contribute. In some measure, serving as a participant in a research study always has to take the form of a gift. Which makes the demand that the gift be freely given and fully acknowledged all the more important.

Among the means of reciprocity are small symbols that show appreciation: a handwritten note, or even just a sincere "thank-you!" Pride also is its own reward when participants feel that they have contributed to the search for knowledge (or to finding solutions for practical problems), though that wears thin when the required investment of time or effort is large. Qualitative researchers often find that giving a respectful, nonjudgmental ear to participants' accounts of their experiences can have important value as a return for cooperation. An opportunity to satisfy curiosity, or for participants to learn something about themselves (or even about research) also may have some place in an honest exchange. In the end, however, the researcher always is left to answer two hard questions. For whose benefit is this work being done, and where are the interests of my subject in the calculus by which I find the answer?

The Ethics of Writing

PLAGIARISM

Ideas, and the words that express those ideas, are the valuables of scholarship. The people who create them have a right to receive credit for them. When one person appropriates the ideas or text of another person and presents them as his or her own, it is theft. The technical term is plagiarism, but it is theft, and the ethics of scholarship make no provision for petty crime—it is all grand theft.

Yes, grey areas exist where ideas, phrases, and even entire ways of thinking about things pass into the public domain where acknowledging their origin no longer is obligatory. And yes, the distinction between a paraphrase in your words and one that derives too much from the original author is a judgment call. For problems of that kind we leave you to other resources—and your conscience.

What we are talking about here is thievery, and that includes failure to use quotation marks where they belong, omitting citations that credit material found in someone else's work, shoddy carelessness in preparing the list of references, and failure to obtain permission for the use of figures, tables, or even illustrations from another document—whether published or not. In each of those, doing the right thing does not involve knowing the niceties of custom or the precise reading of an obscure rule. You know exactly what is ethical without any coaching. All you need to remember is what your mother said: *"Don't cheat!"* If you need more motivation than that, you might consider the proposition that it is prudent to treat the property of others as you hope they will treat yours.

PROVIDING ALL THE FACTS

The purpose of a proposal, you will remember, is to help other people understand what you plan to do. To accomplish that, they need all the relevant facts, not just those favorable to your inclinations. Deliberate omission of information hostile to some part of your proposal is dishonest. Accidental omission of important information (that includes simply not having learned it) is incompetence. Either way, an incomplete account defeats one of the main purposes in writing the proposal—to provide the basis for obtaining good advice.

MANUFACTURING THE FACTS

Once the study is under way, frequent opportunities will occur to fabricate data (creating it rather than collecting it), and falsify data (tampering with it to make it appear to be what it is not). Although obviously a violation of ethical practice, it is surprising how reasonable such fraud can seem. If you are collecting data on a subject over five days, and she happens to miss the third day, and your final record sheet shows scores of 10, 20, (?), 40, and 50, what is so unreasonable about inserting the 30 *except that it is a lie?*

Temptations like that are not rare in research. In fact, such situations are more the rule than the exception. In the rush to finish before a deadline, how reasonable will a small lie seem to you? In your response will reside the answer to another question: What kind of scholar do you want to become? (In case you wondered, in many forms of data analysis there are appropriate ways to deal with missing data. All you need to do is use the correct procedure and then be honest—describing in your report exactly how data were handled.)

Inappropriate use of data is no different than making it up. Using raw scores when you know they should be transformed before analysis is just another kind of falsification. Data dredging—repeatedly changing your analysis when results do not come out as anticipated—is another way to fudge. Use the data you have, use it correctly, and tell the reader exactly what you did. With those simple rules, it is hard to go wrong.

Other falsehoods do not directly involve the data. For example, it may be tempting to describe testing procedures as more rigorous than you actually were able to maintain or to report taking the precautions against contamination that you had proposed, when, in fact, it proved impossible to do so. It may be easy to allow the reader to infer that a standard protocol was used unchanged, when, in fact, it had to be modified, or to give the impression that your selection of observation sites was random, when, in fact, you had to pick the ones closest to your office. All are breaches of ethics, all undercut the value of your research, and all serve to create an insidious pollution in the atmosphere of science.

Discussion of your findings provides one last temptation to tilt the facts in a way that favors your personal interests, but falls short of an honest accounting. The researcher has a perfect right to emphasize the results that seem most important. That power is abused, however, when disconfirming data are left out of the discussion, or are included without a clear notation of their implications.

Graduate students can be particularly vulnerable to the natural attraction of selective reporting. There often is subtle pressure to present the results that advisors expect. If having to find a way to deal with equivocal or counter-intuitive findings is likely to delay graduation, the temptation to simply "not have them" grows ever more attractive. The choice to do the right thing can be inconvenient, expensive, and even painful. No experienced investigator would claim that research is a rose garden.

ETHICS IN PUBLICATION

Sending off the manuscript to a journal, mailing your abstract to the review committee for a national conference, finding your name in the table of contents, those are golden moments—and any researcher who no longer finds them so should consider a long vacation. The route to those wonderful moments, however, is strewn with ethical pitfalls for the unwary novice. There is a lot to know about the rules that govern ethics in publication, and much of that is beyond the purview of this handbook.

As an example, in the case of research studies to which a number of people contribute, there are rules (both written and unwritten) about whose names appear on the report, in what order they appear, and who should be acknowledged but not given status as an author. Unfortunately, these rules come in versions established by universities, journals, scholarly organizations, government agencies, laboratories, and even individual professors. The best we can do is to advise that you make it a point to find out the regulations (or local conventions) that apply in your circumstance. In such matters as whose name will appear on publications and who (or what entity) will have ownership of research products, it is prudent that you locate this information *early* in the proposal development process—and for this purpose, formal documents are always more appropriate than informal conversations.

We will note here only three of the many ethical concerns related to publication, one of them because it is among the first and most obvious, and two because they are well-disguised pitfalls that may not be recognized for the dangers they present. First, can you submit your manuscript to more than one journal at the same time? The short answer is: No, don't ever do it. If you have a fertile mind you will recognize at once that there are dozens of questions that surround that simple rule. For example, can you submit a manuscript to a journal after the abstract for the same study was published in a conference proceedings? (The answer is yes.) For each of these subsidiary problems you will have to find what is considered ethical in the particular situation. Just do not forget the basic rule—duplicate submissions are absolutely prohibited, and the event of duplicate publication brings swift and Draconian consequences.

A second temptation will come early in your study, and it is that timing that gives it both great attraction and serious danger. Almost every researcher we know has been tempted to submit an abstract to a prestigious conference (to be held well after the proposed conclusion of the study), when the analysis has not been finished, or even when all the data are not yet in hand. The motive is understandable. Researchers are excited about their work, and always anxious to join the great conversation that represents scholarship in their field. Writing up an abstract that is incomplete or that projects anticipated results seems a minor transgression, but one thing can lead to another. What if the final analysis contradicts your confident projection? What if the work slows down and still is incomplete when the conference date arrives? Among embarrassing alternatives are withdrawing the paper, or making a public confession. Worse, however, there will be temptation into serious violation of ethics, such as covering your tracks by faking results, or downplaying findings that don't harmonize with the earlier abstract. Cooking up an abstract so you can reserve a place on the program is risky business. Our advice is to do what you know is the right thing—just wait until next year.

A third pitfall lies waiting beyond presentations and journal articles, in a seemingly risk-free document—your resumé. Most beginners in academe do a bit of padding by including fairly minor accomplishments that later will be omitted as publication lists begin to lengthen. But this practice has limitations and points at which it becomes dishonesty rather than innocent enthusiasm. Employers and promotion committees have become increasingly restive about the kind of unethical padding that has proliferated in academic resumés. Among the truly dishonest inclusions are abstracts from presentations that are given a title different from an ensuing published report—so that the two appear to be different studies, when they are not. Another is listing research articles and/or grant proposals in a way that allows the reader to assume you were a coinvestigator, when in fact you contributed only a minor part to the submission. Contributions to the "Brief Research Notes" sections of journals are found displayed as though they were major achievements.

All such forms of padding are not innocent enthusiasm, they are dishonesty. Happily, a simple procedure can be adopted that will keep you safe from any complaint about your resumé—and still allow you to take credit for everything. Put your accomplishments in categories headed by labels that clearly describe what each contains, and cross-reference where citations represent the same piece of work.

Personal and Professional Relationships

A very fine distinction separates violations of research ethics (that include most of what has been discussed to this point), and ethical misconduct. For a helpful discussion that defines those and other categories in the domain of ethics, see *Responsible Science*, a publication prepared by the Panel on Scientific Responsibility and the Conduct of Research (1992). It is that latter category of misconduct, which includes the ethics of how scholars treat each other in their personal and professional relationships, to which we will now attend.

RELATIONSHIPS WITH FACULTY MENTORS

As described by Roberts (1993), in the ideal situation, the relationship between graduate student and major professor gradually matures until at the completion of the degree the student and professor have become colleagues. Unfortunately, what is ideal is not always real. Some dysfunctions in professor/student relationships are no more than the collision of personality styles, the abrasion of conflicting intellectual interests, or the tensions of differing personal politics. Those are painful, and even harmful if not addressed, but they do not necessarily involve unethical behavior by anyone. Certain types of interpersonal behavior, however, are not acceptable because they are dangerous, or violations of what is equitable, or both.

First among these are instances in which pressure is put upon a student to go beyond the expected academic or professional relationship. In our judgment, any attempt by a faculty member to coerce a student into an expanded relationship is inappropriate.

Perhaps not obvious as a form of ethical misconduct is pressure from faculty that urges students to perform tasks that are not part of the academic program—and that they do not wish to do. These subtle abuses include requesting errand service, assigning attendance at social functions, and even the expectation of jogging together. In most collegial relationships such activities are normal. People who work closely together often exchange favors and socialize. The problem is that the relationship between professors and students is not truly collegial. There is an enormous imbalance of power. In the most innocent and well-intended invitations, students often find the hidden force of coercion.

The point at which inappropriate pressures shade into reasonable requirements is a grey area. An important part of any graduate program is gaining research experience by hands-on engagement. Working with faculty members on their projects can be a valuable source of such training. There are limits to be observed, however, and care needs to be taken so that apprenticeship does not become servitude in disguise.

When the task performed is so narrow as to yield no new skill or knowledge, when the student's own work has to be unreasonably delayed, and when the topic of inquiry is not remotely related to the student's specialization, the line between education and abuse has been crossed. By then it may be too late to extricate yourself comfortably. For that reason we suggest prior discussion of all such research opportunities with other faculty advisors, the prospective research mentor, and other graduate students.

Much more serious examples of abusing the faculty-student imbalance of power are all the forms of sexual harassment. The form taken may range from subtle comments to direct demands for sex. Although it is obvious that what one person considers as offensive another person may regard as repartee or humor, that understanding

does not make remarks with sexual connotations any more acceptable or any less serious as breaches of ethical conduct. Students have
an absolute right to be free of such discomforts. Subtle or glaring,
intended or inadvertent, sexual harassment is wrong and not to be
tolerated.

If you encounter such problems, we suggest confronting them
immediately, rather than allowing them to fester. Some faculty members may not understand that you find something troubling, and a
private discussion may set everything straight. Repeated incidents
or any invitation or pressure for a sexual relationship should be
brought to the attention of someone you can trust—another faculty
member, the department chair, the dean, or perhaps the best choice
of all, the university ombudsperson.

It is to everyone's advantage that student/professor relationships
stay at the formal level of teacher and pupil. If you want a men-
tor/mentee relationship to turn into something more, we urge that
you acquire a new mentor before allowing that to happen. Human
relationships are complex, but those that attempt to bridge stations
of unequal power are doubly so.

Where goodwill reigns and a modicum of sensitivity is the norm,
the relationship between professor and student is not a mine field of
hidden risks. It is the place for a rare and invaluable kind of human
exchange. Given even reasonable nurture and protection, it will
flourish and grow—into collegiality.

DISCOVERY AND OBLIGATION

What if it really happens? What if you discover or have strong
reason to suspect unethical behavior on the part of a colleague or
faculty member? Our first advice is to think carefully, very carefully,
about how to protect yourself from involvement or reprisal. Also
consider the terrible consequences of an accusation that proves false.
Whether or not you take action will be a matter of conscience, and
your conscience should tell you that cheating in research can never
be condoned or tolerated. What course of action you choose, however, will be a function of circumstance, prudence, and courage.

Talking with the person(s) involved is one course of action. If you
judge that to be unreasonable, then you must find other options. In
most universities appropriate authorities are available, and again the

ombudsperson will know who they are. Any institution that receives federal research funds will have procedures for investigating violations of research ethics. In some instances there are provisions to protect the "whistle blower," though that is not always possible.

In the end, anyone accused of a violation has a proper claim to due process, and even well-intentioned reports of ethical violations that cannot be sustained when investigated will rebound to the discomfort (and often disadvantage) of the accuser. Again, take the time to review the pages of *Responsible Science* (1992) before you act. Doing the right thing may not be easy, but at least it can be done the right way.

None of us can decline to take responsibility. Every study is part of a shared enterprise—the work of scholarship. When anyone does not do what is right, everyone is harmed.

3

Developing the Thesis or Dissertation Proposal

Some Common Problems

The general purposes and broad format of the proposal document have now been presented. There remain, however, a number of particular points that cause a disproportionate amount of difficulty in preparing proposals for student-conducted research. In some cases, the problems arise because of real difficulty in the subtle and complex nature of the writing task. In other cases, however, the problems are a consequence of confusion, conflicting opinions, and ambiguous standards among research workers themselves and, more particularly, among university research advisors.

As with many tasks involving an element of art, it is possible to establish a few general rules to which most practitioners subscribe. Success in terms of real mastery, however, lies not in knowing, or even following, the rules but in what the student learns to do within the rules.

Each student will discover his or her own set of special problems. Some will be solved only through practice and the accumulation of experience. While wrestling with the frustrations of preparing a proposal, the student should try to remember that the real fascination of research lies in its problematic nature, in the search for serviceable hypotheses, in selecting sensitive means of analyzing data, and in the creative tasks of study design.

Some of the problems graduate students face cannot be solved simply by reading about them. What follows, however, is an effort to alert you to the most common pitfalls, to provide some general suggestions for resolution of the problems, and to sound one encouraging note: Consultation with colleagues and advisors, patience with the often slow process of "figuring out," and scrupulous care in writing will overcome or circumvent most of the problems encountered in preparing a research proposal. In the midst of difficulty, it is useful to remember that problems are better encountered when developing the proposal than when facing a deadline for a final copy of the report.

The problems have been grouped into two broad sections: "Before the Proposal: First Things First" and "The Sequence of Proposing: From Selecting a Topic to Forming a Committee." Each section contains a number of specific issues that may confront the student researcher and provides some rules of thumb for use in avoiding or resolving the attendant difficulties. Readers should skim through the two sections selectively, because not all of the discussions will be relevant to their needs. Chapter 4 ("Content of the Proposal: Important Considerations"), Chapter 6 ("Style and Form in Writing the Proposal"), and Chapter 7 ("The Oral Presentation") deal with specific technical problems and should be consulted after completing a review of what follows here.

Before the Proposal:
First Things First

MAKING YOUR DECISION:
DO YOU REALLY WANT TO DO IT?

The following idealized sequence of events leads to a thesis or dissertation proposal.

1. In the process of completing undergraduate or master's level preparation, the student identifies an area of particular interest in which he or she proposes to concentrate advanced study.
2. The student selects a graduate institution that has a strong reputation for research and teaching in the area of interest.
3. The student identifies an advisor who has published extensively and regularly chairs graduate student research in the area of interest.

4. Based on further study and interaction with the advisor, the student selects and formulates a question or hypothesis as the basis for a thesis or dissertation.

As we do not live in the best of all possible worlds, few students are able to pursue the steps of this happy and logical sequence. For a variety of reasons, most students have to take at least one of the steps in reverse. Some even find themselves at the end of several semesters of study just beginning to identify a primary area of interest, in an institution that may be less than perfectly appropriate to their needs, and assigned to an advisor who has little or no experience in that particular domain. For this unfortunate state of affairs, we offer no easy solution. We do believe that one significant decision is, or should be, available to the student—the decision to do, or not to do, a research study. Faced with conditions such as those described above, if the option is available, the more rational and educationally profitable course may be to elect not to undertake a research study. You can determine whether this option is available before the school is selected, or at least before the program of study is selected.

There are sound reasons to believe that experience in the conduct of research contributes to graduate education. There also are good and substantial reasons to believe that other kinds of experiences are immeasurably more appropriate and profitable for some students. The question is, "Which experience is right for you?"

If you are, or think you might be, headed for a career in scholarship and higher education, then the decision is clear. The sooner you begin accumulating experience in research activities, the better. If you are genuinely curious about the workings of the research process, interested in combining inquiry with a career of professional service, or fascinated by the problems associated with a particular application of knowledge to practice, again the decision is clear. An experience in research presents at least a viable alternative in your educational plans.

Lacking one of these motives, the decision should swing the other way, toward an option more suited to your needs. Inadequately motivated research tends not to be completed or, worse, is finished in a pedestrian fashion far below the student's real capacity. Even a well-executed thesis or dissertation may exert a powerful negative influence on the graduate experience when it has not been accepted by the student as a reasonable and desirable task.

One problem touches everyone in graduate education, faculty and students alike—the hard constraints of time. Students want to finish their degree programs in a reasonable period of time. The disposition or circumstance of some, however, may define reasonable time as "the shortest possible time." Others find the thought of any extension beyond the standard number of semesters a serious threat to their sense of adequacy. For students such as these, a thesis or dissertation is a risky venture.

Relatively few research studies finish on schedule, and time requirements invariably are underestimated. Frequent setbacks are almost inevitable. This is one aspect of the research process that is learned during the research experience. Haste in research is lethal to both quality of the product and worth of the experience. If you cannot spend the time, deciding to initiate a research project endangers the area of inquiry, your advisor, your institution, your education, your reputation, and any satisfaction you might take in completing the task. In short, if you can't afford the time, then don't do it at all.

CHOOSING YOUR TURF:
ADVISORS AND AREAS

Once a firm decision has been made to write a thesis or dissertation, the choice of an advisor presents a less difficult problem. Here, area of interest dictates selection because it is essential to have an advisor who is knowledgeable. Further, it always is preferable to have one who is actively publishing in the domain of interest.

Competent advisement is so important that a degree of student flexibility may be required. It is far better for students to adjust their long-range goals than to attempt research on a topic with which their advisor is completely unfamiliar. It may be necessary for the thesis or dissertation to be part of the advisor's own research program. As long as the topic remains within the broad areas of student interest, however, it is possible to gain vital experience in formulating questions, designing studies, and applying the technology and methods of inquiry that are generic to the domain.

It is desirable for student and advisor to interact throughout the development of the proposal, beginning with the initial selection and formulation of the question. On occasion, however, the student may bring an early stage proposal to a prospective advisor as a test of his or her interest or to encourage acceptance of formal appointment as advisor. Experience suggests that this strategy is most likely to produce immediate results if the proposal is in the primary interest area of the advisor. If the proposal involves replication of some aspect of the advisor's previous research, the student may be amazed at the intensity of attention this attracts.

FINDING YOUR QUESTION: WHAT DON'T WE KNOW THAT MATTERS?

Before launching into the process of identifying a suitable topic for inquiry, we suggest a short course of semantic and conceptual hygiene. The purpose of this small therapy is to establish a simple and reliable set of terms for thinking through what can sometimes be a difficult and lengthy problem—what do I study?

All research emerges from a perceived problem, some unsatisfactory situation in the world that we want to confront. Sometimes the difficulty rests simply in the fact that we don't understand how things work and have the human itch to know. At other times we are confronted by decisions or the need for action when the alternatives or consequences are unclear. Such perceived problems are experienced as a disequilibrium, a dissonance in our cognition. Notice, however, they do not exist out in the world, but in our minds.

That may sound at first like one of those "nice points" of which academics are sometimes fond, but for the purposes of a novice researcher, locating the problem in the right place and setting up your understanding of exactly what is unsatisfactory may represent much more than an arbitrary exercise. Thinking clearly about problems, questions, hypotheses, and research purposes can prevent mental log jams that sometimes block or delay clear identification of what is to be investigated.

The novice will encounter research reports, proposals, and even some well-regarded textbooks that freely interchange the words "problem" and "question" in ways that create all sorts of logical confusion (as in "The question in this study is to investigate the problem of . . ." or "The problem in this study is to investigate the question of . . . "). The problem is located alternately in the world or in the study, the distinction between problems and questions is unclear, and what is unsatisfactory in the situation is not set up as a clear target for inquiry.

We suggest that you be more careful as you think through the question of what to study. Define your terms from the start and stick with them, at least until they prove not to be helpful. The definitions we prefer are arbitrary, but it has been our experience that making such distinctions is a useful habit of mind. Accordingly, we suggest that you use the following lexicon as you think and begin to write about your problem.

Problem—the experience we have when an unsatisfactory situation is encountered. Once carefully defined, it is that situation, with all of the attendant questions it may raise, that can become the target for a proposed study. Your proposal, then, will not lay out a plan to study the problem but will address one or several of the questions that explicate what you have found "problematic" about the situation. Note that in this context neither situation nor problem is limited to a pragmatic definition. The observation that two theories contradict each other can be experienced as a problem, and a research question may be posed to address the conflict.

Question—a statement of what you wish to know about some unsatisfactory situation, as in the following: What is the relation between. . . ? Which is the better way to. . . ? What would happen if. . . ? What is the location of. . . ? As explained below, when cast in a precise, answerable form, one or several of these questions will become the mainspring for your study—the formal research question.

Purpose—the explicit intention of the investigator to accumulate data in such a way as to answer the research question posed as the focus for the study. The word "objective" is a reasonable synonym here. Although only people can have intentions, it is common to invest our research design with purpose (as in "The purpose of this study is to determine the mechanism through which . . .").

Hypothesis—an affirmation about the nature of some situation in the world. A tentative proposition set up as a convenient target for an investigation, a statement to be confirmed or denied in terms of the evidence.

Given this lexicon, the search for a topic becomes the quest for a situation that is sufficiently unsatisfactory to be experienced as a *problem*. The proposal has as its *purpose* the setting up of a research *question* and the establishing of exactly how (and why) the investigator intends to find the answer, thereby eliminating or reducing the experience of finding something problematic about the world. Problems lead to questions, which in turn lead to the purpose of the study and hypotheses. Table 3.1 shows the question, purpose, and hypotheses for a study. Note that the hypotheses meet the criteria established in Chapter 1 and are the most specific.

The research process, and thus the proposal, begins with a question. Committed to performing a study within a given area of inquiry and allied with an appropriate advisor, students must identify a question that matches their interests as well as the resources and constraints of their situation. Given a theoretically infinite set of possible problems that might be researched, it is small wonder that many students at first are overwhelmed and frozen into indecision. The "I can't find a problem" syndrome is a common malady among graduate students, but fortunately one that can be cured by time and knowledge.

Research questions emerge from three broad sources: logic, practicality, and accident. In some cases the investigator's curiosity is directed to a gap in the logical structure of what already is known in the area. In other cases, the investigator responds to the demand for information about the application of knowledge to some practical service. In yet other cases serendipity operates and the investigator is stimulated by an unexpected observation, often in the context of another study. It is common for several of these factors to operate simultaneously to direct attention to a particular question. Personal circumstance and individual style also tend to dictate the most common source of questions for each research worker. Finally, all of the sources depend on a more fundamental and prior factor—thorough knowledge of the area.

It is this latter factor that accounts for the "graduate student syndrome." Only as one grasps the general framework and the specific details of a particular area can unknowns be revealed, fortuitous observations raise questions, and possible applications of knowledge become apparent. Traditional library study is the first step toward the maturity that permits confident selection of a research question. Such study, however, is necessary but not sufficient. In any active area of inquiry the current knowledge base is not in the library—it is in the invisible college of informal associations among research workers.

The working knowledge base of an area takes the form of unpublished papers, conference speeches, seminar transcripts, memoranda, dissertations in progress, grant applications, personal correspondence, telephone calls, and electronic mail communications, as well

TABLE 3.1 Problem, Question, Purpose, and Hypotheses

Problem – Does extensive teacher planning really pay off in terms of student learning, or even student learning behaviors?

Question – Are there relationships between teacher thought processes during planning and student time-on-task?

Purpose – The purpose of this study is to examine the relationships between different categories of teacher thought processes during planning and student time-on-task in high school algebra classes.

Hypotheses (note that directional hypotheses are used for hypotheses 1-3 and that even hypothesis 4, stated in the null form, could be based on pilot data).

    1. The number of student skill level planning decisions and student time-on-task are positively related.

    2. The number of management planning decisions and student time-on-task are positively related.

    3. Noninstructional planning decisions and student time-on-task are negatively related.

    4. The total number of planning decisions is not related to student time-on-task.

as conversations in the corridors of conference centers, restaurants, hotel rooms, and bars. To obtain access to this ephemeral resource the student must be where the action is.

The best introduction to the current status of a research area is close association with advisors who know the territory and are busy formulating and pursuing their own questions. Conversing with peers, listening to professorial discussions, assisting in research projects, attending lectures and conferences, exchanging papers, and corresponding with faculty or students at other institutions are all ways of capturing the elusive state of the art. In all of these, however, the benefits derived often depend on knowing enough about the area to join the dialogue by asking questions, offering a tangible point for discussion, or raising a point of criticism. In research, as elsewhere, the more you know, the more you can learn.

While establishing a network of exchange may seem impossible to young students who view themselves as novices and outsiders, it is a happy fact that new recruits generally find a warm welcome within any well-defined area of intensive study. Everyone depends on informal relationships among research colleagues, and this rapport is one source of sustaining excitement and pleasure in the research enterprise. As soon as you can articulate well-formulated ideas about possible problems, your colleagues will be eager to provide comment, critical questions, suggestions, and encouragement.

In the final process of selecting the thesis or dissertation problem there is one exercise that can serve to clarify the relative significance of competing questions. Most questions can be placed within a general model that displays a sequence of related questions—often in an order determined by logic or practical considerations. Smaller questions are seen to lead to larger and more general questions, methodological questions are seen necessarily to precede substantive questions, and theoretical questions may be found interspersed among purely empirical questions. The following is a much simplified but entirely realistic example of such a sequential model. It begins with an everyday observation and leads through a series of specific and interrelated problems to a high-order question of great significance.

> OBSERVATION: Older adults generally take longer than young adults to complete cognitive tasks, but those who are physically active seem to be quicker mentally, especially in tasks that demand behavioral speed.
>
> 1. What types of cognitive function might be related to exercise?
> 2. How can these cognitive functions be measured?
> 3. What are the effects of habitual exercise on one of these types of cognitive function—reaction time?
> 4. Are active older adults faster on a simple reaction time task than sedentary older adults?
> 5. Are active older adults faster on a more complex reaction time task, such as choice reaction time, than older sedentary adults?
>
> QUESTION: What effect does habitual exercise have on choice reaction time in older adults?

By making the twists and turns of speculation visible in the concrete process of sequential listing, previously unnoticed possibilities may be revealed or tentative impressions confirmed. In the simple example given above, the reader may immediately see other questions that could have been inserted or alternative chains of inquiry that branch off from the main track of logic. Other diagrammatic lists of questions about exercise and cognitive function might be constructed from different but related starting points. One might begin, for example, with the well-established observation that circulation is superior in older individuals who exercise regularly. This might lead through a series of proximal experiments toward the ultimate question, "What is the *mechanism* by which exercise maintains cognitive function?"

Building such diagrams will be useful for the student in several other ways. It is a way of controlling the instinct to grab the first researchable question that becomes apparent in an area. Often such questions are inferior to what might be selected after more careful contemplation of the alternatives. A logical sequence can be followed for most questions, beginning with "What has to be asked first?" Once these serial relationships become clear it is easier to assign priorities.

In addition to identifying the correct ordering and relative importance of questions, such conceptual models also encourage students to think in terms of a series of studies that build cumulatively toward more significant conclusions than can be achieved in a one-shot thesis or dissertation. The faculty member who has clear dedication to a personal research program can be a key factor in attracting students into the long-term commitments that give life to an area of inquiry.

Researchable questions occur daily to the active researcher. The problem is not finding them but maintaining some sense of whether, and where, they might fit into an overall plan. While this condition may seem remote to the novice struggling to define a first research topic, formulating even a modest research agenda can be a helpful process. The guidance of a sequential display of questions can allow the student to settle confidently on the target for a proposal.

The Sequence of Proposing:
From Selecting a Topic to Forming a Committee

A PLAN OF ACTION:
WHAT FOLLOWS WHAT?

Figure 3.1 can be useful for the novice if one central point is understood. A tidy, linear sequence of steps is not an accurate picture of what happens in the development of most research proposals. The peculiar qualities of human thought processes and the serendipity of retrieving knowledge serve to guarantee that development of a proposal will be anything but tidy. Dizzying leaps, periods of no progress, and agonizing backtracking are more typical than is a continuous, unidirectional flow of events. The diagram may be used to obtain an overview of the task, to establish a rough time schedule, or to check retrospectively for possible omissions, but it is not to be taken as a literal representation of what should or will happen.

To say that development of a proposal is not a perfectly predictable sequence is not to say, however, that it is entirely devoid of order. Starting at the beginning and following a logical sequence of thought and work has some clear advantages. When the proposal has been completed, a backward glance often indicates that a more orderly progression through the development steps would have saved time and effort.

For instance, although the mind may skip ahead and visualize a specific type of measure to be used, Step 11 ("Consider alternative methods of measurement") should not be undertaken until Step 6 ("Surveying relevant literature") is completed. Many methods of measurement may be revealed and noted while perusing the literature. Sometimes suggestions for instrumentation materialize in unlikely places or in studies that have been initially categorized as unlikely to yield information concerning measurement. Additionally, reported reliabilities and validities of alternative procedures will be needed before any final selection can be made. Thus a large commitment of effort to consideration of alternative methods can be a waste of time if it precedes a careful survey of the literature.

For simplicity, many important elements have been omitted from Figure 3.1. No reference is made to such pivotal processes as developing a theoretical framework, categorizing literature, or stating hypotheses. Further, the detailed demands that are intrinsic to the writing process itself, such as establishing a systematic language, receive no mention. What is presented are the obvious steps of logic and procedure—the operations and questions that mark development toward a plan for action. Finally, the reader who begins to make actual use of the diagram will find that the sequence of steps at several junctures leads into what appear to be circular paths. For example, if at Question F a single form of inquiry does not present itself as most appropriate, the exit line designated "NO" leads back to the previous procedural step of considering alternative forms of inquiry. The intention in this arrangement is not to indicate a trap in which beginning researchers are doomed forever to chase their tails. In each case the closed loop suggests only that when questions cannot be answered, additional input is required (more study, thought, or advice), or that the question itself is inappropriate to the case and must be altered.

For the most part, Figure 3.1 will be self-explanatory. In the pages that follow, however, we have selected a few of the steps and questions for comment, either because they represent critical junctures in the proposal process or because they have proven particularly troublesome for our own advisees. It will be helpful to locate in the diagram sequence each of the items selected for discussion so that the previous and succeeding steps and questions provide a frame for our comments.

Step 3: Narrow down. What do I want to know? Moving from general to specific is always more difficult for the beginner than is anticipated. It is here that the student first encounters two of the hard facts of scientific life: logistic practicality and the perverse inscrutability of seemingly simple events. Inevitably, the novice must learn to take one small step, one manageable question, at a time. In other words, the proposal must conform in scope to the realistic limitations of the research process itself. At their best, research tools can encompass only limited bits of reality; stretched too far, they produce illusion rather than understanding.

It may be important to think big at first, to puzzle without considering practicality, and to allow speculation to soar beyond the confines of the sure knowledge base. From such creative conceptual exercises, however, the researcher must return to the question, "Where, given my resources and the nature of the problem, can I begin?" Delimiting questions such as "In which people?" "Under what conditions?" "At what time?" "In what location?" "By observing which events?" "By manipulating which variables?" serve the necessary pruning function.

Step 5: Identify reasons answer is important. This step places the proposed research in scientific-societal perspective. The study should contribute to the generation or validation of a theoretical structure or subcomponent or relate to one of the several processes by which knowledge is used to enhance professional practice. The trick here is to justify the question in terms appropriate to its nature. Inquiry that is directed toward filling a gap in the structure of knowledge need not be supported by appeals to practical application (even though later events may yield just such return). Inquiry that arises

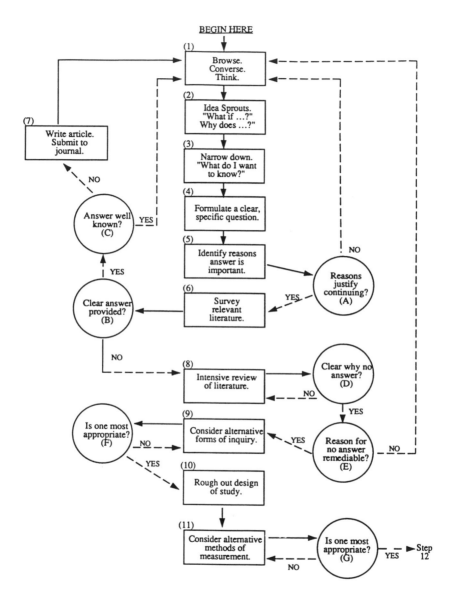

Figure 3.1. Twenty Steps to a Proposal

directly from problems in the world of practice need not be supported by appeals to improve understanding of basic phenomena (even

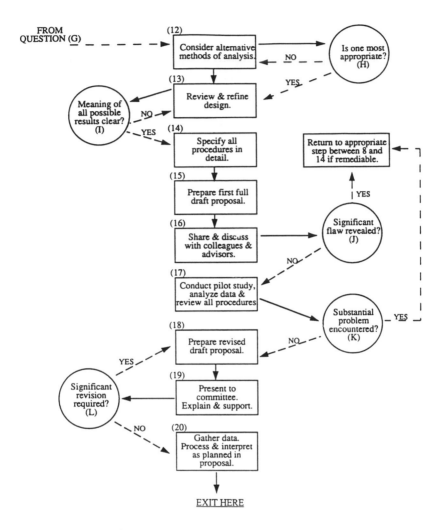

Figure 3.1. Continued

NOTE: Boxes represent major procedural steps; unbroken lines trace the main sequence of those steps. Circles represent the major question to be confronted; the broken lines lead to the procedural consequences of the alternative YES or NO answers.

though later events may lead to this). Each kind of question has its own correct measure of importance. The task of distinguishing the trivial from the substantive is not always easy; do not make it even more difficult by attempting to apply the wrong standard.

Question A: Reasons justify continuing? In examining a list of reasons that support the importance of a question, the issue of worth may be viewed from several dimensions: worth to the individual contemplating the answer and worth to the profession, to the academic community, and ultimately to society. Question A, "Reasons justify continuing?" is the question that the researcher must answer in terms of personal interests and needs. The world is full of clearly formulated and specific questions that may not, once seen in their formal dress, seem worth the effort of answering. Because researchers are human, perfectly legitimate questions may seem dull, interesting veins of inquiry may peter out into triviality, and well-defined issues may fail to suit for no better reason than a clash with personal style. On the other hand, some questions are supported by the researcher's immediate need to enhance teaching in a vital subject area or to quench curiosity about a long-held hunch.

The basic rule is to be honest before proceeding. If you really don't care about answering the question, it may be better to start again while the investment still is relatively small.

Step 6: Survey relevant literature. A preliminary scanning of the most obvious, pertinent resources, particularly reviews of the literature, is a way of husbanding time. It is far better to abandon a line of thought after several weeks of selective skimming than to work one's way via slow, thorough digestion of each document to the same conclusion after several months of effort.

Conscientious students sometimes feel vaguely guilty about such quick surveys. Keeping in mind the real purpose, which is to identify questions that already have satisfactory answers, is one way of easing such discomfort.

Question E: Reason for no answer remediable? In some cases the literature contains an empty area because the state of technology, the available knowledge framework, ethical considerations in completing the study, or the logistic demands peculiar to the question have made it impossible or unreasonable to conduct appropriate forms of inquiry. So long as the gap in knowledge seems to exist because no one has yet defined the question or become interested in pursuing the answer, it is reasonable to proceed. There are other reasons for empty or ambiguous areas in the literature, however, and they signal caution before proceeding.

Question I: Meaning of all possible results clear? The tighter the logic, the more elegant the theoretical framework, the more closely the design is tailored to produce clarity along one dimension—in short, the better the quality of the proposal—the greater the risk that the proposer will be lured into an unfortunate presumption: that the result of the study is known before the data are in hand. That student researchers sometimes are confronted by the stunning news that their treatment produced a reverse effect is in itself neither surprising nor harmful. Being unable to make an intelligent interpretation of such a situation, however, is unfortunate and in most cases unnecessary.

Unanticipated results raise a fundamental question that the investigator must confront. Does the finding truly reflect what is resident in the data, or is it only an artifact of the analysis? If there is any doubt about the appropriateness of the analysis, particularly if the procedures were not perfectly aligned with the research question, the latter possibility must be considered. If reexamination of the analysis provides no accounting for findings that are sharply incongruent with expectations, another explanation must be sought. All of this is made more difficult if the possibility of discrepant findings has never been contemplated. A strong proposal, constructed in an orderly, step-by-step sequence, will enhance the likelihood that the student can manage the unexpected with at least a degree of dignity.

By serious consideration of alternative outcomes at the time of constructing the proposal, it may be possible to include elements in the study that will eliminate ambiguity in some of the most likely results. One method of anticipating the unexpected is to follow through the consequences of rejecting or failing to reject each hypothesis of the study. If the hypothesis was rejected, what is the explanation? How is the explanation justified by the rationale for the study? What findings would support the explanation? Conversely, if the findings of the study fail to provide a basis for rejection, what explanations are to be proposed? At the least, some careful preliminary thought about alternative explanations for each possible result will serve as a shield against the panic that produces such awkward post hoc interpretations as "no significant differences were observed because the instruments employed were inadequate."

Step 16: Share and discuss with colleagues and advisors. There is a well-known syndrome displayed by some who attempt research, characterized by the inclination to prolong the period of writing the final report—indefinitely. Some people simply cannot face what they perceive to be the personal threat implied in opening their work to challenge in the public arena. These individuals are terribly handicapped and only rarely can become mature, productive scholars. An early sign of this is seen in students who cannot bring themselves to solicit advice and criticism for their proposals.

Sometimes students experience severe criticism because they present their ideas before they have been sufficiently developed into a conceptual framework that represents careful preparation. Many professors avoid speculative conversations about "half-baked" ideas that have just arrived in a blinding flash of revelation to the student. Few professors, however, refuse a request for advice concerning a proposal that has been drafted as the culmination of several weeks of hard thought, research, and development. Even at that, having one's best effort devastated by pointed criticism can be an agonizing experience. Nevertheless, the only alternative is to persist in error or ignorance, and that is untenable in research.

If the student is fortunate enough to be in a department that contains a vigorous community of inquiring minds, with the constant give and take of intellectual disputation, the rough and tumble soon will be regarded as a functional part of producing good research. The novice will solicit, if not always enjoy, the best criticism that can be found.

The notion that it is vaguely immoral to seek assistance in preparing a proposal is at best a parody of real science and at worst, as in the form of an institutional rule, it is a serious perversion arising from ignorance. Research may have some game-like qualities, but a system of handicaps is not one on them. The object of every inquiry is to get the best possible answer under the circumstance, and that presumes obtaining the best advice available. It is hoped that the student will not be held to any lesser standard.

It should be obvious that students, after digesting and weighing all the criticism received, must still make their own choices. Not all advice is good and not all criticism is valid. There is only one way to find out, however, and that is to share the proposal with colleagues whose judgments one can respect, if not always accept.

Step 19: Present to committee. Explain and support. Presentation of your proposal may take place before a thesis or dissertation committee on an occasion formally sanctioned by the graduate school, or at an informal gathering in the advisor's office. In either instance, the purpose served and the importance assumed will depend on both local traditions and the relationships that have evolved to that point among the chairperson, committee members, and the student.

If, for example, the chairperson has closely monitored the developing proposal and is satisfied that it is ready for final review and approval, the nature of the meeting is shaped accordingly. In addition, if other committee members have consulted on the proposal at various stages of writing, the meeting may serve primarily as an occasion for final review and a demonstration of presentation skills, rather than evaluation, extensive feedback, and judgment. When these conditions do not apply, the meeting assumes far greater significance, in itself, and the length and nature of the presentation will be affected.

Whatever the circumstance, both a prudent respect for the important function the committee members must perform and a proper desire to demonstrate the extent to which the efforts of your advisors have been effective make careful preparation and a good presentation an absolute necessity. Much of our advice about that is contained in Chapter 7. For the present purpose we want to underscore the following points.

1. The more you can work with committee members before an official meeting, the more that meeting can focus on improving (and appreciating) your proposal—rather than just on understanding it.
2. As committee members talk with you and with each other at the meeting, it is natural that new insights and concerns will surface. So long as those are accurately recorded, and so long as there is clear provision for how the committee will manage subsequent revisions in the proposal, that process is all to your advantage. The object is not simply to get the proposal (as it stands) accepted, it is to create the best possible plan for your dissertation or thesis.
3. Where you have had to make difficult choices, accept compromises in method for pragmatic reasons, or leave some final decision(s) for a later point in time, it is best to bring such matters directly to the attention of your committee. Don't wait to be questioned. Take the initiative and lay out the problematic aspects for your advisors as you go through the presentation. You need not make the proposed study appear to be mired in difficulty. Propose solutions and give your rationale. But never ignore or gloss over what you know requires more attention—and the help of your committee.
4. If the proposal is approved with the understanding that certain revisions or additions will be made, the best procedure is to obtain signatures on documents while at the meeting. The signed forms can then be held by your chairperson until he or she has approved the final draft.

Step 20: Gather data, process, and interpret as in proposal. This is the payoff. A good proposal is more than a guide to action, it is a framework for intelligent interpretation of results and the heart of a sound final report. The proposal cannot guarantee meaningful results, but it will provide some assurance that, whatever the result, the student can wind up the project with reasonable dispatch and at least a minimum of intellectual grace. If that sounds too small a recompense for all the effort, consider the alternative of having to write a report about an inconsequential question, pursued through inadequate methods of inquiry, and resulting in a heap of unanalyzable data.

ORIGINALITY AND REPLICATION:
WHAT IS A CONTRIBUTION TO KNOWLEDGE?

Some attention already has been given to considerations that precede the proposal, the critical and difficult steps of identifying and delimiting a research topic. One other preliminary problem, the question of originality, has important ramifications for the proposal.

Some advisors regard student-conducted research primarily as an arena for training, like wood-chopping that is expected to produce muscles in the person who holds the axe, but not much real fuel for the fire. Whatever may be the logic of such an assumption, students generally do not take the same attitude. Their expectations are more likely to resemble the classic dictum for scholarly research, to make an original contribution to the body of knowledge.

An all-too-common problem in selecting topics for research proposals occurs when either the student or an advisor gives literal interpretation to the word "original," defining it as "initial, first, never having existed or occurred before." This is a serious misinterpretation of the word as it is used in science. In research, the word "original" clearly includes all studies deliberately employed to test the accuracy of results or the applicability of conclusions developed in previous studies. What is not included under that rubric are studies that proceed mindlessly to repeat an existing work either in ignorance of its existence or without appropriate attention to its defects or limitations.

One consequence of the confusion surrounding the phrase "original contribution" is that misguided students and advisors are led to ignore one of the most important areas of research activity and one

of the most useful forms of training for the novice researcher—
replication. That replication sometimes is regarded simply as rote
imitation, lacking sufficient opportunity for students to apply and
develop their own skills, is an indication of how badly some students
misunderstand both the operation of a research enterprise and the
concept of a body of knowledge.

The essential role of replication in research has been cogently
argued (Borg & Gall, 1989). What has not been made sufficiently
clear, however, is that replication can involve challenging problems
that demand creative resolution. Further, some advisors do not appreciate the degree to which writing proposals for replicative studies
can constitute an ideal learning opportunity for research trainees.

In direct replication, students must not only correctly identify all
the critical variables in the original study, but also create equivalent
conditions for the conduct of their own study. Anyone who thinks
that the critical variables will immediately be apparent from a reading of the original report has not read very widely in the research
literature. Similarly, an individual who thinks that truly equivalent
conditions can be created simply by "doing it the same way" just has
not tried to perform a replicative study. Thorough understanding of
the problem and, frequently, a great deal of technical ingenuity are
demanded in developing an adequate proposal for direct replication.

As an alternative to direct replication, the student may repeat an
interesting study considered to have been defective in sample, method,
analysis, or interpretation. Here the student introduces deliberate
changes to improve the power of a previous investigation. It would
be difficult to imagine a more challenging or useful activity for
anyone interested in both learning about research and contributing
to the accumulation of reliable knowledge.

In writing a proposal for either kind of replicative study, direct or
revised, the student should introduce the original with appropriate
citation, make the comments that are needed, and proceed without
equivocation or apology to the proposed study. Replicative research
is not, as unfortunate tradition has it in some departments, slightly
improper or something less than genuine research.

The cross-validation study is another type of investigation that
sometimes is characterized as unoriginal, and even may be confused
with replication. An excellent example of a cross-validation study
has been provided by Willoughby and Bixby (1991). Cross-validation
studies most frequently appear in conjunction with or following

prediction studies, in which the investigator attempts to determine an equation by which to predict a variable or variables. The equations that are derived for the sample used, however, may have been affected by chance correlations and errors of measurement to the extent that the investigator cannot be sure how predictive the selected set of variables would be for other samples.

Two techniques of cross validation are used. In one technique the investigator computes a predicted score for each subject—on the basis of the equation derived from the original study—and then correlates predicted scores with the scores that actually were measured in the second sample. In some situations the total sample is split into two groups to provide equal samples for the cross validation. If a very high correlation is obtained between those predicted scores and the measured scores in an entirely different sample, the original set of independent variables with their given weights has been validated as being generally predictive of the dependent variable. A second technique is to use the second sample to derive a new set of regression weights and a new multiple R statistic for the originally selected independent variables.

Another situation in which cross validation is used involves studies in which an investigator selects from a large pool of test items those that significantly discriminate between two or more groups. Again, chance plays a role in the differentiation of the groups—perhaps creating spuriously large differences or an inflated correlation between the criterion and the sample on which the selection of items was based. In studies of this type, cross validation on additional groups is required.

Irrespective of the situation in which cross validation is used, or the technique used to accomplish it, it should be readily apparent that cross validation does not require a completely original effort. Yet it is a technique sorely needed in the behavioral sciences where the body of knowledge would be expanded and refined much more rapidly if many of the hundreds of theses undertaken each year were careful cross validations or replications rather than inexperienced and misguided attempts at originality.

Given the limitations of research reports, it often is useful to discuss the source study for the replication or cross validation with the original author. Most research workers are happy to provide greater detail and in some instances raw data for inspection or reanalysis. In a healthy science, replication is the most sincere form of flattery. A proposal appendix containing correspondence with the author of the original report, or data not provided in that report, often can serve to interest and reassure a hesitant advisor.

GETTING STARTED:
PRODUCING THE FIRST DRAFT

The student who has never written a research proposal commonly sits in front of a desk and stares at a blank piece of paper or an empty video monitor for hours. The mind is brimming with knowledge gleaned from the literature, but how does one actually get started? The concept of "a research proposal" conjures up ideas of accuracy, precision, meticulous form, and the use of a language system that is new and unpracticed by the neophyte researcher. The demands can suddenly seem overwhelming. The student should realize that this feeling of panic is experienced by nearly everyone, not only those who are new to the writing endeavor but those who are skilled as well. Fanger (1985) expressed it beautifully: "I have come to regard panic as the inevitable concomitant of any kind of serious academic writing" (p. 28). For anyone temporarily incapacitated by a blank page or empty monitor, the following suggestions may be helpful.

Make an outline that is compatible with the format selected to present the communication tasks listed in Chapter 1. An initial approval of the outline by the advisor may save revision time later. Gather the resource materials, notes, and references, and organize them into groups that correspond to the outline topics. For instance, notes supporting the rationale for the study would be in one group, and notes supporting the reliability of an instrument to be used would be in another group.

Once the outline is made and the materials gathered, tackle one of the topics in the outline (not necessarily the first) and start writing. If the section to be written is labeled "The Problem," try imagining that someone has asked, "What is the problem of this study?" Your task is to answer that question. Start writing. Do not worry about grammar, syntax, or writing within the language system. Just write. In this way you can avoid one of the greatest inhibitions to creativity—self-criticism so severe that each idea is rejected before it becomes reality. Remember, it is easier to correct than to create. If all the essential parts of a topic are displayed in some fashion, they can later be rearranged, edited, and couched within the language system. With experience, the novice will begin thinking in the language system and forms of the proposal. Until that time, the essential problem is to begin. Awkward or elegant, laborious or swift, there is no substitute for writing the first draft.

If you have access to a microcomputer with a word processing program, the same steps hold, but the revisions will be much easier. If you do not have your own computer, some academic departments and most universities have facilities that students can use for little or no cost. Locating these facilities and learning a word processing program will make the writing task much easier. One way to approach writing on a word processor is to use the outline feature, which allows you to develop your outline and then go back and progressively fill in the detail under each heading. Learn to use this feature. The effort needed to learn its use will be repaid many times over. Word processing programs, which now provide the opportunity to edit, rearrange text easily, and store manuscript copy for future revision, offer great economy. Further, there is a significant psychological advantage in the ease with which revised drafts can be produced. This encourages the author to make revisions that might otherwise be set aside under the press of limited time.

SELECTING YOUR THESIS
OR DISSERTATION COMMITTEE

Master's thesis committees vary in number from one professor to a committee of five or six faculty members. A doctoral dissertation committee typically consists of four to six members. In some instances, all committee members are from within the department of the student's major. In other instances, the committee is multidisciplinary, with faculty representing other departments on campus.

At most universities, students have some opportunity to request specific faculty members for their committee. If the student does have some freedom to exercise choice, committee membership should be designed to maximize the support and assistance available. A student interested in the study of behavioral treatment of drug abuse in young upwardly mobile women, could tap the value of different faculty perspectives and skills by blending members from several departments. For this purpose individuals with multiple interests are particularly useful. For example, a faculty member in the psychology department might be selected both for statistical competence and interest in behavior modification, someone in the school of social work might bring epidemiological expertise regarding drug usage, and a faculty member in the school of public health might be a part of the committee because of expertise in both experimental design and therapeutic compliance techniques.

Because students know from the beginning of the graduate program that faculty will eventually have to be selected for such a committee, it behooves them to be thinking about these matters during the selection of elective courses throughout the program. If a choice has to be made between two professors for an elective course, and one of them is more interested in the student's probable area of research, that may carry the day in determining which course to take. Although it is not essential that students have taken their committee members' class, it is easier to ask a known faculty member to serve on your committee. They are likely to take a greater interest in your work, and you have a good idea of their standards and methods of scholarship.

4

Content of the Proposal

Important Considerations

The topics covered in this chapter are designed to assist the true beginner. Most experienced proposal writers may want to go directly to Chapter 7 or simply skim this chapter for review.

REVIEWING THE LITERATURE: FINDING IT FIRST

Areas of inquiry within the disciplines exist as ongoing conversations among those who do the work of scholarship. The published literature of an area constitutes the archival record of those conversations: research reports, research reviews, theoretical speculation, and scholarly discourse of all kinds. You join the long conversation of science as you join any other, by first listening to what is being said, and only then formulating a comment designed to advance the dialogue.

The metaphor of scholarship as an extended conversation works well at a variety of levels—because at heart it is an accurate representation. The process of locating the voices of individual conversants, for example, is called *retrieval*. That involves searching through the accumulated archive of literature to find out what has been said (when, by whom, and on the basis of what evidence). The process of listening carefully to the ongoing discourse about a topic of inquiry is called *review*. That involves studying items previously retrieved until both the history and current state of the conversation are understood. It does not stretch the metaphor too far to observe that writing the proposal is a step in preparing yourself to have your own voice be heard—to do research and enter what you learn into the long conversation.

Retrieval, review, proposing and conducting research, and even report writing, are tasks that have their own sets of requisite technical skills. Each also has a place for art and instinct as well as intelligence and accumulated knowledge. This chapter deals with what goes into the proposal (content) once the topic and terms of discourse have been defined. It follows, then, that it must begin with what you have learned by listening in on the conversation—a review of the literature. In your review, you will establish what has been said to this point as the basis for proposing your own contribution. Retrieval, however, comes first in the order of things. You can't review what you haven't found. That brings us to the technical skill and fine art of searching the literature.

We will not burden you with the specifics of a particular search procedure. The demands made by proposals differ widely, as do the background and skills of each proposal writer. Further, the facilities for retrieval vary enormously at different institutions and, of course, each discipline and sub-specialty has its own peculiar mechanisms for searching the literature. What we can do here is set forth the small number of general rules, which, if observed from the outset, have the power to make any retrieval effort more efficient.

Knowing what you need to know is the obvious first step in formulating a retrieval strategy. Knowing how much you really need to know, however, is a vital second step—and one not always properly appreciated by the novice in research. Discussion with your advisor, consultation with colleagues who have written proposals, inspection of proposals previously accepted by the graduate school, and the preliminary reading already done during the process of identifying the topic of your proposed study will all serve to identify what you need to know—and thereby the literature you will seek. Normally that includes research reports and reviews related to your questions or hypotheses. This literature provides information about research methodology in the area and items dealing with both theory and application as they are related to your study.

Deciding how much you need to know is a more complex decision—in part because you often cannot answer that question until after some retrieval and review already has been accomplished. This is a matter of defining the purpose to be served by what you retrieve. Acquiring a broad overview of previous work in an area leads to one kind of retrieval strategy. If your purpose is to know what a small set of senior scholars have reported in the last two years, the strategy will be different, as will be the case if your purpose is to do an exhaustive search in which every scrap of fugitive literature is doggedly pursued until acquired.

What we suggest is that you talk with your advisor about the question of "how much?" and that you stay in touch with him or her on that topic as you proceed. The notion that every search of the literature needs to be exhaustive is one of the more destructive mythologies that persists in graduate student culture. When you have enough sense of the conversation to argue persuasively that the target for your proposed study is sound, and that the methods of inquiry are correct, you know enough for the purpose of the proposal.

Over a longer period of time you may have plenty of motivation to read more widely and deeply than anything demanded by your proposal, but that is a different matter. For the present, it is wise to acquire some sense of how much you need know so that you can shape the size of your review task accordingly—and thereby know what and how much to retrieve. Until you have done some retrieval and review, it is likely that neither you nor your advisor will be able to set that target with precision, but some careful preliminary thought will serve you well.

Retrieval Rule 1. Do not begin by going to the library and starting to search for literature. Talk first to your advisor (or entire thesis or dissertation committee) and research colleagues who have some familiarity with the area of your proposal. Make a list of what they think you should read. Locate the items, skim them, and record full citations for all that appear to be appropriate. These form the core of your retrieved literature base. Go over the reference lists in the items that appear to be most directly relevant to your needs and make those citations the priority for retrieval when you return to the library.

Retrieval Rule 2. When you go to the library, do not begin by starting to search for literature. Talk first to the reference specialists who can identify the retrieval systems that are most likely to be productive for your topic. Retrieval is one part sweat and two parts knowing where to look.

For nearly every scholar, the marvels of computerized retrieval are available. The data bases that any given system can access, however, differ in important and subtle ways. Asking for expert help can save hours. Swift, accurate, flexible, and powerful beyond anything we could have dreamed only a decade ago, computer retrieval systems are, nonetheless, only as good as their indexing structures, and those are just as full of limitations and idiosyncratic quirks as any of the printed indexes with which everyone is familiar.

That observation leads to two items of advice. First, plan to devote a considerable amount of retrieval time to learning how each system works. Second, by all means use computerized systems whenever they are available, but do not automatically assume that manual search is without value. In other words, all but a very small number of highly technical topics can profit by a visit to whatever is the equivalent to the *Reader's Guide to Periodical Literature* in your particular subject area.

Retrieval Rule 3. From the outset, think of your retrieval effort as consisting of a series of stages. It is unlikely that you will (or should) march through them in perfect sequence; it is more a matter of moving back and forth among the stages in ways that will make best use of your time.

Stage 1: Identification—Find and record citations that seem potentially relevant. This is work done with indexes, bibliographies, reference lists, and, increasingly, with the computer.

Stage 2: Confirmation—Determine that the items identified can be obtained for use. This is work done with the library holdings of serials and books, reprint services, interlibrary loan personnel, microfiche files, and the telephone.

Stage 3: Skimming and Screening—Assess each item to confirm that it actually contains content to be reviewed (to be read and studied with care). This is work that demands enough mastery of the system language and the constructs related to your topic to recognize what is and is not of potential use. Much of this (though not all) can be accomplished without taking the resource item into your physical possession. This means time in the stacks and time at the microfiche reader. The most important retrieval skill here is the ability to resist the temptation to stop the work of skimming and screening and immerse yourself in the conversation.

Stage 4: Retrieval—Acquire the literature. This is work done by checking out books, copying articles from journals, ordering microfiche and reprints, and initiating requests for interlibrary loans. Not everything must be (or should be) retrieved. There is a strong argument for not having every article immediately at hand when you are drafting the review of literature, and one way to insure that is to take notes from references that then stay in the stacks.

Stage 5: Review—Read and study the literature that records the conversation about your topic. Subsequent sections of this chapter will deal with how to use what you learn to build your proposal.

Retrieval Rule 4. From the first moment of your search, keep a log of all the words used to name what you have to learn about. These will become the key words used by indexing systems (often they are specifically designated as key words by the authors) for accessing their holdings. Building a key word list is like acquiring a set of master keys to a large building. They can open doors in a variety of locations, and without them you can wander for hours without gaining entry to anywhere you want to be. In almost every case, the novice will be astonished at the variety of words and phrases employed to file away items that appear to be identical.

Retrieval Rule 5. Always take maximum advantage of other people's work. For that reason, research reviews in your area always should have the highest priority in your search plan, as should annotated bibliographies and the reference list at the back of every article and book you retrieve. For the same reason, your first stop in the library should be *Dissertation Abstracts International* (and *Masters Abstracts*). What could be a better search strategy than reading the reviews of literature crafted by students who have worked on similar problems? Dissertations are the *Yellow Pages* of research retrieval. From the start, let your fingers do a lot of the walking.

Retrieval Rule 6. Record a complete citation for every item you identify. Whether with index cards or a computer program that alphabetizes and sorts by key words, keep a complete running record of what you find—whether immediately reviewed, or not. No frustration can match that of having to backtrack to the library for a missing volume or page number.

Retrieval Rule 7. Whatever notes you may take during the stages of Skimming and Screening or Review, never write anything down in which there could be the slightest confusion at a later date as to whether the words are your own—or those of another author. If you take down a quote, take it verbatim and attach the proper page citation. If you write anything other than a direct quote, make absolutely sure it is a paraphrase in your own words. There is no place for anything in between those two species of notes.

If you follow these seven rules, if you build a reasonable sense of how much you really need to know, and if you persist, you may have one of the most wonderful epiphanies a scholar can experience. As you look down a page of references, you will recognize all the names, and the voices of their conversation will fill your ears. At that moment, you are current and you are ready to take part. Given the pace of work in many areas of science that moment will be brief, but savor it! That is the sweet fruit of retrieval.

REVIEWING THE LITERATURE: WRITING THE RIGHT STUFF

By much deserved reputation, the reviews of literature in student research proposals are regarded as consisting of clumsy and turgid prose, written as *pro forma* response to a purely ceremonial obligation in the planning format. Even when carefully crafted with regard to basic mechanics they make dull reading, and when not so prepared they are excruciating torture for most readers. Much of this problem arises from a misunderstanding of the task served by reviewing the literature, and none of it need be true.

To begin, the common designation used in proposals, "review of the literature," is a misleading if not completely inappropriate title. A research proposal is not the place to review the body of literature that bears on a problematic area, or even the place to examine all the research that relates to the specific question raised in the proposal. A variety of methods for "reviewing the literature" do exist, such as best evidence synthesis, critical reviews, and even meta-analysis, but they are rarely appropriate for proposals. Analyses of that kind may be useful documents publishable in their own right. Indeed, some journals such as the *Review of Educational Research* are exclusively devoted to such critical retrospectives on scholarship. The task to be performed in the proposal, however, is different. It is not inferior to the true review, it simply is different.

In writing a research proposal, the author is obligated to place the question or hypothesis in the context of previous work in such a way as to explain and justify the decisions made. That alone is required. Nothing more is appropriate and nothing more should be attempted. Although the author may wish to persuade the reader on many different kinds of points, ranging from the significance of the question to the appropriateness of a particular form of data analysis, sound proposals devote most of the literature review to explaining (a) exactly how and why the research question or hypothesis was formulated in the proposed form and (b) exactly why the proposed research strategy was elected. What is required to accomplish these tasks is a step-by-step explanation of decisions, punctuated by reference to studies that support the ongoing argument. In this the writer uses previous work, often some critique of previous work, and sometimes some exposition of the broad pattern of knowledge as it exists in the area to appeal for the reader's acceptance of the logic represented in the proposed study.

Whatever particular arguments must be sustained in the review of the literature, there is no place for the "Smith says this . . ." and "Jones says that . . ." paragraph-by-paragraph recital that makes novice proposals instruments for dulling the senses. This is the place to answer the reader's most immediate questions: What is it the author wants to know, and why has this plan been devised to find the answer? In a good review, the literature is made to serve the reader's query by supporting, explicating, and illuminating the logic now implicit in the proposed investigation.

It follows, then, that where there is little relevant literature, or where decisions are clear-cut and without substantial issues, the review should be brief. In some cases the examination of supporting literature may best be appended or woven into another section of the proposal. To write a review of literature for the sake of having a review in the document is to make it a parody and not a proposal.

Remember, the writer's task is to employ the research literature artfully to support and explain the choices made *for this study,* not to educate the reader concerning the state of science in the problem area. Neither is the purpose of the section to display the energy and thoroughness with which the author has pursued a comprehensive understanding of the literature. If the author can explain and support the question, design, and procedures with a minimum demand on the reader's time and intellect, then he or she will be more than sufficiently impressed with the applicant's capabilities and serious purpose.

None of this is intended to undervalue the task that every researcher must face, that of locating and thoroughly assimilating what is already known. To do this the student must experience what Fanger (1985) described as "immersion in the subject" by reading extensively in the areas that either are directly or indirectly related to the topic of study. This may lead at first to a sense of frustration and confusion, but perseverance usually leads out of the wilderness to the point at which what is known about the topic can be seen in the light of what is not known. The goals of the proposed study can be projected against that backdrop.

The proposal is the place to display the refined end products of that long and difficult process. It is not uncommon, for example, for the study's best support to emerge from a sophisticated understanding of gaps in the body of knowledge, limitations in previous formulations of the question, inadequate methods of data collection, or inappropriate interpretation of results. The review of the literature section then becomes a vehicle for illustrating why and how it all can be done better. What readers need, however, is not a full tour retracing each step the author took in arriving at the better mousetrap, but a concise summary of the main arguments properly juxtaposed to the new and better plan for action.

Most students will agonize over the many studies discovered that, while fascinating and perhaps even inspiring during the immersion process, in the final stages of writing turn out to fail the test of critical relevance and therefore merit exclusion from the proposal. It is tempting to see discarded studies and unused note cards as wasted time, but that misses the long view of learning. The knowledge gained through synthesis and evaluation of research results builds a knowledge base for the future. The process of immersion in the literature provides not only the information that will support the proposal, but the intellectual framework for future expertise. What may appear in the crush of deadlines and overload stress to have been pursuit down blind alleys, ultimately may provide insights that will support new lines of thought and future proposals.

Writing the section on related literature often is no more complex than first describing the major concepts that led you to your research question or hypothesis and then describing the supporting research findings already in the literature. It may be as simple as hypothesizing that A is greater than C. Why do you hypothesize that A is greater than C? Because evidence suggests that A is greater than B, and B is greater than C, therefore it is reasonable to hypothesize that A must be greater than C.

In the review of related literature, you express these conceptual relationships in an organized fashion and then document them with previously reported studies. For example, the first section would include the most important studies indicating that A is greater than B, and the second section would include studies that suggest that B is greater than C. The literature section of your proposal would conclude by showing that, given this information, it is reasonable to hypothesize that A is greater than C.

Look at the example in Table 4.1, which also is represented diagrammatically in Figure 4.1. In this table the general research question is posed, followed by the specific hypothesis through which the question will be answered. They are shown here merely to establish the frame of reference for the outline. In this example of the development of the related literature, three major concepts are necessary to support the legitimacy of this hypothesis. In Table 4.1, the question suggests that the way physical fitness and cognitive function are related is through a change in brain aerobic capacity as a result of training. If this is a reasonable question to ask, one would have to show that there have been some prior studies in which physical fitness level has been related to some measure of cognitive function (concept I). Second, some evidence that cognitive function might be altered by aerobic functional capacity of the brain should be shown (concept II). Finally, some evidence should exist that physical movement can alter blood flow shifts in the brain, and that blood flow shifts are related to aerobic capacity (concept III).

Generally, the major concepts are supported by two or three subtopics, all of which lead to the formalization of the main concept. For example, the concept that reaction time and physical fitness level are related (I) can be supported in three different ways, by showing (a) that reaction time is faster in physically fit persons than in sedentary persons, (b) that physical training enhances reaction time, and (c) that reaction time in those on the lowest end of the physical fitness continuum is the slowest of all. Each of these subtopics is supported by the findings from several studies, as shown in the third stage outline section of the table.

Writing the related literature section is much easier if an outline is developed in stages of increasingly greater detail, as shown in

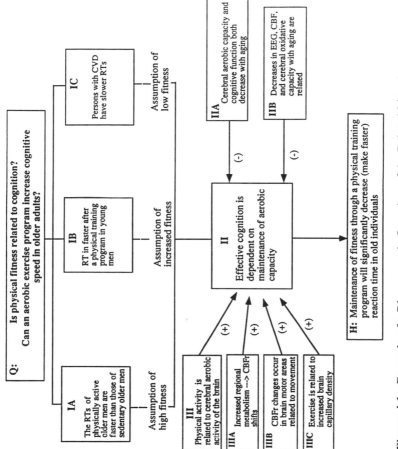

Q: Is physical fitness related to cognition?
Can an aerobic exercise program increase cognitive speed in older adults?

IA
The RTs of physically active older men are faster than those of sedentary older men

Assumption of high fitness

IB
RT in faster after a physical training program in young men

Assumption of increased fitness

IC
Persons with CVD have slower RTs

Assumption of low fitness

II
Effective cognition is dependent on maintenance of aerobic capacity

IIA
Cerebral aerobic capacity and cognitive function both decrease with aging

(–)

IIB
Decreases in EEG, CBF, and cerebral oxidative capacity with aging are related

(–)

III
Physical activity is related to cerebral aerobic activity of the brain

(+)

IIIA
Increased regional metabolism --> CBF shifts

(+)

IIIB
CBFr changes occur in brain motor areas related to movement

(+)

IIIC
Exercise is related to increased brain capillary density

(+)

H: Maintenance of fitness through a physical training program will significantly decrease (make faster) reaction time in old individuals

Figure 4.1. Example of a Diagrammatic Overview of the Related Literature

TABLE 4.1 Preparing the Related Literature Section

QUESTION: Is physical fitness related to cognition in older adults? More specifically, can an aerobic exercise program increase cognitive processing speed in older adults?

HYPOTHESIS: Maintenance of fitness through a physical training program will significantly decrease (make faster) reaction time in old individuals.

First Stage Outline: Develop the Concepts that Provide the Rationale for the Study

I. Reaction time is related to physical fitness level.

II. Maintenance of cognitive function is dependent on maintenance of aerobic capacity in the brain.

III. The aerobic capacity of brain tissue is affected by physical activity-related regional cerebrovascular changes.

Second Stage Outline: Develop the Subtopics for Each Major Concept

I. Reaction time is related to physical fitness level.

    A. Comparisons of the reaction time of physically active and inactive subjects

    B. Training effects on reaction time

    C. Reaction time of those in poor physical condition (cardiovascular disease, hypertension)

II. Maintenance of cognitive function is dependent on maintenance of aerobic capacity in the brain.

    A. Relationship of cognitive function and brain aerobic capacity in aging individuals

    B. Relationship of a neurological measure of brain function, electroencephography (EEG), to cerebral blood flow and cerebral oxygen uptake in older subjects

III. The aerobic capacity of brain tissue is affected by physical activity-related regional cerebrovascular changes.

    A. Increased metabolism in specific regions leads to cerebral blood flow shifts to those regions.

    B. Regional blood flow shifts in motor areas of the brain are related to physical movement.

    C. Exercise is related to changes in brain capillarization.

Table 4.1, prior to the actual writing. Once the outline is developed, this section of the proposal can be written in a straightforward

TABLE 4.1 Continued

Third Stage Outline: Add the Most Important References That Support Each Subtopic

   I. Reaction time is related to physical fitness level.

      A. Physically active individuals have faster reaction times than do sedentary individuals (Botwinick & Storandt, 1974; Chodzko-Zajko & Ringel, 1987; Clarkson-Smith & Hartley, 1989; Dustman et al., 1990; Emmerson, Dustman & Sheaver, 1989; Spirduso, 1975; Spirduso & Clifford, 1977; Stones & Kozma, 1988).

      B. Reaction time is faster after a physical training program (Dustman et al., 1984; Gibson, Karpovitch, & Gollnick, 1961; Matsui, 1971; Tweit, Gollnick, & Hearn, 1963; Rickli & Edwards, 1991; Spirduso & Farrar, 1981; but see Blumenthal & Madden, 1988; Blumenthal et al., 1991; Madden et al., 1989).

      C. Cardiovascular-diseased patients have slower reaction time than normal individuals (Abrahams & Birren, 1980; Benton, 1977; Birren, Woods, & Williams, 1980; Hicks & Birren, 1970; Simonson & Enzer, 1941; Speith, 1965).

  II. Maintenance of cognitive function is dependent on maintenance of aerobic capacity in the brain.

      A. Both cognitive function and aerobic capacity decrease with age (Simonson, 1965; Welford, 1977).

      B. EEG, cerebral blood flow, and cerebral oxidative capacity decrease with age are related (Fitzpatrick et al., 1976; Hevischaft & Junze, 1977; Ingvar, Sjelund, & Ardo, 1976; Obrist, 1975).

 III. The aerobic capacity of brain tissue is affected by physical activity-related regional cerebrovascular changes.

      A. Increased regional metabolism leads to blood flow shifts (Crossman & Szafran, 1956; Injer, 1978; Szafran, 1965).

      B. Regional blood flow shifts to motor areas of the brain are related to physical movements being controlled (Halsey, Blanenstein, Wilson, & Wills, 1979; Ingvar & Skinjk, 1978; Lassen, Ingvar, & Skinhoj, 1978).

      C. Exercise is related to changes in brain capillarization (Black et al., 1990; Isaacs et al., 1992).

manner, with little backtracking necessary. If meticulous care is taken in selecting each reference, an enormous amount of time will be saved in the long run.

TABLE 4.2 Steps in Writing the Related Literature Section

---

1. Determine the major concepts (generally no more than two or three) that are pertinent to the proposed research question. That is, what are the concepts that must be true in order for your question to be appropriate or your hypothesis tenable?

2. List concepts either in descending order of importance or in terms of logical presentation. That is, does one concept have to be understood before another can be introduced?

3. Prepare an outline with these major concepts as the major headings (such as the one in Table 4.1, concepts I, II, III).

4. Under each major heading list the articles that are most directly related (authors and dates only).

5. If the articles under a major heading cluster themselves and suggest a subheading, then arrange the clusters (and their subheadings) under the major heading in logical order. For example, you might note that of nine studies pertaining to the notion of a relationship between reaction time and physical fitness, in five of these reaction times of animals were reported, whereas in the other four studies the reaction times were from humans. The interpretation of these studies, when clustered in terms of type of subject, might be different and have a substantial bearing on the potential outcome of the proposed research.

6. Without referring to the details in the articles, summarize in one paragraph the combined findings of each cluster of studies. For example, in concept I.A. of Table 4.1, the summary might be that reaction time of physically active men and women is faster than that of sedentary individuals, as long as the subjects are over 60 years old. The summary of concept I.B. might be that aerobic training improves reaction time, but strength training in older individuals does not improve reaction time. At some point you will have to discuss the interpretation to be made from different results of physical fitness on reaction time, depending on the way physical fitness as an independent variable is measured.

Another easy way to conceptualize the organization of the related literature is to diagram it, as shown in Figure 4.1. In this figure, the question (Q) is shown in the first box, and then the major components of the rationale are shown as they relate to each other. Component I refers to the behavioral observations that have been reported in the research literature. Component II refers to the literature in which the effects of aging on cerebral aerobic capacity and cognitive function

TABLE 4.2 Continued

---

7. Write an introductory paragraph explaining what the two or three major areas are and in what order they will be discussed. Explain why the order used was selected, if that is important. Explain why some literature may be omitted if it might seem logical to the reader that it would be included.

8. Write a statement at the end of each section summarizing the findings within each cluster of studies. Show how this summary of findings relates to those of the cluster of studies described in the following paragraphs.

9. Write a paragraph at the end of each major topic that summarizes the major points, supports the cohesiveness of the subtopics, and establishes the relevance of these concepts to the proposed research question.

10. Write a paragraph at the conclusion that draws together all of the major summarizing paragraphs.

11. Read the paragraphs and subject them to the "Guidelines for Evaluation of Related Literature Section" (Table 4.3).

12. After all of these concepts and subtopics have been carefully introduced, described, and summarized, return to the beginning and insert the documentation for each of the concepts in the proper location. That is, document the statements made in each of the paragraphs by describing the studies leading to them or verifying them.

13. Each time a reference is inserted, place the complete citation in a special file for eventual compilation of a reference list.

14. After a week has passed, reread the related literature section and again use the "Guidelines for Evaluating the Related Literature Section" that are provided in Table 4.3. Make whatever revisions seem necessary and wait one more week.

15. Read the entire related literature section for coherence, continuity, and smoothness of transition from one concept to another. Check carefully for accuracy of all citations and edit for mechanics.

---

are described. Because these relationships have negative outcomes, they are shown with a negative sign. Component III refers to all literature that provides support for a relationship between physical activity and cerebral aerobic activity. In this case, these are all positive relationships, which are shown with plus signs. Finally, the last box depicts how all of these relationships lead to the hypothesis (H) of the study.

TABLE 4.3 Guidelines for Evaluating the Related Literature Section

After you have written the first draft of the related literature section, answer the questions below. Mark the manuscript where the answers to each of these questions are located.

1. Is there a paragraph outlining the organization of the related literature section?
2. Does the order of the headings and subheadings represent the relative importance of the topics and subtopics? Is the order of headings logical?
3. Are there summary paragraphs for each of the two or three major sections and an overall summary at the end?
4. Is the relation of the proposed study to past and current research clearly shown in the summary paragraphs?
5. What new answers (extension of the body of knowledge) will the proposed research provide?
6. What is distinctive or different about the proposed research compared with previous research? Is this clearly stated? Is this introduced in the first few paragraphs?
7. What are the most relevant articles (no more than five) that bear on this research? Underline these references. Are they listed under the first topical heading?
8. Are these articles presented in a way that denotes their importance? Are some cited so many times they lose power through repetition?
9. Has the evaluation of these key articles been presented succinctly in terms of both procedures and interpretation of results?
10. Have the results from your own pilot studies been interwoven into the synthesis of the related literature?

Both the outline and diagram format can be very helpful in conceptualizing the related literature. The entire process can be summarized in the 15 steps in Table 4.2. Table 4.3 contains guidelines for evaluating the related literature section.

SPADEWORK:
THE PROPER USE OF PILOT STUDIES

The pilot study is an especially useful form of anticipation, and one too often neglected in student proposals. When it comes to convincing the scholarly skeptic (often your own advisor), no argument can be so effective as to write, "I tried it and here is how it worked."

It is difficult to imagine any proposal that could not be improved by the reporting of actual preliminary work. Whether it is to demonstrate instrument reliability, the practicality of procedures, the availability of volunteers, the variability of observed events as a basis for power tests, subjects' capabilities, or the investigator's skills, the modest pilot study is the best possible basis for making wise decisions in designing research.

The pilot study, for example, is an excellent means by which to determine the sample size necessary to discover significant differences among experimental treatments.[1] Sample size estimation or "power analysis" recently has become commonplace in quantitative research. Although it always has been an important component of good research, it has become more frequently used because of the availability of easy-to-use books and computer programs. A particularly useful introduction to power analysis, replete with examples and tables, is *How Many Subjects?* (Kraemer & Thiemann, 1987). In addition, a number of computer programs are available—some of which only require the user to answer a few questions before calculating sample size. Because software is being updated quickly, we suggest inquiring at your institution's statistical consulting office or computer center to find out what is available.

Pilot data and a few decisions (primarily related to the error rates you want for the study) allow researchers to estimate the sample size needed to find significance, if in fact it exists in the data. It is possible that the estimated sample size required will be so large as to be prohibitive, in which case, method and measurement tools should be reexamined. In the ideal case, a power analysis will inform the researcher of an appropriate sample size based on permissible error and the data—not just from arbitrary guessing. It is better to find the appropriate sample size in advance, rather than after the fact. Both a sample size that precludes a significant finding and the use of more subjects than needed are wastes of time and effort.

The use of even a few subjects in an informal trial can reveal a fatal flaw before it can destroy months of work. The same trial may even provide a fortunate opportunity to improve the precision of the investigation or to streamline cumbersome methods. For all these reasons, students and advisors should not insist on holding stringent, formal standards for exploratory studies. A pilot study is a pilot study; its target is the practicality of proposed operations, not the creation of empirical truth.

Examples of purposes that pilot studies might serve include the following:

1. To determine the reliability of measurement in your own laboratory
2. To ensure that differences that you expect to exist, do in fact exist—that is, if you are studying the different effects of gender on motivation, make sure the gender difference exists
3. To "save" a sample that is difficult to obtain until the real research project is undertaken—that is, it is prudent to test available subjects until procedural bugs are worked out before testing world-class athletes
4. To determine the best type of skills to use as an independent variable; for example, effects of different ankle braces on knee mobility—test jumping vertically, horizontally, and while running, then select one.

The presentation of pilot study results sometimes does create a troublesome problem. Readers may be led inadvertently to expect more of pilot work than it can reasonably deliver. Their concerns with the limitations may distract from its limited use in the main line of the argument being advanced by the author. Accordingly, the best course is to make no more of the pilot study than it honestly is worth—most are no more than a report of limited experience under less than perfectly controlled conditions—and do so only when the report will best illuminate the choices made in the proposal.

Brief reference to pilot work may be made in supporting the broad research strategies selected consequent to the review of research. Some pilot studies may, in fact, be treated as one of the works worthy of review. More commonly, however, the results of exploratory studies are used in supporting specific procedures proposed in the section dealing with methodology.

When the pilot study represents a formal and relatively complete research effort, it is proper to cite the work in some detail, including actual data. When the preliminary work has been informal or limited, it may be introduced as a footnote to the main text. In the latter case, it may be desirable to provide a more detailed account of the work in a section of the appendix, leaving the reader the choice of pursuing the matter further if desired.

MURPHY'S LAW:
ANTICIPATING THE UNEXPECTED

Murphy's Law dictates that, in the conduct of research, if anything can go wrong, it probably will. This is accepted by experienced researchers and research advisors but rarely is considered by the novice. Within reasonable limits, the proposal is the place to provide for confrontation with the inexorable operation of Murphy's Law. Subject attrition cannot be prevented, but its effects can be circumscribed by careful planning. The potentially biasing effects created by nonreturns in questionnaire studies can be examined and, to some degree, mitigated by plans laid carefully in the proposal. The handling of subjects in the event of equipment failure is far better considered at leisure, in writing the proposal, than in the face of an unanticipated emergency. Field research in the public schools can provide a range of surprises, including indisposed teachers, fire drills, and inclement weather, all better managed by anticipation than by snap decisions forged in the heat of sudden necessity.

Equipment failure may interrupt carefully timed data collection sequences, or temporary computer breakdowns may delay data processing and analysis. At best such accidents will do no more than alter the time schedule for the study. At worst they may require substitutions or substantive changes in the procedures. Each step of the research process should be studied with regard to potential difficulty, and plans in the event of a problem should be stated in the appropriate place within the proposal. For instance, if unequal subject attrition occurs across groups, the type of analysis to be used with unequal *N*s should be stated in the analysis section of the proposal.

It is impossible to anticipate everything that can happen. A good proposal, however, provides contingency plans for the most important problems that may arise in the course of conducting the study.

ANTICIPATING THE ANALYSIS:
DO IT NOW

The proposal is the proper place to reveal the exact nature of the analysis, as well as anticipated plans in the event of emergency. For many students, especially master's candidates, the analysis, if statistical, may represent new knowledge recently acquired and not fully digested. In addition, the customary time limitation of 12 to 16 months, by which the master's candidate is bound, adds to the difficulty. The candidate may even be in the middle of a first formal course in techniques of data reduction and analysis during the same period of time used for constructing the proposal. Consequently, students find themselves in the awkward position of having to write lucidly about their analytic tools without yet knowing the entire armamentarium available. As untenable as this position is, and as much sympathy as may be generated by the student's advisor or friends, the omission of a full explanation of the analysis in the proposal may prove to be disastrous. Countless unfortunates have found themselves with shoe boxes full of unanalyzable data, all because the analysis was supposed to take care of itself. A step-by-step anticipation of the analysis to be used is also a double-check on the experimental design.

Descriptive, survey, and normative studies require extensive data reduction to produce meaningful quantitative descriptions and summaries of the phenomena of interest. Techniques for determining sample characteristics may be different from those anticipated on the basis of pilot results, or the study sample may be skewed, resulting in the need to discuss techniques for normalizing the data.

Statistical techniques are founded on assumptions relating to sample characteristics and the relationship between that sample and its respective population. The methods one intends to use to determine whether the sample meets the assumptions implicit in the anticipated analysis should be clearly stated. For example, many statistical techniques must be used only when one or more of the following assumptions are met: (a) normal distribution of the sample, (b) random and independent selection of subjects, (c) linear relationships of variables, (d) homogeneity of variance among groups (in regression analysis, this is called homoscedasticity), (e) independence of sample means and variances, and (f) units of measure of the dependent variable on an interval or ratio scale.

Accordingly, the process of selecting a statistic brings with it a number of subsequent questions. What methods will be employed to determine that assumptions have been met? What analyses will be used in the event the assumptions are not met? Will the planned

Hypothesis	Variables	Analysis
1. The self-concept of 7-year-olds is higher than that of 5-year-olds.	Sum of self-concept subscales	MANOVA with follow-up if age factor is significant
2. The self-concept of 9-year-olds is higher than that of 7-year-olds.	Sum of self-concept subscales	MANOVA with follow-up if age factor is significant
3. There is no difference between rural or suburban children's self-concept for 5- and 7-year-olds.	Sum of self-concept subscales	MANOVA interaction effect with follow-up if significant
4. Nine-year-old suburban children will have higher self-concept than 9-year-old rural children.	Sum of self-concept subscales	MANOVA interaction effect with follow-up if significant
5. The self-concept of 7-year-olds is higher than that of 5-year-olds.	Peer Sociability Index	MANOVA with follow-up if age factor is significant
6. The self-concept of 9-year-olds is higher than that of 7-year-olds.	Peer Sociability Index	MANOVA with follow-up if age factor is significant
7. Suburban children will have higher peer sociability than urban children.	Peer Sociability Index	MANOVA with follow-up if location factor is significant

Figure 4.2. Example of a Table Showing How Each Hypothesis Will be Tested

NOTE: This is presented for illustrative purposes. An actual study may have additional hypotheses.

analyses be appropriate in the event subjects are lost so that there are unequal numbers of subjects or trials in the different conditions?

The analysis section of the proposal should be outlined to correspond with the objectives of the study so that each analysis will yield evidence relating to a corresponding hypothesis. In addition, the reader should be able to determine how all data collected are to be analyzed. An efficient way of accomplishing this is by using a graphic model similar to the one shown in Figure 4.2.

If data are to be presented in tabular or graphic form in the completed report, an example of one such table, including predicted figures, often will be helpful to the reader. The purpose of a table or figure in a research report is to summarize material and to supplement the text in making it clearly understandable. Tables and graphic presentation may serve the same purpose in a proposal.

Because of their display quality, the inclusion of tables in the proposal may expose errors of research design. For instance, some committee readers may not detect the use of an incorrect error term from a reading of the text, but one glance at the degrees of freedom column in an analysis of variance table will reveal the error. In analysis of variance comparisons, inclusion of several tables may expose the presence of nonindependent variables.

If the analysis activity of the project is studied carefully in advance, many headaches as well as heartaches may be avoided. It may seem to take an inordinate amount of time to plan the analysis, but it is time that will not have to be spent again. As the analyses are completed, the results can immediately be inserted in the prepared tables, and the researcher can complete the project with a feeling of fulfillment rather than a frantic scramble to make sense out of a puzzle for which some of the pieces may prove to be missing.

THE STATISTICAL WELL: DRINKING THE GREATEST DRAUGHT

Students usually can expect help from their advisors with the design of statistical analysis. At minimum, an experienced advisor will have some suggestions about the type of analysis that would be most appropriate for the proposed investigation. Many departments include specialists who have statistical consultation with graduate students as a primary part of their professorial responsibility. Other departments work closely with outside statistical and computer consultants who may be in departments of educational psychology, psychology, computer science, or business administration.

The student should not, however, operate under the faulty impression that when the data are collected they can be turned over to a handy statistical expert who, having an intimate relationship with a computer, will magically transform raw data into a finished form of findings and conclusions. Just as the student cannot expect the analysis of data to take care of itself, neither can the student expect a statistical consultant to take care of it.

The assistance of a statistician or computer consultant, invaluable though it may be, ordinarily is limited to the technology of design and data analysis and help with using a packaged statistical program on a computer. The conceptual demands of the study and the particular form and characteristics of the data generated are the investigator's province—to be explained to the consultant, not vice versa. Likewise, the interpretation of results is a *logical*, not a technical, operation and thus is a responsibility for which only the investigator is properly prepared.

On Finding a Friendly Computer

A variety of interrelated decisions must be addressed as the student contemplates the analysis phase of the study. First, what statistical tools are needed to analyze the data correctly? Then, after the statistical methods are selected, what is the most efficient way to do the analysis? (Note that it is not a good idea to reverse the order of these two questions.) At one time, students had few choices with regard to methods of analysis. Either they calculated the statistics themselves on hand or table calculators, or they used the university computer to complete the analysis. Today, personal microcomputers have become commonplace and for most a variety of statistical programs are available. In addition, statistical packages for university mainframe computers have become far more versatile. Part of research planning involves making choices among a growing number of attractive options for analysis.

The first step in selecting a computer and program to analyze your data is to find out what computers and packages are available. The student's advisor, other graduate students, and the university computer center can be helpful. Many universities will have both mainframe and microcomputer consultants to help students and faculty and may have agreements with software companies that greatly reduce the cost of the software. The first step is to eliminate all packages (and computers) that will not allow you to do the desired analysis. This may involve more than assuring yourself that the proposed statistical operation is available. For instance, you should be interested in the number of subjects and variables the program or computer can handle, whether data can be stored for reanalysis at a later date, and, should data assume an unexpected form, whether other tests that might be needed are available with the same computer and package.

Fortunately, the most common and powerful statistical packages (Biomedical Computer Programs [BMDP], Statistical Analysis System [SAS], and Statistical Package for the Social Sciences [SPSS]) now are available for both mainframe and microcomputers. The packages can accommodate relatively large data sets for analysis and storage (the limits, of course, will depend on the configuration of the microcomputer if one is being used for the analysis), perform virtually any statistical test researchers require, and are available on most university campuses. Although some may find these packages slightly more difficult to master than those designed to perform a specific task on one type of microcomputer, several benefits accrue from learning to use one or more of the large statistical packages. Among these advantages are:

1. The ability to transfer data and programs between a microcomputer and mainframe computer provides added flexibility for analysis—particularly if data sets are too large for the microcomputer—without learning a new program.
2. If the data need to be reanalyzed, it is very likely that the package can complete the analysis without the time-consuming problem of reformatting data.
3. Familiarity with a commonly used program will serve a student well when moving on to an academic appointment—the packages are available on most campuses and little start-up time will be wasted on learning a new program to analyze data.

Whether you choose a microcomputer or a mainframe computer, it is absolutely essential to backup your files. This can be accomplished on a mainframe computer by using a tape cartridge or downloading the files to your microcomputer and by simply saving microcomputer files on both the hard disk and a diskette or on multiple diskettes. No matter how diligent you are about saving and backing up your files, you also should save a hard copy (a printout of your data) in more than one place. This applies equally to word processing text for the proposal document. As a matter of practice, have a printout of the data in at least two places. An extra word of caution—pay attention to the computer manual's nagging reminders to save frequently. Remember, data are like eggs, they are most secure when stored in more than one basket.

Selecting the wrong statistical package and computer rarely is fatal in the research process. The selection of a computer or package that does not meet all your needs may require additional time for entering data or may delay completion of the analysis. A little careful planning, however, may eliminate waste and reduce aggravation at a later date.

The Care and Nurture of Consultants

To obtain technical help from an advisor or consultant, the student should be prepared to provide basic concepts about the content domain of the investigation, including a concise review of what is to be studied, a clear picture of the form data will take, and a preliminary estimate of alternative designs that might be appropriate to the demands of the proposed research. In addition, whether advice concerning design, statistics, or computer programming is sought from the student's project advisor, from a departmental specialist, or from an expert source external to the department, basic rules exist that must be considered if the student is to glean the most information and help for the smallest cost in valuable consultation time.

Rule 1: Understand the consultant's frame of reference. As with any other situation involving extended communication, it is useful to know enough about the language, predilections, and knowledge base of the consultant to avoid serious misunderstandings and ease the process of initiating the transaction. Research consultants are professionals whose primary interest is in the process of research design, statistical analysis, and the application of computers in research. They use a system language unique to statistics and data management and appreciate those who understand at least the rudiments of this vocabulary. Correspondingly, your consultant will not necessarily understand the system language to be used in the proposal, nor the peculiar characteristics of the data. For example, it cannot be assumed that the consultant knows that some of your data consist of repeated measures. Similarly, it would be unlikely for a statistician to know whether these data are normally distributed across trials.

The consultant cannot be expected to make decisions that relate to the purpose of the study, such as those regarding the balance between internal and external validity. Some designs may maximize the validity of the differences that may be found, but correspondingly trade off external validity, and thus the generalizability of the findings. Decisions concerning the acceptability of such research designs must be made by the proposer of the study. The grounds for such a determination rest in the purpose of the study and thus in conceptual work completed long before the consultation interview.

Consultants can be expected to evaluate a proposed experimental design, assist in selection from a group of alternative designs, suggest more efficient designs that have not been considered, and propose methods for efficiently completing the analysis. Often they can be most helpful, however, if preliminary models for design and statistical analysis have been proposed. This provides a starting place for discussion and may serve as a vehicle for considering characteristics of the data that will impose special demands.

Consultants can provide information about computer programs, the appropriateness of a particular program for the proposed design, and the entry techniques into these programs. Again, some preliminary preparation by the student can make the consultant's advisory task easier and work to guarantee an optimal selection of procedures for processing raw data. This preparation might include talking with other students presently engaged in computer use, reviewing material on computer language and packaged statistical programs, and visiting the computer center for an update on available services.

Normally, the statistics and computer specialists in a university setting are besieged by frantic graduate students and busy faculty colleagues, all in addition to the demands of their own students. Further, they may be responsible for the management of one or more functions in their own administrative unit or in the computer center. Finally, as active scholars they will be conducting their own research. Both the picture and the lesson should be equally clear to the student seeking assistance. Statisticians and computer scientists are busy people. They can provide effective assistance only when investigators come with accurate expectations for the kind of help a consultant can properly provide and come fully prepared to exercise their own responsibilities in the process.

Rule 2: Learn the language. The system languages of measurement, computer science, experimental design, and both inferential and descriptive statistics are used in varying degrees in the process of technical consultation for many research proposals. No one, least of all an experienced consultant, expects fluent mastery in the novice. The student must, however, have a working knowledge of fundamental concepts. These ordinarily include measures of central tendency and variability, distribution models, and the concept of statistical significance. Basic research designs, such as those described in introductory research method books, should be familiar to any novice.

It is, of course, preferable to complete at least one statistics course before attempting any study that will demand the analysis of quantitative data. If, as sometimes is the case, the student is learning basic statistics concurrent with the preparation of the proposal, special effort will have to be concentrated on preparing for consultations concerning design and analysis. The situation will be awkward at best, although many advisors will remain sympathetic and patient if students are honest about their limitations and willing to exert heroic effort once it becomes clear which tools and concepts must be mastered.

Beyond the problem of mastering enough of the language to participate in useful discussion is the more subtle problem of understanding the particular analysis and techniques selected for the study. The student must not drift into the position of using a statistical tool or a measurement technique that really is not understood—even one endorsed and urged by the most competent of advisors. Ultimately, the student will have to make sense out of the results obtained through any analysis. At that point, shallow or incorrect interpretations will quickly betray a failure to understand the nature of the analysis. The student also will have to answer questions about the findings long after the advisor is not around. Expert technical advice can be an invaluable asset in devising a strong proposal, but in the final analysis, such advice cannot substitute for the competence of the investigator.

Rule 3: Understand the proposed study. If the novice researcher does not understand the study sufficiently to identify and ask important and explicit questions, that lack is a major obstacle to a successful consultation. Only when the consultant understands the questions of central interest in the study is it possible to translate them into the steps of statistical analysis and selection of the appropriate computer program. Even if you employ a consultant only to help you with data preparation and analysis, if you cannot communicate exactly what you want, you may get back a printout from an analysis that is irrelevant to your needs. Further, a host of specific constraints associated with the nature of the study will condition the advisor's decision about which analysis to recommend.

The student should be ready to provide answers to each of the following questions:

1. What are the independent variables of the study?
2. What are the dependent variables of the study?
3. What are the potential confounding variables of the study?
4. What is the measurement scale of each variable (nominal, ordinal, interval, or ratio)?
5. Which, if any, of the variables are repeated measures?
6. What are the reliability and validity of the instruments used to produce the scores for each variable?
7. What are the population distribution characteristics for each of the variables?
8. What difference between dependent variables would be of *practical* significance?
9. What are the monetary, safety, ethical, or educational risks involved if a Type I error is made?
10. What is the nature of the loss if a Type II error is made?

In summary, before consulting with a technical specialist the student must be able to express exactly what the study is to be designed to accomplish, identify the help needed in producing such a design, and provide all the explicit details the consultant will need in formulating advice.

THE SCIENTIFIC STATE OF MIND:
PROOF, TRUTH, AND RATIONALIZED CHOICES

Scientific inquiry is not so much a matter of elaborate technology or even rigorous method as it is a particular state of mind. The processes of science rest, in the end, on how scientists regard the world and their work. Although some aspects of scientific thinking are subtle and elusive, others are not. These latter, the basic attitudinal prerequisites for the conduct of scientific inquiry, are reflected in the way a novice speaks and writes about proposed research. More directly, the proposal will reflect the degree to which the author has internalized critical attitudes toward such matters as proof, truth, and publicly rationalized choices.

What matters is not the observance of particular conventions concerning phrasing, but fundamental ways of thinking that are reflected in the selection of words. When, for example, students write, "The purpose of this study is to prove (or to demonstrate) that . . .," there always is the dangerous possibility that the intent is to do just that—to prove what they have decided must be true.

Such phrasing cannot be dismissed simply as awkward or naive. Students capable of writing such a sentence without hearing at once its dangerous implications are students with a fundamental defect in preparation. They should be allowed to go no further until they apprehend both the nature of proof and the purpose of research in the scientific enterprise, for clearly neither is understood.

Proof, if it exists at all in any useful sense, is a probabilistic judgment based on an accumulation of observations. Ordinarily, only a series of careful replications can lead to the level of confidence implied by the word "proved." Research is not an attempt to prove or demonstrate, it is an attempt to ask a careful question and to allow the nature of things to dictate the answer. The difference between "attempting to prove" and "seeking proof" is subtle but critical, and a scientist must never confuse the two.

If scientists have no illusions about proof, it is wrong, nonetheless, to believe that they never care about the direction of results obtained from their research. As humans, they often are painfully aware of the distinction between results that will be fortunate or unfortunate for their developing line of thought. As scientists, however, they recognize the irrelevance (and even the danger) of allowing personal convenience or advantage to intrude in the business of seeking knowledge. In the end, researchers must sit down before their facts as children and allow themselves to be instructed. The task lies in arranging the context for instruction so that the answers to questions will be clear, but the content of the lesson must remain in the facts as revealed by the data.

A second critical sign of the student's ability to adopt the scientific viewpoint is the general way the matter of truth is treated in the proposal. When students write, "The purpose of this study is to discover the actual cause of . . .," there is danger that they think it is possible to do just that—to discern the ultimate face of reality at a single glance. The most fundamental remediation will be required if such students ever are to understand, much less conduct, scientific inquiry.

Experienced researchers seek and revere veridical knowledge; they may even choose to think of research as the search for truth, but they also understand the elusive, fragile, and probabilistic nature of scientific truth. Knowledge is regarded as a tentative decision about the world, always held contingent on the content of the future.

The business of the researcher is striving to understand. Correspondingly, a high value is placed on hard-won knowledge. Truth is held gently, however, and the experienced investigator speaks and writes accordingly. It is not necessary to lard a proposal with reservations, provisos, and disclaimers such as "it seems." It is necessary to write with respect for the complexity of things and with modesty for what can be accomplished. The researcher's highest expectation for any study is a small but perceptible shift in the scale of evidence. Most scientific inquiry deals not in the heady stuff of truth, "establishing actual causes," but in hard-won increments of probability.

A third sign by which to estimate the student's scientific maturity is the ability (and willingness) to examine alternative interpretations of evidence, plausible rival hypotheses, facts that bid to discomfort the theoretical framework, and considerations that reveal the limitations of the methodology. It is important not only to lay out the alternatives for the reader, but to explain the grounds for choice among them. The student who neither acknowledges alternatives nor rationalizes choices simply does not understand research well enough to bother with a proposal.

The mature researcher feels no compulsion to provide perfect interpretations or to make unassailably correct choices. One does the best one can within the limits of existing knowledge and the present situation. The author of a proposal is compelled, however, to make clearly rationalized choices from among carefully defined alternatives; this is one reason readers outside the scientific community find research reports tedious in their attention to detail and explanation. It is the public quality of the researcher's reasoning that makes a community of scientific enterprise possible, not the construction of a facade of uniform certainly and perfection.

Student-conducted research often contains choices that must be rationalized less by the shape of existing knowledge and the dictates of logic and more by the homely facts of logistics: time, costs, skills achieved, and available facilities. The habit of public clarity in describing and rationalizing choices must begin there, with the way things are. An honest accounting of hard and often imperfect choices is a firm step for the student toward achieving the habits of a good researcher—the scientific state of mind.

Note

1. Statistical significance, of course, is not synonymous with scientific significance in terms of the evolution of knowledge, or practical significance in terms of solving professional problems. Statistical significance largely depends on sample size and selection of an *alpha* level (the level of confidence necessary to reject the null hypothesis). It can be demonstrated between almost any two groups using almost any variable selected, if the sample size is large enough and the power of the test sufficiently high. Such differences between groups may be statistically significant but scientifically trivial and professionally worthless. The pilot study is an excellent device by which the probability of a Type I error may be estimated and an appropriate sample size selected. In this way the investigator can increase the probability that a statistically significant result also will reflect a difference of scientific and practical significance.

5

Preparation of Proposals for Qualitative Research

Different Assumptions

When this guide first reached print (1976), the probability that readers would elect a qualitative study for their dissertation or grant proposal was small. Only students in sociology or anthropology would have been likely to know that such an option even existed. In that year, most graduate students and young scholars would have begun their apprenticeship in research with studies cast in the familiar mode of natural science.

Those studies would have presumed views of the world and the process of inquiry that were then so pervasive in the disciplines of natural science (and applied professional fields such as education and medicine) as to be called simply "the scientific method." It was an orderly, understandable, and innocent time. There was one way to do good research, one learned it, and did it. Because science is not a static set of prescriptions, however, the natural evolution of the enterprise produced some dramatic alterations in that landscape.

What changed was not the viability of the natural science tradition. Experimental and quasi-experimental designs remain the choice for many kinds of inquiry. What changed was our growing understanding that experiments and the search for objective reality are not the only way to do science—and certainly not the only means deserving to be called scientific. Other assumptions about reality lead to other systems of inquiry—and to new possibilities for graduate student research.

The years since the first edition of *Proposals That Work* have seen an explosion of interest in another way of knowing, a vantage point on the world that allows assumptions that are impossible in the natural science model for inquiry. This scientific paradigm[1], what we refer to in this guide as "qualitative" research, has a long history of use in the social sciences, but until recently was not a significant part of mainstream scholarship, or research training, in other disciplines and professional areas.

In less than two decades, we have witnessed the luxurious growth of new methods (and new applications for old methods) and the burgeoning of a new knowledge base in the literature. Where, at the end of the 1960's, only a handful of relatively obscure books and journal articles dealing with qualitative research existed, suddenly a mountain of print appeared containing discussions of theory, new models of design, and debate about technical applications. More important, there emerged a growing corpus of research reports that displayed the uses of qualitative inquiry.

In response to all of this scholarly ferment, it was necessary in 1987 to add a chapter on qualitative proposals for the second edition of this guide. Now, only 6 years later, that chapter requires both substantial revisions and a completely new listing of available resources. Even with this effort to stay current, novices in qualitative research will have to look to local sources for the latest advances.

THE PURPOSE OF THIS CHAPTER—
AND SOME WARNINGS

Many readers now will be aware of qualitative research, at least as a possible alternative for studies in their area of interest. Others already will have decided to use that paradigm as the theoretical basis for their research plan—and thus their proposals. Accordingly, the purpose of this chapter is to serve the needs of both groups, directing the former to resources that will help in deciding what kind of research to do and assisting the latter in organizing the ideas and materials needed to begin a qualitative proposal.

We recognize that some users of this guide will be unfamiliar with (or unclear about) qualitative research. For their use, we will provide a brief description. First, however, we must establish several caveats that apply to all readers.

Because use of this type of inquiry is relatively new in some areas of scholarship, the field is anything but tidy. Qualitative research is characterized by a good deal of messy disagreement among scholars. For this chapter, we have established some of our own definitions, with the full expectation that many scholars would find them unsatisfactory. This guide, however, is not written for established researchers who already know how to prepare proposals.

At the outset, there is no agreement on a universal label for this kind of research. In the literature of social science and education, such terms as *interpretive, naturalistic, fieldwork, case study,* and *ethnography* are used to designate what we here call *qualitative research.* Some of those terms reflect important distinctions in the minds of people who employ them. In contrast, we have selected the label *qualitative research* as an arbitrary convenience. It is intended to be generic and should not be assigned any particular theoretical or ideological connotation.

For those interested in the many varieties (or traditions) under the generic umbrella of qualitative research, there has been a recent and very lively discussion about that topic. The literature containing this provides not only an economical way to survey the field of qualitative research but a sense of the tensions that attend the process by which scholars begin to stake out territorial claims in a new enterprise.

The most accessible example of this discourse is a series that began with reviews by Jacob (1987, 1988), followed by responses from Atkinson, Delamont and Hammersley (1988), Buchmann and Floden (1989), and Lincoln (1989), and a final riposte by Jacob (1989). Even the reader with only a rudimentary background in social science will find these are not overly difficult. Obtaining such an overview of the diversity within qualitative research will have the salutary effect of reminding you to hold your commitments lightly— until you have a complete map of the territory.

Given a paradigm so rich with possibilities for inquiry, why have we opted here for such generic treatment? The answer is because all forms of qualitative research with which we have experience make some demands on the planning process that are different from those encountered in quantitative[2] designs—and for the purposes of this guide that is what matters. A simple dichotomous division into qualitative and quantitative is practical, if inelegant. We leave to others the task of discerning all the fine distinctions within and between those two broad categories of research.[3]

A BRIEF DESCRIPTION
OF QUALITATIVE RESEARCH

What is qualitative research and how is it done? On first hearing, the answer seems disarmingly simple. It is a systematic, empirical strategy for answering questions about people in a bounded social context. Given any locus for interaction, it is a means for describing and attempting to understand the observed regularities in what people do, say, and report as their experience.

Qualitative researchers raise the primordial question, "What's going on here?" Venues for their work might include a religious community, a school or classroom, a playground, or a school district undertaking the process of textbook selection. Alternatively, the experience of being a first-year teacher, an older adult returning to attend a community college, a Little League coach, or a case worker in a social agency might be the focus for a study. In each instance it is the total context that creates what it means to be present, to be a participant, to be a member, and to have a role to play. It is that context and those meanings that the qualitative researcher seeks to capture.

Some of the activities employed to collect data resemble those used by social scientists engaged in quantitative research. What differentiates qualitative inquiry from conventional science are the assumptions held by the investigator—how he or she thinks about the world—not the methods of data collection. It is in the researcher's beliefs about what is real and how we come to know things, that the paradigmatic differences lie.

In qualitative research, the focus of attention is on the perceptions and experiences of the participants. What individuals say they believe, the feelings they express, and explanations they give are treated as significant realities. In that sense, this is a profoundly relativistic view of the world. The researcher is not seeking the kind of verifiable and absolute "truth" that functions in a cause and effect model of reality. The working assumption is that people make sense out of their experiences and in doing so create their own reality. In qualitative research, understanding both the content and construction of such multiple and contingent realities is regarded as central to answering the question, "What's going on here?"

This kind of research is descriptive in that text (recorded words rather than numbers) is the most common form of data. Thus, interview transcripts, field notes from direct observation, diaries, and documents are primary forms of information. Qualitative inquiry also is analytic or interpretive in that the investigator must discern and then articulate often subtle regularities within those data. For that reason, data reduction, organization, manipulation, and display are central activities in the research process.

Most qualitative research (though not all) is naturalistic in that the researcher enters the world of the participant as it exists and obtains data without any deliberate intervention designed to alter the setting. Even in the case of phenomenological interviewing, a qualitative research form that does not require the physical presence of the investigator in the subject's home environment, an important objective is the reconstruction of experience as it has been lived by the participant in his or her natural setting.

Detailed descriptions of context and what people say or do form the basis for inductive rather than deductive analysis. That is, theory is created to explain the data, rather than data being collected to test preestablished hypotheses. The investigator may begin with some preliminary questions in mind, or may allow some foreshadowing of problems and relationships to direct the initial focus of attention. Otherwise, however, researchers try to avoid imposing presumptions and preconceived structures. The growth of understanding begins with trying to figure out how the *participants* understand the setting.

THE FINAL CAVEATS

With that brief description of qualitative research, we reach the last warnings to be observed in what follows. First, the purpose of this chapter is *not* to provide advice for those who plan to use interviews, questionnaires, critical incident collection, content analysis of documents, or even systematic field observations, in what otherwise are traditional quantitative study designs. Aside from the technical demands peculiar to each, such methods of data collection and analysis present no special problems for the proposal. Reference to standard textbook sources, training experiences, and consultant advice will provide the support needed to make appropriate use of those tools in a proposed study.

Parts of other chapters in this guide are designed primarily to help in preparing proposals for quantitative research. The concern in this chapter, however, is with the writing of proposals that make use of such familiar data gathering methods as interviews and field observations in the framework of qualitative inquiry. That, as they say in Oz, is a horse of a different color.

Finally, everyone should understand that some options for research lie beyond the simple dichotomy of qualitative and quantitative. A third paradigm, critical theory, is well-established in both the social sciences and education. Except for the brief comment below, we will not attempt here to treat with the implications of critical theory for the production of a research proposal. If you would like an introduction to that paradigm that is reasonably easy to digest, we suggest Carr and Kemmis (1986), Maguire (1987), Thomas (1992), and Whyte (1990). Chapters dealing directly or indirectly with critical theory also may be found in the collections edited by Eisner and Peshkin (1990), and LeCompte, Millroy, and Preissle (1992).

As with its two paradigmatic neighbors, critical theory shelters a number of inquiry forms that are only loosely (and not always comfortably) related. Participatory, empowering, action, materialist, and feminist research traditions are among the present occupants. What they share is a concern for the ways that power is distributed and maintained in social settings.

On the surface, that kind of interest appears not to require a new set of assumptions about research. As the concern begins to shape the relationship between the researcher and the researched, however, it begins to have important implications for both method and what one regards as the nature of truth. In some forms of critical theory, research becomes a vehicle for redistributing power and improving the life circumstances of the participants. At that point, where the imagined line between politics and scholarship begins to blur, you can be sure that we have moved into new territory.

Those who do what is called feminist research have made some claims to separate status as a paradigm distinct from critical theory. We take no side in this, but suggest that if you are interested in the way gender enters into inquiry you take a short excursion into the often lively literature that examines the topic. For this, we would begin with two vantage points from Great Britain, Roberts (1981) and Stanley and Wise (1983), adding Harding (1987), Lather (1988), and Stacey (1988) if your interest persists. Chapters dealing with the feminist approach to qualitative research also may be found in the collections edited by Eisner and Peshkin (1990), and LeCompte et al. (1992).

RESOURCES FOR QUALITATIVE RESEARCH

This chapter once served to direct novice researchers to the small number of references that could assist in preparing a proposal for a qualitative study. Now our function is to serve primarily as a guide through the thickets of literature, pointing out likely places to begin or resources that provide attention to particular topics. That is a happy change in function.

Our recommendations have been divided into 12 topical areas that, although they obviously must overlap in many respects, should allow you to find references that attend to most of the major questions the proposal will raise. The order in which the topics are listed is significant. We have tried to list first those resources that would be used by someone at the earliest stage and then add in serial order the investments in reading that would have to precede a final commitment. Readers who have at least working familiarity with qualitative research should simply browse through the lists and select what meets their present need.

At the outset, we draw to your attention four major resources that, while represented in the 12 categories below, constitute by themselves the most important repositories for information about qualitative research. What you do not find in our listings you can locate in these resources.

The International Journal of Qualitative Studies in Education began publication in 1988 and now represents an invaluable resource for locating original reports, research reviews, theoretical and methodological articles, and book reviews. Issued quarterly by Taylor and Francis, Ltd., the journal is available in most larger institutional libraries, or may be obtained from the publisher's Philadelphia office.

In 1986, Sage Publications initiated a series in Qualitative Research Methods (John Van Maanen presently serves as the Series Editor). Rapidly approaching the thirtieth volume at the time of this writing, the collection is one of the most comprehensive efforts ever undertaken to provide support for qualitative research. Packaged in the form of paperbound monographs of 50-100 pages in length, the series provides students with a resource that is both inexpensive and carefully targeted on troublesome aspects in the planning and execution of qualitative studies.

For more than two decades, the journal *Educational Researcher* has been the primary forum for what has been called the "paradigm wars" (Gage, 1989). This lively and informative debate over the nature, uses, virtues, limitations, and evolution of qualitative research reflects the way scholars gradually accommodate to new possibilities for inquiry. Issued nine times each year by the American Educational Research Association, the journal is available to students for a small annual membership fee.

The handbook format has become a standard means for periodically collecting and reviewing research in various disciplines. In education, the *Handbook of Research on Teaching* (see Erickson, 1986), and the *Handbook of Research on Curriculum* (see Walker, 1992) both give significant attention to qualitative research. Although less ambitious in scale, the *Handbook of Qualitative Research in Education* (see LeCompte et al., 1992) provides the first collection of its kind. Eighteen chapters cover current boundaries of the field, issues in the execution of studies, and applications of qualitative research.

TWELVE CATEGORIES
FOR REFERENCE SOURCES

1. *Introduction*—If you really are starting from the beginning, then short articles by Fetterman (1987a), Peshkin (1988b), Rogers (1984), and Wilson (1977) will provide a gentle introduction. If it sounds interesting, next would come a tutorial designed for the orientation of novice researchers (Locke, 1989), and finally the special issue of *Theory Into Practice* devoted to qualitative issues in educational research (Chandler, 1992).

2. *User-Friendly Textbooks*—There is no point in going further without some sense of what it takes to become a qualitative researcher and what kinds of skills are needed to design studies, collect and analyze data, and write reports. An old favorite for this purpose is Bogdan and Biklen (1982), although both Glesne and Peshkin (1992) and Delamont (1992) are a decade younger and just as friendly. If you are inclined to the idea of doing a case study, Merriam (1988) is the best introductory

book available, as Seidman (1991) is for interviewing. Finally, Fetterman (1989), Lofland and Lofland (1984), and Spradley (1980) provide basic introduction to social science versions of qualitative research—in inexpensive paperback form. If you decide to go further with qualitative research, you will be returning to one or several of these texts as you work on the proposal. For now, just browse and get acquainted.

3. *Specimens*—Journals such as *The International Journal of Qualitative Studies in Education, Qualitative Sociology,* and the *American Educational Research Journal* are the best places to find examples of what qualitative research can produce. If you have difficulty locating useful specimens, texts by Dobbert (1982), Reason and Rowen (1981), and Spindler (1982) contain some that have been reprinted in abbreviated form. Collections edited by Burgess (1985) and Shaffir, Stebbins and Turowetz (1980) have the added virtue of containing accounts of what it is like to do qualitative research.

4. *Theory*—Books on the theoretical foundations of qualitative research are notoriously difficult—and for the uninitiated, ponderously dull. Sooner or later, however, you have to make a start. Instead of going to the epistemological roots of the paradigm, we suggest starting at an intermediate level by consulting texts written by people concerned about ways of keeping the practice of method faithful to the theory of philosophical foundations. For this, Lincoln and Guba (1985) have written the standard in the field, and Patton (1990) provides useful counterpoint. If you become serious about qualitative research, there will be many more hard theoretical rows to hoe. For the present, however, this is enough.

5. *The Debate*—It is impossible to have conversations with more than one or two scholars without discovering the lively controversy that surrounds qualitative research. You should learn early on where the hot spots are located (if only to avoid them in friendly discourse). For this, almost any issue of *Educational Researcher* over the last two decades will provide exemplars. Gage (1989), Rizo (1991), and Salomon (1991) are the best of the recent forays. Eisner and Peshkin (1990) have collected a number of excellent essays on the continuing debate and Hammersley (1992) now has provided a critique of the critiques.

6. *About Qualitative Proposals*—If you have gone this far, you probably are going to write a proposal for qualitative research. As of yet, there is not a substantial literature on this subject, so your best bet may be to locate some successful proposals and give them close attention. We can recommend, however, two resources: Marshall and Rossman's specific treatment of the subject *Designing Qualitative Research* (1989), and Chapter 5 "The Research Plan" in Volume 1 of Werner and Schoepfle's set, *Systematic Fieldwork* (1987a). Although very different as texts, the

two complement each other nicely. The former deals with formats that will be familiar to educational researchers (including the doctoral dissertation) and those doing applied studies, while the latter is pitched toward grant applications to federal agencies for the support of ethnographic field studies. Included are proposal guidelines for the National Institute of Mental Health and the National Endowment for the Humanities are examined.

The strength of the Marshall and Rossman text is in the guidance it provides for thinking through how to choose a problem, determine its worth, and decide whether it is doable in practical terms. In its limited confines, it can only provide an introduction to the problems of choosing a design, selecting methods of data collection, and setting up procedures for data analysis. Taken in the context of their much larger two-volume set, Werner and Schoepfle have the advantage on design, method, and analysis. Their chapter on proposals contains a particularly interesting treatment of sampling in field studies.

7. *Ethics*—We put ethics here, before the categories dealing with methodological issues and procedures, because we believe it is more important. As we note in Chapter 2, the topic gets short shrift in research training of all kinds and, sad to say, that is just as true of qualitative research. Aside from a passing encounter with the human subjects review committee, most beginners give scant thought to matters of how they wish to treat their participants—until they walk headlong into the nasty dilemmas that abound in qualitative research. You should not go further until you have consulted several of the following: Burgess (1989), Flinders (1992), Glesne (1989), Kimmel (1988), Reece and Siegel (1986), Sieber (1992), or Soltis (1989), or the substantial sections devoted to ethics in Eisner and Peshkin (1990), and LeCompte et al. (1992). It is our honest belief that you may someday have cause to be thankful if you will now take time to read widely and think carefully about ethical issues in qualitative research.

8. *Methodological Issues*—By this point, many of you will have accumulated nagging doubts about a number of issues in qualitative research. Some of these were addressed in the sources listed for *Theory* above, but the following items will extend and refine those discussions. The matter of general standards is addressed by Howe and Eisenhart (1990) and Lincoln and Guba (1990), while the familiar issues of validity and reliability have been treated by Guba (1981), Lather (1986), LeCompte and Goetz (1982), and Phillips (1987). Excellent discussions of how to manage problems related to the sensitive issues of subjectivity and anonymity have been provided, respectively, by Peshkin (1988a) and Shulman (1990). Finally, all of these difficult issues (plus others, such as generalizability) are given substantial treatment in the collections edited by Eisner and Peshkin (1990), Fetterman (1987b), and LeCompte et al. (1992).

9. *Interviewing*—Because this is a particularly common form of data collection, interviewing is accorded a chapter in nearly every qualitative research methods text. In that regard, Lofland and Lofland (1984), Patton (1990), and Werner and Schoepfle (1987a) are particularly good. The specialized texts, however, have the advantage of detail and focus. This is most clearly evident in Seidman's (1991) treatment of phenomenological interviewing, a thoughtful book that teaches much about the craft of inquiry, as well as how to converse with people. A short paper by Weber (1986) has saved many proposal writers who found themselves uncomfortable with the inequity implied in interview situations. A collaborative relationship provides a different vantage-point for thinking about, and doing, interviews. Books by Douglas (1985), McCracken (1988), and Spradley (1979) provide sound treatment of interviewing as a tool in the social sciences. Finally, Krueger (1988), Morgan (1988), and Stewart and Shamdasani (1990) introduce the focus group as an interesting alternative to the traditional group interview format.

10. *Computers*—Few first-time investigators have any conception of the volume of data generated by a qualitative study of even modest scope. As soon as they do, the notion of putting a computer to work in managing, manipulating, sorting, and displaying data becomes enormously attractive. If you do not have an intimate relationship with your local computer, a good place to begin is with the collection edited by Fielding and Lee (1991). Somewhat more technical treatments are provided in Tesch's *Qualitative Research: Analysis Types and Software Tools* (1990), the ongoing series of columns on computer applications published in the *International Journal of Qualitative Studies in Education* between 1988 and 1990, and the special issues of *Qualitative Sociology* published as numbers 3 and 4 of volume 14 (see: Tesch, 1991a, 1991b).

11. *Data Analysis*—Whether you use a computer or a pair of scissors and some shoeboxes, analysis requires a plan, and the place to sketch out the initial shape of that plan is in the proposal. If you wish to consider the method of analysis called "constant comparison," you will find Grove (1988) particularly lucid on the topic of an otherwise arcane procedure. Miles and Huberman (1984) and Werner and Schoepfle (1987b) provide great detail and extensive examples, but Delamont's introductory text (1992) contains a chapter in which the analysis is envisioned on a scale that is closer to what the average novice can contemplate.

12. *Writing and Publication*—Nearly every author of a qualitative research text has enough opinions about how to write qualitative research reports to fill a chapter. Few chapters, however, are very impressive as writing

or contain much that seems particularly helpful as advice. Our counsel is to cultivate assiduously those colleagues who are known to have solid editorial skills, and then make shameless use of their assistance. In preparation for that, monographs by Atkinson (1992), Richardson (1990), and Wolcott (1990) in the Sage Qualitative Research Methods series, and the articles by Chilcott (1987) and Smith (1987) may yield some helpful guidance as you set out on the road to publication.

THE DECISION TO GO QUALITATIVE

The decision to undertake a qualitative study brings two types of problems: those that are external and mostly antecedent to the proposal, and those that are internal as part of content within the proposed design. While some of these difficulties overlap both areas, it will be convenient here to treat them separately.

The external problems that precede the writing of a proposal begin with the author as a person. Every graduate student who is tempted to employ a qualitative design should confront one question, "Why do I want to do a qualitative study?" and then answer it honestly. Some novice researchers, traumatized by a fourth-grade encounter with fractions, see qualitative research as a way of avoiding numbers in general and statistics in particular. So long as question and method are well matched, a choice made on such personal grounds is neither improper nor dysfunctional. Personal biography is a wise consideration in locating questions and methods about which one can be enthusiastic. Unfortunately, having an aversion to math is not the same as having the personal capacities and intellectual interests demanded in the conduct of qualitative research. Avoiding statistics is not so much a *bad* reason for electing to do a field ethnography as it is a motive that is *irrelevant* to locating the kind of research that you will perform well. Having the interest, ability, and patience to acquire qualitative research skills is a far more relevant foundation than discovering you have a bad case of math anxiety.

In the same vein, a student who elects qualitative research because it appears to be either relatively "quick" in terms of time commitment or "easy" in terms of intellectual demands has, in the first instance, simply never talked with anyone who has completed such a study and, in the second instance, not read published reports of qualitative research with much care. Field studies are never quick and rarely are completed within the projected time lines. The analysis of qualitative data demands a sustained level of creative thought rarely required once data are collected in a quantitative study. Qualitative research may be enormously valuable for scientific purposes, and immensely satisfying to the investigator, but quick and easy it is not.

Finally, some individuals find themselves drawn to qualitative forms of inquiry because they are unable to accept the initial assumptions that underlie quantitative research. They simply feel more comfortable, in personal or intellectual terms, with the view of knowledge and reality presumed in qualitative research. Such dispositions may constitute a sound basis for establishing preferences in research style. Close examination of how, whether, and when one "knows" something is a discipline that might profitably be practiced by all research workers.

Whatever one's predilections concerning such matters as objectivity, truth, and reality, it still is necessary to match method to question. Ideology or personal preference in epistemology do not make it possible to fit round methods into square questions. If you are committed to doing qualitative research, then you are limited to questions that yield best to that scientific paradigm. Determination of the method of inquiry before identification of the question always bears that restriction.

A second preproposal problem centers on the investigator's ability to move out of the quantitative mode of thought. For many graduate students the process of becoming comfortable with the qualitative way of thinking about problems requires adopting a view of the world that is alien to the fundamental canons of empirical thought. For most of us, the assumptions of quantitative research have been presented and learned as "science" through at least a dozen years of school and university education. That if something truly exists, it must exist in some number, and exist "out there" in some finite form, is more than the unspoken premise of quantitative research. It is an assumption that people in Western cultures often accept about what is real and what is not real in the world.

To operate comfortably with the proposition that people construct reality, thus allowing truth to reside as much in our heads as "out there," demands a sharp alteration in habitual modes of thought. Even partially accomplished, this is difficult for most and, as experience warns us, is impossible for some. It is important that this be confronted during the early apprenticeship stage, when patient and sympathetic mentors can assist in the difficult transition of habitual perceptions and familiar concepts into a new mode of thought.

Dealing with the researcher as a person leads inevitably to a more immediate and obvious problem; finding sources for training and support. Courses and internships in qualitative research methods are rare at many institutions and unavailable at others. When such opportunities do exist, they most commonly occur as upper-level graduate experiences in social science departments. As such they are not always accessible to students with backgrounds in other fields. In sum, both students and professorial advisors may find themselves far more alone than they might wish.

While a degree of self-education is possible for both advisors and the solitary student, it is best to have no illusions about how difficult that process might become. Because preparation for qualitative research often is most effective and efficient when it takes the form of apprenticeship, with intensive field experiences and closely supervised data analysis at the heart of the training process, the student without such opportunities must confront some serious questions. In terms of outcomes, will such effort be cost-effective? Will the best solution require transfer to a more hospitable department or institution? Is there sufficient time to invest in both extensive preparation and a lengthy study? Hard questions, but better raised now than later!

Finally, in some departments (or whole institutions) qualitative research is not yet an acceptable form of inquiry. Individual professors may undertake to enlighten or reeducate their colleagues, or to work for revision of graduate school policies (written or unwritten), but individual graduate students are likely to find themselves overmatched in any such effort. A realistic appraisal of the political territory, including the existence of precedents and the fate of similar efforts, should come before the final commitment to prepare a full-scale proposal. Have potential committee members or needed consultants seen a prospectus or mini-proposal and indicated their willingness to participate? Have qualitative studies actually been accepted by the graduate school? What questions were raised about previous qualitative proposals by review groups at department or school levels? How has the human subject review committee responded to qualitative designs in the past? Those are the practical kind of questions that should be raised.

Given some reassurance that a path might be cleared through the problems of obtaining institutional support and approval, the focus of concern shifts from the external preliminaries of identifying a research question, selecting a mode of inquiry, and developing research skills, to the actual task of writing a proposal. We come here to the concerns that are internal because they are intrinsic to the paradigm. In this second broad arena the problems to be surmounted relate to the special characteristics of qualitative research. The proposal still serves the same functions; but with a new form of inquiry, old problems may require new responses.

NEW RESPONSES TO FAMILIAR PROBLEMS

Many of the elements of research that concern the author of a quantitative proposal are present in qualitative designs, but they often demand quite different responses. Issues related to framing an appropriate initial question, reliability and validity of data, generalizability of results, replicability, sources of error, management and reduction of data, and interpretation of results are just as much central of an effective qualitative study as they are to a classical laboratory experiment, but the nature of the issues pertaining to each may assume an unfamiliar form.

As an example of how familiar elements of quantitative research take on new meaning in qualitative designs, consider the role of the investigator relative to the process of inquiry. Personal distance from both subjects and data is the key to objectivity in any experiment. Often heroic measures are taken to prevent the introduction of observer bias or subject reactivity. Similar concerns arise in qualitative research, but there the response must assume a quite different form. In a nonparticipant field observation study, for example, the investigator *is* the primary research instrument. Intimate and extended contact with human data sources at the level of direct personal interaction is the only way to make use of the sensitive capacities of that tool.

Direct presence as part of the research process means that the entire biography of the investigator—values, habits of perception, intellectual presumptions, and personal dispositions—becomes potentially relevant to gathering, analyzing, and understanding the data. There is no strategy that can eliminate the routing of data through the perceptual processes of the investigator. All that can be done is to understand enough about the nature of those processes so as to control the most serious threats to capturing an accurate picture of the world as understood by the resident(s) in the setting. At the level of the proposal, this means the task is to assure advisors that the author is both exquisitely aware of what will be brought to the study setting and reasonably well practiced at the skill of using the self as a research instrument without intruding personal dispositions that distort rather than illuminate the data.

From this it should be clear that the issue of investigator bias as a source of error in qualitative research is a different kind of concern than the problem encountered in more familiar quantitative designs. More to the point here, it requires an entirely different form of control. What has been said in previous chapters about the general functions and uses of the proposal will serve equally well for qualitative designs. What has been said about particular research elements, however, will not apply in many instances. New responses are required for old problems.

THE QUALITATIVE PROPOSAL:
AN OPEN CONTRACT

For graduate students, the most troublesome problems encountered in preparing a proposal for qualitative research often do not involve learning how to respond to unfamiliar methodological demands. The more serious difficulties have their origins in the context and expectations for graduate education. The first of these contextual problems is related to the nature of the proposal.

Ordinarily, the author works to achieve a level of specification and anticipation in the proposal that will bring it as near to a "closed contract" as conditions permit. In contrast, the nature of qualitative research demands an "open contract." Unlike the typical quantitative investigation, the qualitative research worker sometimes must move back and forth between data sources and ongoing data analysis *during the period of data collection.* Initial questions are progressively narrowed or, on occasion, shifted entirely as the nature of the living context becomes apparent through preliminary analysis. While this sort of in-process shift of focus or change in method is less typical of interview-based case studies than of field enthnographies, all subspecies of qualitative research commonly undergo some form of refinement during the period of active investigation.

Accordingly, although all proposals must begin with some clear question or set of questions that can be answered only by describing and understanding a bounded slice of the world, neither the specific focus of inquiry nor the exact and final form of method and analysis can be specified in advance for most qualitative studies. In whatever discussion the proposal provides, the initial set of questions and procedures must be established, at least in general or tentative terms. When, however, it is an essential part of the research process to be responsive to the ongoing process of data acquisition, it is difficult to describe precisely what you plan to do in advance. Unfortunately, in many graduate programs that is the expectation advisors bring to the proposal.

There are two ways to deal with this sensitive problem. The first is to engage in enough careful piloting of method and analysis to permit discussion of the matters that normally concern advisors— initial focus, study site and subjects, obtaining access, number and type of data sources, ethical concerns, forms of data processing and display, and demonstration of needed research skills. Not only can information from a preliminary study help meet the concerns of advisors, pilot work allows the researcher to shape the proposal around concrete experiences rather than speculation. This can yield greater conceptual strength as well as improvements in logistic efficiency.

The second alternative is to create a largely speculative proposal, using the literature to foreshadow themes and provide examples of method. At the least, this strategy permits demonstration of the author's familiarity with existing research, ability to think carefully about the problems of field investigation, and capacity to lay out intentions in broad terms. Such theoretical discourse may be sufficient for a committee that is familiar with the qualitative paradigm and confident that the novice's level of preparation will be equal to the demands of the proposed study. Under these conditions, however, it can be anticipated that advisors will be far less helpful in conceptualizing the study or in suggesting useful strategies for data analysis. The concrete products of a good pilot study are a better basis for consultation than even the most elegant of theoretical speculations.

THE QUALITATIVE PROPOSAL: REVIEWING THE LITERATURE

If qualitative proposals deviate from the norm as contracts for future action, they may deviate even more sharply in the specific area of the literature review. Some functions in this section of the proposal will be familiar, if not identical, replications of those present in the quantitative model. These include seating the study in the foundational literature of the paradigm, citing works that explain and legitimate the particular methods proposed for use, using scholarly works to create a frame of constructs and theory for the particular area of study, and demonstrating how the proposed research would fit into the ongoing dialogue of science.

The unique difference in the use of literature will lie in decisions that may be made concerning use of research reports dealing with the same or closely related questions. There may be sound reasons not to read that literature, at least not until after pilot work is complete, or possibly until a preliminary analysis of the data from the main study is available. The rationale for this departure from expected use of background material is not difficult to appreciate.

Remembering that the investigator *is* the primary instrument on which qualitative research must depend for acquisition of data, it is clear that such an instrument must be fully open to the print of other people's view of their world without imposing the freight of the observer's own perceptions. For that purpose, there are obvious advantages to beginning study without knowledge of conclusions reached by others working in the same context. The necessary critical comparison of results with the published literature may best be left to the final stage of the research process.

Under the best of conditions the problem of what to read often proves to be more complicated than the novice anticipates. In some cases the most helpful information about appropriate methods can only be found embedded in the very reports the student might wish to eschew. In other cases, advisors may argue that whatever contamination might devolve from reviewing previous research presents no more risk than the collection of values and beliefs already present in the novice's head and thereby may urge use of every possible resource in constructing the proposal.

Resolution of these dilemmas will be neither simple nor perfectly satisfying to all parties. The only certain rule applies here as in any other proposal. The author *is* obligated to do a thorough search of the literature so that decisions about the timing and nature of its use will relate to the complete body of potentially relevant resources. As with quantitative proposals, whether related research is grouped in a separate review section or is used as needed throughout the proposal is an individual choice.

THE QUALITATIVE PROPOSAL:
COMING CLEAN

Another problem encountered in qualitative proposals is the task of "coming clean" about the ways in which personal biography will influence the research process. All researchers, quantitative as much as qualitative, bring significant personal baggage to the tasks of inquiry. It may be possible to pretend that the investigator's person can effectively be isolated from the processes of quantitative research. This pretense, however, is never possible in qualitative research.

Clear threats to accurate perception in terms of previous experience in the research setting, personal values, characteristic assumptions, and obvious bias must be addressed directly in the proposal. This is not done in an attempt to cleanse one's self of personal viewpoint and become neutral relative to the subject of study. Most qualitative researchers hold objectivity to be an illusion, a human state that is both impossible and undesirable to achieve. What the investigator brings to the setting can become a positive part of the research process, but only if it is recognized as an inextricable background for every step from question to conclusion. Coming clean thus means the creation of awareness, not the divestiture of self.

While concerns such as observer bias do have analogues in quantitative research, they are here a more pervasive problem, and one for which there are seldom simple solutions. For example, one common instance of the problem of investigator biography occurs when graduate students, who themselves are former teachers or school administrators, design a study that requires them to return to the context of public education and play the role of unbiased spectator. The first attempts to observe often trigger an avalanche of judgments about right or wrong, effective or ineffective, and desirable or undesirable, all based on the observer's past experiences in similar settings. This unbidden flood of evaluation poses a severe impediment to seeing, much less understanding, the world as experienced by the present participants. This particular problem is difficult to overcome and is precisely why it sometimes is best to select problems in a context with which the investigator has had little previous experience.

The proposal should provide evidence that factors of personal background have been scrupulously examined, understood, and accommodated by clear provisions for self-monitoring at each stage of the study. It often is possible to make plans to control for the influence of biography at the stages of data-gathering and data analysis. It may be desirable, for example, to cross-check the investigator's perceptions and decisions with a colleague whenever it is evident that personal dispositions might interact with bias-sensitive research tasks.

THE QUALITATIVE PROPOSAL:
ETHICAL CONCERNS

As indicated in Chapter 2, ethical concerns are not unique to qualitative proposals but may be more complex and troublesome. Issues concerning the ethics of qualitative research continue to stimulate debate and concern, perhaps most so among those who have extensive experience with the paradigm. To resolve these, novices may need lengthy discussion with advisors, and certainly will require long dialogue with their conscience.

The issues here are not all abstract, subtle, gradual, or distant from the person of the investigator. They can be sudden, painful, and fraught with genuine risk. How does the researcher weigh morality and pragmatic concerns when a study participant is observed in an illegal action? What does the observer do when an informant suddenly demands access to field notes? What is ethical behavior when circumstances appear to require that the investigator take an active part in the very events for which nonparticipant observation is the desired role? What is the right response when a school principal accuses the program evaluator of collusion with teachers for the purpose of subverting district policy? What action represents ethical behavior when the guarantee of subject anonymity is irretrievably breached after 20 in-depth interviews have already been conducted?

Whenever investigators enter into the daily lives of others at the level of intrusion required for qualitative study, significant problems of ethics are raised. Because the potential for direct harm is less obvious and the issues are more subtle than those typically encountered in quantitative research, ethical problems are easier to overlook in the proposal—and thereby are doubly serious.

The obligation to protect the best interest of subjects has compelling force in the qualitative paradigm. To complete a successful study requires that one or several residents in the study context welcome the investigator as a guest and a trusted confidant. Subjects who, by sharing their intimate version of events, are not exposed to some risk or disadvantage are the exception rather than the rule. This is most commonly the case in terms of possible repercussions on relationships with other people in the setting. It is all too easy for an informant to be regarded as a tattletale. The ideal rule of ethical conduct requires that whenever the researcher has a choice between using or not using material that is valuable to the study, but that may make the subject vulnerable, the interest of the subject must be selected over that of the investigation. It is much easier to subscribe to this, however, than it is to carry it out when interesting information must be lost.

At the least, such problems place heavy responsibility on the visitor for sensitive protection of sources. That the novice researcher understands this should be evident in every part of the proposal: the choice of language, the constraints accepted, the security devised to protect data, the establishment of informed consent at entry, the negotiation of subject rights, and the provision of genuine reciprocity with participants. The definition of what is right and acceptable conduct may be treated as a matter that is relative to context; for different circumstances there may be different rules of behavior. Determining these definitions with great care, however, is not an optional element in the proposal. Attention to ethical problems is an essential obligation in the planning of all research.

THE QUALITATIVE PROPOSAL: PUTTING IT TOGETHER

Once the unique problems—the open contract, use of the literature, personal biography, and ethical questions—have been considered, the more general tasks of proposal writing can be addressed in the specific forms they assume for qualitative study. Each author will devise a list of tasks based on his or her training and experience, and the particular nature of the proposed study.

The following items seem to rise to the top of many priority lists:

1. Developing a language or set of constructs for talking about the question to be pursued
2. Identifying appropriate data sources, and methods of gathering information
3. Setting boundaries for the investigation determining what is inside and what is beyond the limits of the study

4. Determining strategies to ensure the trustworthiness of data
5. Establishing procedures that will leave a clear trail, allowing others to know with reasonable precision how and why decisions were made at each stage of the study
6. Developing procedures for data management, reduction, and display
7. Identifying at least the first steps in data analysis
8. Laying plans for negotiating entry into the field of study.

ON COMBINING PARADIGMS

At this point it is appropriate to make note of one of the most interesting options available to the scholar who is interested in qualitative techniques. It obviously is possible to gather qualitative and quantitative forms of data within the same study. Whether it also is possible to analyze those data from perspectives that genuinely represent the two distinctive world views, combining results in some truly meaningful fashion, is the subject of continuing and energetic debate (Howe, 1988; Phelan, 1987; Smith & Heshusius, 1986).

Whatever the conclusion of that long dialogue among scientists, it is a fact that a growing number of published studies do include both qualitative and quantitative elements. Further, there is evidence that designs employing such combinations have made important contributions to program evaluation, organizational studies, and policy development. Even if quantitative data are not gathered, the investigator may still have to weigh the advantages and disadvantages of the quantification of qualitative information as part of the data reduction process.

The salient question here is whether an attempt to combine qualitative and quantitative paradigms is an appropriate undertaking for a beginner in research. Certainly examples can be found in almost every academic and professional literature. Novices can inspect these and form their own conclusions about the complexity of the process and the quality of the result.

Our experience as advisors suggests simply that if doing one kind of research is difficult, doing two kinds at once may be doubly so. The line between what is courageous and what is foolhardy is not always easy to discern. The importance of ending up on the right side of that line, however, is clear and compelling. The work of a novice, like any other, must meet a basic test. It must be done well, with correct use of both the techniques of data acquisition and modes of data analysis common to the scientific paradigm(s) employed. With that in mind, both the power of the design and the capability of the designer become legitimate concerns in planning any study. The resulting rule is clear and simple. Propose only the study you honestly believe you are prepared to execute.

To close on a note of optimism, it is fair to observe that decisions about each of these planning steps are more "forgiving" than they tend to be in quantitative research. The selection of a study site, for example, probably is not as critical as the novice is inclined to believe. There is a strong tendency after reading impressive field studies to believe that the great site produced the fine study. Experienced qualitative research workers, however, are more inclined to credit careful planning, perceptive analysis of data—and luck. None of the decisions made for the proposal are likely to make or break a first effort, even though they are decisions that must be made. Our advice is to plan as carefully as possible, but to keep a healthy respect for the surprises to be encountered and the inevitable adjustments that must be made in the best laid plans.

Notes

1. A scientific paradigm is a particular way of thinking about meaning in the context of inquiry. Just as each person has a cognitive schema for making sense of the world of daily experience, groups of scientists have particular ways of making sense of their scientific world. The area of paradigmatic epistemology is beyond the scope of this guide, but acquaintance with the concepts and issues therein will be part of the essential preparation of any young scholar. For readers not yet introduced to research paradigms we recommend the work of Kuhn (1970), Smith and Heshusius (1986), and Tuthill and Ashton (1983) as appropriate places to begin. The latter two are particularly helpful because of their close attention to education and the ways in which research paradigms differ in the physical and social sciences.

2. Our use of the term "quantitative" also is arbitrary. The use of numbers in research, per se, does not serve to distinguish one kind of paradigm from another— both quantitative and qualitative investigations may employ quantification. The quantitative (or positivist) paradigm is marked by particular ontological and epistemological assumptions that differ sharply from those forming the philosophical roots of the qualitative approach to inquiry.

3. Readers who would like to have an overview of research approaches in education will find a useful survey in an essay by Shulman (1981) that examines the questions and methods typical of each. The taxonomy of qualitative approaches may be extended beyond what has been touched on in the present chapter by including artistic as well as scientific modes of inquiry (Thornton, 1987).

6

Style and Form
in Writing the Proposal

The writing style of the thesis or grant proposal may be the most important factor in conveying your ideas to graduate advisors or funding agencies. Even experienced researchers must critically evaluate their writing to ensure that the best laid plans are presented in a clear, straightforward fashion. The sections that follow represent primary concerns for proposal writers.

PRAISING, EXHORTING,
AND POLEMICIZING: DON'T

For a variety of motives arising principally from the reward system governing other writing tasks, many students use their proposal as an opportunity to praise the importance of their discipline or professional field. Some use exhortative language to urge such particular points of view as the supposed importance of empirical research in designing professional practice. Others use the proposed research as the basis for espousing the virtues of particular social or political positions.

There is no need or proper place in a research proposal for such subjective side excursions. The purpose of a proposal is to set forth for a reader the exact nature of the matter to be investigated and a detailed account of the methods to be employed. Anything else distracts and serves as an impediment to clear communication.

As a general rule, it is best to stick to the topic and resist the temptation to sound "properly positive and enthusiastic." Do not attempt to manipulate the opinions of the reader in areas other than those essential to the investigation. The simple test is to ask yourself this question, "Does the reader really need to consider this point in order to judge the adequacy of my thinking?" If the answer is "no," then the decision to delete is clear, if not always easy, for the author.

QUOTATIONS:
HOW TO PICK FRUIT
FROM THE KNOWLEDGE TREE

Too often, inexperienced writers are inclined to equate the number of citations in a paper with the weight of the argument being presented. This is an error. The proper purposes served by the system of scholarly citation are limited to a few specific tasks. When a document has all the citations needed to meet the demands of those few tasks, it has enough. When it contains more citations, it has too many and is defective in that regard. Reviewers deem the use of nonselective references as an indication of poor scholarship, an inability to discriminate the central from the peripheral and the important from the trivial in research.

The proper uses of direct quotation are even more stringently limited than the use of general citations for paraphrased material. The practice of liberally sprinkling the proposal with quoted material—particularly lengthy quotations—is more than pointless, it is self-defeating. The first truth is that no one will read them. The second truth is that most readers find the presence of unessential quotations irritating and a distraction from the line of thought being presented for examination. When quotations are introduced at points for which even general citations are unnecessary, the writer has reached the limit of disregard for the reader.

There are two legitimate motives for direct use of another scholar's words: (a) the weight of authoritative judgment, in which "who said it" is of critical importance, and (b) the nature of expression, in which "how it was said" is the important element. In the former instance, when unexpected, unusual, or genuinely pivotal points are to be presented, it is reasonable to show the reader that another competent craftsperson has reached exactly the desired conclusion, or observed exactly the event at issue. In the latter instance, when another writer has hit on the precise, perfect phrasing to express a difficult point, it is proper to employ that talent on behalf of your own argument. The rule to follow is simple. If the substance of a quotation can be conveyed by a careful paraphrase, followed, of course, by the appropriate credit of a citation, with all of the clarity and persuasive impact of the original, *then don't quote*. In almost all instances it is best for the proposer to speak directly to the reader. The intervention of words from a third party should be reserved, like heavy cannon in battle, for those rare instances when the targets are specific and truly critical to the outcome of the contest.

A beneficial technique for students who recognize their own propensity toward excessive quotation is to use the critical summary form of note-taking. In this format, after carefully recording a full citation, each article is critically examined and then paraphrased on reference cards in the student's own words. During note-taking, a decision is made on whether the aesthetics of phrasing or the author's importance in terms of authority justify the use of direct quotation. Except in rare instances, quoted material is not transferred to the note cards. Thus direct quoting becomes less tempting during the subsequent writing phase when the student has recourse to notes. This technique also prevents unintentional plagiarism.

If using a computer for note storage and retrieval, similar precautions should be taken. When retrieving information from the computer, you should make certain that each item can clearly be identified either as your paraphrase or as a direct quote. It is possible to lose this information as you switch back and forth between notes, computer, and proposal document. One way to ensure identification, which can be used both on the computer and on handwritten note cards, is to use quotation marks for all direct quotes, listing the page number on which the text was found in parentheses immediately after the closing quotation mark. As you work between notes, computer, and writing of the proposal, transfer all this to your draft.

CLARITY AND PRECISION:
SPEAKING IN SYSTEM LANGUAGE

The language we use in the commerce of our everyday lives is common language. We acquired our common language vocabulary and grammar by a process that was gradual, unsystematic, and mostly unconscious. Our everyday language serves us well, at least as long as the inevitable differences in word meanings assigned by different people do not produce serious failures of communication. The language of science, specifically the language of research, is uncommon. The ongoing conversation of science, for which a research proposal is a plan of entry, is carried on in system languages in which each word must mean one thing to both writer and reader. Where small differences may matter a great deal, as in research, there must be a minimum of slippage between the referent object, the word used to stand for the object, and the images called forth by the word in the minds of listeners and readers.

The rules of invariant word usage give system languages a high order of precision. Minute or subtle distinctions can be made with relative ease. Evaluative language can be eliminated or clearly segregated from empirical descriptive language. More important, however, the language of research affords the reliability of communication that permits scientists to create a powerful interdependent research enterprise rather than limited independent investigations. When a chemist uses the system language of chemistry to communicate with another chemist, the word "element" has one and only one referent, is assigned to that referent on all occasions, is used for no other purpose within the language system, and consistently evokes the same image in the minds of everyone, everywhere, who has mastered the language.

Various domains of knowledge and various research enterprises are characterized by differing levels of language development. Some disciplines, such as anatomy or entomology, have highly developed and completely regularized language systems whereas others, particularly the behavioral sciences, employ languages still in the process of development. Irrespective of the area of investigation, however, the language of any research proposal must, as a minimum requirement, be systematic within itself. The words used in the proposal must have referents that are clear to the reader, and each must consistently designate only one referent. When the investigation lies within a subject area with an existing language system, then, of course, the author is bound to the conventions of that system.

Obviously, the researcher should be familiar with the system languages that function in the area of proposed investigation. Reading and writing both the specific language of the subject matter area and the more general languages common to the proposed methodology (statistics, experimental design, psychometrics, computer languages, etc.) are clear requirements for any study. Less obvious, however, is the fact that research proposals, by their exploratory nature, often demand the extension of existing language into new territory. Operations, observations, concepts, and relationships not previously specified within a language system must be assigned invariant word symbols by the investigator. More important, the reader must carefully be drawn into the agreement to make these same assignments.

Advisors and reviewers misunderstand student proposals far more often then they disagree with what is proposed. The failure of communication often occurs precisely at the point where the proposal moves beyond the use of the existing system language. This problem involves a failure of careful invention rather than a failure of mastering technique or subject matter. The following rules may be of some help as the student attempts to translate a personal vision of the unknown into the form of a carefully specified public record.

1. Never invent new words when the existing system language is adequate. If the referent in established use has a label that excludes what you do not want and includes all that you do want, then it needs no new name.

2. If there is reasonable doubt as to whether the word is in the system or the common domain, provide early in the proposal the definition that will be used throughout. Readers may give time and attention to deciphering the intended meaning unless you put their minds at ease.

3. Words that have been assigned system meaning should not be used in their common language form. For example, the word "significant" should not be used to denote its common language meaning of "important" in a proposal involving the use of statistical analysis. The system language of inferential statistics assigns invariant meaning to the word "significant"; any other use invites confusion.

4. Where a system language word is to be used in either a more limited or a more expanded sense, make this clear when the word first is introduced in the proposal. If the norms for local style requirements permit, this is one of the legitimate uses of footnotes to the text.

5. Where it is necessary to assign invariant meaning to a common language word in order to communicate about something not already accommodated within the system language, the author should choose with great care. Words with strong evaluative overtones, words with a long history of ambiguity, and words that have well-entrenched usage in common language make poor candidates for elevation to system

status. No matter how carefully the author operationalizes the new definition, it is always difficult for the reader to make new responses to familiar stimuli.

6. A specific definition is the best way to assign invariant meaning to a word. When only one or two words require such treatment, this can be accomplished in the text. A larger number of words may be set aside in a section of the proposal devoted to definitions. The best definition is one that describes the operations that are required to produce or observe the event or object. For example, note how the following words are assigned special meaning for the purpose of a proposal.

   a. Common language word is assigned invariant use:
   Exclusion will be deemed to have occurred when both of the following happen: The student no longer is eligible to participate in extracurricular activities under any provision of school district policy, and the student's name is stricken from the list of students eligible for extracurricular activities.

   b. System language word is employed with limitations not ordinarily assigned:
   The curriculum will be limited to those after-school activities that the current *School District Manual* lists as approved for secondary school students.

   c. System language word is operationalized by describing a criterion:
   Increased motivation will be presumed when, subsequent to any treatment condition, the time spent in any extracurricular activity rises more than 10% of the previous weekly total.

   d. Common language word is operationalized by describing a criterion:
   Dropouts are defined as all participants who fail to attend three consecutive activity meetings.

   e. System language word is operationalized by describing procedure:
   Reinforcement will refer to the procedure of listing all club members in the school newspaper, providing special hall passes for members, and listing club memberships on school transcripts.

   f. Common language word is operationalized by describing procedure:
   Instruction will consist of five 10-minute sessions in which the club sponsor may employ any method of teaching so long as it includes no fewer than five attempts for each student to complete the activity.

EDITING: THE CARE AND NURTURE OF A DOCUMENT

A proposal is a working document. As a primary vehicle for communication with advisors and funding agencies, as a plan for action, and as a contract, the proposal performs functions that are immediate and practical, not symbolic or aesthetic. Precisely because of these important functions, the proposal, in all of its public appearances at least, should be free from distracting mechanical errors and the irritating confusion of shoddy format.

At the privacy of your own desk, it is entirely appropriate to cross out passages, add new ones, and rearrange the order of paragraphs. The series of rough drafts are part of the process through which a proposal evolves toward final form. When, however, the proposal is given to an advisor, sent to a funding agency, or presented to a seminar, the occasion is public and calls for an edited, formally prepared document. The document should be easy to read—the proposer should use a good typewriter or printer and, when required, a new ribbon. If you use a dot matrix printer make certain the text can be read without visual strain.

Every sentence must be examined and reexamined in terms of its clarity, grammar, and relationship with surrounding sentences. A mark of the neophyte writer is the tendency to resist changing a sentence once it is written, and even more so when it has been typed. A sentence may be grammatically correct and still be awkward within its surroundings. The tough test is the best test here. If, in reading any sentence, a colleague or reviewer hesitates, stumbles, or has to reread the sentence to understand the content, then the sentence must be examined for possible revision—no matter how elegant, obvious, and precise it seems to the author.

Aside from meticulous care in writing and rewriting, the most helpful procedure in editorial revision is to obtain the assistance of colleagues to read the proposal for mechanical errors, lack of clarity, and inadequacies of content. An author can read the same error over and over without recognizing it, and the probability of discovery declines with each review. The same error may leap at once to the attention of even the most casual reader who is reading the proposal for the first time. One useful trick that may improve the author's ability to spot mechanical errors is to read the sentences in reverse order, thus destroying the strong perceptual set created by the normal sequence of ideas.

Although format will be a matter of individual taste or departmental or agency regulation, several general rules may be used in designing the layout of the document:

1. Use double-spacing, substantial margins, and ample separation for major subsections. Crowding makes reading both difficult and unpleasant. *Always* number pages so that readers can quickly refer to a specific location.

2. Make ample use of graphic illustration. A chart or simple diagram can improve clarity and ease the difficult task of critical appraisal and advisement.

3. Make careful and systematic use of headings. The system of headings recommended in the *Publication Manual of the American Psychological Association* (1983) is particularly useful for the design of proposals.

4. Place in an appendix everything that is not immediately essential to the main tasks of the proposal. Allowing readers to decide whether they will read supplementary material is both a courtesy and good strategy.

IN SEARCH OF A TITLE:
FIRST IMPRESSIONS AND
THE ROUTE TO RETRIEVAL

The title of the proposal is the first contact a reader has with the proposed research. First impressions, be they about people, music, food, or potential research topics, generate powerful anticipations about what is to follow. Shocking the reader by implying one content domain in the title and following with a different one in the body of the proposal is certain to evoke a strong negative response. The first rule in composing a title is to achieve reasonable parity between the images evoked by the title and the opening pages of the proposal.

For the graduate student, the proposal title may well become the thesis or dissertation title and therefore calls for careful consideration of all the functions it must serve and the standards by which it will be judged. The first function of the title is to identify content for the purpose of retrieval. Theses and dissertations are much more retrievable than was once the case. In fact, they have become a part of the public domain of the scholar. The increasing use of microfiche and microfilm has made the circulation of unpublished documents many times faster and far broader in geographic scope. Titling research has become, thereby, an important factor in sharing research.

In less sophisticated times, titles could be carelessly constructed and the documents would still be discovered by diligent researchers who could take the time to investigate items that appeared only remotely related to their interests. Today, scholars stagger under the burden of sifting through enormous and constantly increasing quantities of material apparently pertinent to their domain. There is no recourse other than to be increasingly selective in documents actually retrieved and inspected. Hence, each title the researcher scans must present at least a moderate probability of being pertinent, on the basis of the title alone, or it will not be included on the reading list for review. In short, the degree to which the title communicates a concise, thorough, and unambiguous picture of the content is the first factor governing whether a given report will enter the ongoing dialogue of the academic community.

Word selection should be governed more by universality of usage than by personal aesthetic judgment or peculiarly local considerations. Computer retrieval systems, on which more and more scholars are depending for leads to related studies in their research field, classify titles according to a limited set of key words. As we discussed in Chapter 4, researchers construct search plans that will identify all studies categorized by key words known to be associated with their area of interest. Thus both readers and writers of research reports must describe the research in similar terms or, in too many instances, they will not reach each other.

The title should describe as accurately as possible the exact nature of the main elements in the study. Although such accuracy demands the use of specific language, the title should be free of obscure technical terms or jargon that will be recognized only by small groups of researchers who happen to pursue similar questions within a narrow band of the knowledge domain.

Components Appropriate for Inclusion in the Title

The elements most commonly considered for inclusion in the title are the dependent and independent variables, the performance component represented by the criterion task or tasks, the treatment or treatments to be administered, the model underlying the study, the purpose of the study (predicting, establishing relationships, or determining differences), and any unusual contribution of the study.

Dependent and independent variables ordinarily should be included, although they may be presented under a more general rubric. For instance, the independent variables of a study might be simple reaction time, discriminatory reaction time, movement time, and reflex time. In the title the four measures might appear as "neuromuscular responses." Similarly, the performance components of the study also may be summarized into a single categorical term.

A clever author can, by careful selection of words, provide information in the title that a theory is being tested by using a word that often is associated with the theory. For instance, the title, "Generalizability of Contingency Management and Reinforcement in Second-Grade Special Education Classes" implies that the investigator is testing the applicability of behavioral theory to a specific population. Much has been communicated by including the single word "generalizability" in the title.

The ultimate purpose of the study in terms of predicting, establishing relationships, or determining differences can be expressed without providing an explicit statement. For example, when variables are expressed in a series, "Anthropometrics, Swimming Speed, and Shoulder-Girdle Strength," relationship generally is implied. If the same study were titled "Anthropometrics and Shoulder-Girdle Strength of Fast and Slow Swimmers," the reader would anticipate a study in which differences were determined.

Any aspect of the study that is particularly unusual in terms of methodology, or that represents a unique contribution to the literature, should be included in the title. A treatment that is unusually long or of great magnitude (e.g., "Longitudinal Analysis of Human Short-Term Memory from Age 20 to 80"), a method of observation that is creative or unusually accurate (e.g., "Hand Preference in Telephone Use as a Measure of Limb Dominance and Laterality"), a sampling technique that is unique (e.g., "Intelligence of Children Whose Parents Purchase Encyclopedias"), and a particular site for measurement that sets the study apart from others (e.g., "Perceptual Judgment in a Weightless Environment: Report from the Space Shuttle") are examples of such aspects.

Components Inappropriate for Inclusion in the Title

Such factors as population, research design, and instrumentation should not be included in the title unless they represent a substantial departure from similar studies. The population, for instance, should not be noted unless it is a population never sampled before, or is in some way an unusual target group. In the title, "Imbedded Figures Acuity in World-Class Chess Masters," the population of the subjects is critical to the rationale for the study. The population in "Running Speed, Leg Strength, and Long Jump Performance of High School Boys" is not important enough to occupy space in the title.

Similarly, research design and instrumentation are not appropriate for inclusion in the title unless they represent an unusual approach to measurement or analysis. The type of research method expressed in "Physiological Analysis of Precompetitive Stress" is common in studies dealing with stress, and surely some other aspect of the study would make a more informative contribution to the title. The approach in "Phenomenological Analysis of Precompetitive Stress," however, represents a unique approach and signals the reader that the report contains information of an unusual kind.

Mechanics of Titling

Mechanically, the title should be concise and should provide comfortable reading, free from elaborate or jarring constructions. Excessive length should be avoided because it dilutes the impact of the key elements presented; two lines generally should be adequate. Some retrieval systems place a word limitation on titles, thus enforcing brevity. Redundancies such as "Aspects of," "Comments on," "Study of," "Investigation of," "Inquiry into," and "An Analysis of" are expendable. It is obvious that a careful investigation of a topic will include "aspects of" the topic, whereas the research report has as its entire purpose the communication of "comments on" the findings of a study. It is pointless to state the obvious in a title.

Attempts to include all subtopics of a study in the title sometimes result in elephantine rubrics. The decision to include or exclude mention of a subtopic should be made less in terms of an abstraction, such as complete coverage, and more in terms of whether inclusion actually will facilitate appropriate retrieval. One useful way to construct a title is to list all the elements that seem appropriate for inclusion, and then to weave them into various permutations until a title appears that satisfies both technical and aesthetic standards.

7

The Oral Presentation

The processes for consideration of your proposal may not require an oral presentation, and the written document may be the only opportunity to explain (and sell) the study. In many universities, however, formal presentation of your ideas for a thesis or dissertation (particularly at the point of an initial prospectus) is a standard expectation, often performed in the context of a graduate seminar. It is less common to have an opportunity to make an oral presentation of a grant proposal, but interviews with site visitors and even command performances before review panels do occur.

Our advice is that if an opportunity occurs to stand up before an audience and talk about what you propose to do—you should take it. Even if your oral presentation is only to your peers in a study or support group, do it! The feedback and exchange of ideas may prove to be invaluable as you shape the final form of the written document. Further, such exercises are excellent preparation for a later thesis or dissertation defense—the final hurdle before graduation at many institutions.

Of equal importance, however, is the valuable training in research presentation skills that will be used when you have later opportunities to share your completed work. Whether with teachers at a local school, with students and faculty at a nearby college, with professional colleagues at a state conference, or in the rarified atmosphere of an international research symposium, talking about your study and findings is an important extension of the research process. Learning to do it with clarity, economy, and confidence will serve both you and your audiences well—and explaining your proposal is the perfect way to develop and refine those skills.

We do not propose to give a tutorial here on public speaking. What we will do, however, is to note those points at which the task of explaining research to a live audience creates demands that require thoughtful preparation. And careful planning is as much needed for presenting a proposed study as for reporting its results.

A slick presentation will not finesse a weak design, but a clear explanation of dilemmas encountered and hard choices yet to be made will improve the quality of assistance you receive. Further, a brisk and economical presentation recruits support because it shows that you understand exactly what is salient for a reviewer's consideration. Best of all, at the other end of the research process, a graceful and lucid discussion of your findings will allow others to share the fruits of your labor—and may even produce invitations to present your work to fellow investigators in exciting and distant venues.

Before launching into a consideration of oral presentations, it will be helpful to review briefly how talking about research is different from writing about it. Each of these differences bears consequences for how the task of speaking is planned and executed.

1. *Time*—The temporal limits for explaining your study to a live audience invariably are more restrictive than the time requirements for accomplishing a written presentation of the same study. Put another way, 20 minutes of a listener's time allow you to cover far less than 20 minutes of a reader's time. The reasons for this are complex and not all of them are obvious, but the end result is a demand for selectivity in content and economy in delivery. Finally, because the listener is not free to go back and hear a presentation over again, as a reader is free to re-study a text, the speaker must achieve absolute clarity on the first attempt.

2. *Interaction*—Oral presentations of research almost always include interchange with the audience. Indeed, in the case of presenting a proposal for a committee or seminar, that exchange is the purpose of the occasion, some or all of the audience having already read your prospectus or full proposal. Questions, comments, advice, and discussion often follow the talk, and sometimes are interspersed within the flow of presentation. This fact not only calls for the use of interactive skills (at the least, the need to think on your feet), but has consequences for planning and delivery as well.

3. *Adjustment*—The speaker can monitor the ongoing reactions of a live audience, responding to the array of nonverbal signals by adjusting pace and content. Boredom, puzzlement, surprise, distraction, and close interest are not visible on the reader's face while you are writing. While you speak, however, all of them can be observed from moment to moment, and such reactions can be useful information. Responding in appropriate ways not only increases the effectiveness of communication, it ties speaker and audience together in a mutual enterprise that is impossible to achieve through the written page.

4. *Anxiety*—If the range of skills demanded for speaking is not wider than the collective span of those needed for writing, at the least, many of them are different. For most students, the skills for making formal oral presentations are much less used, and thereby are less well-honed. The need to display unpracticed skills in a public setting, when added to the normal concern about winning approval or obtaining needed assistance, produces an occasion for anxiety. For some, the number of spontaneous variables at play in a live setting add zest and a sense of rich possibility. For others, a live listening audience simply adds a discomfort for which there is no parallel in the work of writing. For those people, the consequence is a need to prepare in such a way that anxiety (or outright terror) is held within bounds, and becomes facilitating arousal rather than debilitating inhibition.

Those are some of the most distinctive differences between writing and speaking. Their existence means that preparing and delivering an oral presentation involves all the problems of using a new medium to communicate familiar content. Accordingly, we have some advice that may provide users of this handbook with a helpful set of guidelines for getting started. Our suggestions cluster into seven areas that occur in natural sequence: (a) preparing content, (b) preparing materials, (c) practice and revision, (d) preparing the environment, (e) oral presentation, (f) managing interaction, and (g) the aftermath. What we have to say about each of these topics will seem different, in some respects, from what you may have seen in books or heard in public speaking courses. There are several reasons for that, and knowing them may help you digest what is to follow.

First, our advice is tailored to the task of talking about research to other researchers, or, at the least, to people who have working familiarity with scholarship. Customs of language, format, and demeanor allow (or demand) a form of communication that is different from what would be appropriate with another kind of audience.

Although much may be shared among all kinds of public speaking, we are not dealing in this text with a generic form of public discourse. Second, the source here is our own experience as people who have frequent occasion to do oral presentations dealing with research. While that background certainly is helpful in sorting out ideas about what distinguishes effective from ineffective public speaking, it does not provide much occasion to move from specific rules to higher order generalizations. We are not communication specialists, nor are we competent to offer a tutorial on effective use of language. This chapter is about "how to do it," not "how to understand it."

PREPARING CONTENT

In determining what to cover, the particulars of circumstance will dictate most of the decisions. How long do you have? Who will be present and what will they expect you to do? What will the audience already know? What will your listeners need to learn from you in order to play their part in the occasion? For your purpose, what is absolutely essential to explain, and what is not? What content requires emphasis, and what may be given only a passing note? To what extent must you contend with uneven prior knowledge on the part of members of the audience? Is the presentation a follow-up of a previously distributed document (a review leading into discussion), or is it the only access the audience will have to your work? If you can specify the answers to those questions, you will have a rough map of what to include in your presentation. In the process of using that map, the following guidelines will assist in shaping the final product.

1. Don't confuse what you already know with what the members of the audience already know. If there was not something they needed to learn from you, why would you be doing the presentation? The right question to start with is *not*, "What do I want to talk about?" or, "What is in my proposal?" or, "What were my results?" The right questions are, "What don't they know that they need or want to know?" and, "In what order do they need to learn things to make sense of what I have to say?" You are going to lead the listeners through a sequence of logic, or the events of a study, step-by-step. In that sense, a research presentation is teaching, not ritual display. You begin with, stay with, and end with a concern for what you want your audience to learn. That requires a highly selected version of what you know.

2. In deciding what to cover in the time you have available, less often is more. People will understand more, remember more, and make better use (in subsequent discussion) of what you explain, if you explain less. Locate the essentials and make them the center of your presentation. It often will serve you well to note for the audience particular sections of detail you are leaving out (or simply designating by name) and, perhaps, why you are doing so. You even may make clear that you have the material and would be pleased to provide it at another time. That strategy prevents people from being distracted by thoughts about what you are not saying. Having less to talk about allows an easier pace, more opportunity for emphasis, illustration and review, and less tension in the whole process.

   If it is genuinely impossible to communicate what is essential to the purpose of the presentation in the time provided, don't complain about it in your speech. Negotiate an extension of your time, ask for a change in the goals to be accomplished by the presentation, or, as a last resort, make brief public note of what it has been necessary to exclude. Trying to crowd everything in is a lose-lose proposition. It won't work, it will irritate your audience, and it will leave you feeling inadequate.

3. Try to anticipate the needs and reactions of your audience, and build this in as part of your presentation. As with the point made above about noting omissions, there are a number of predictable concerns or needs among audience members that can be dealt with as you proceed. If there is a point about which you are unsure, acknowledge it and invite comment or advice in the following discussion. If there is a point on which you know some of the audience will disagree with what you say, make a polite note of the fact—and perhaps invite subsequent discussion of alternatives. If some people already know something that must be explained for others, recognize the situation and ask those who don't need your tutorial to bear with you. If there has been discussion about a point on a previous occasion, or if there have been revisions in or additions to your work, note them, even if you elect not to discuss them.

All of this serves to assure the audience that you are thinking specifically about them and that you are aware of their unique relationships with the content of your presentation. In addition to helping to maintain their close attention, this strategy allows you to maintain a degree of control (or, at least, influence) over what will be given attention in any discussion that ensues.

PREPARING MATERIALS

Unless you are blessed with the happy facility of perfect memory, the primary task here is to prepare something to guide your presentation. The most obvious purpose of the guide (or script) is to ensure that you say the right things, about the right topics, in the right order. Less obvious are the reasons for trying so hard to get it right—the fact that you have just one chance to achieve transparent clarity, and the fact that making things easy for the audience is the best way to get them to be helpful (and friendly).

It does not matter what form your guide takes, so long as it serves the purpose of getting it right, and is constructed to allow effective delivery of your message. The first rule of delivery is *never read!* The second rule is *if you have to read, never appear to be doing so!* By disconnecting speaker and listeners, reading defeats the purpose of doing an oral presentation. It is impossible for the audience to feel other than insulted. Accordingly, your guide has to take a form that allows you to spend most of your time looking at and reacting to your audience, and only brief instants being reminded of what comes next.

The possibilities for accomplishing this are endless. They range from small note cards with keywords listed in bold type, through pages of text in traditional outline format, to verbatim scripts with key words or phrases highlighted in fluorescent colors. In designing your own guide, however, remember that there are other needs to be serviced beyond having a memory aid. For example, whatever you use should be visible in a way that requires only a quick glance to find your location and pick up a cue to trigger recall of the next sequence. If you want to move about while speaking, then your guide should be comfortably portable. Pages should be boldly numbered in sequence to avoid the unfortunate accident of missing or jumbled notes, and reminders for the use of each visual aid should be inserted exactly where it is to be introduced.

As an example, this is what one of the present authors does for each presentation. A rough script is typed with double spacing. Some sentences are laid out in complete form, while others are indicated just by the opening phrase. All, however, begin at the left margin (essentially, the format is a sequential list of individual sentences). Only the top one third of each sheet is used, the lower two thirds being left entirely blank. Then the typed pages are darkened and enlarged by 10% on a copy machine. (On a computer, all of this could be accomplished by using a larger font and the top half of the page.) Finally a key word or phrase in each sentence is marked with a highlighter pen.

Placed on a lectern, the script, which occupies only the top portion of the page, now rests at a level directly on the speaker's line of sight to the audience. All of the highlighted words are read from peripheral vision, and eye-contact with the audience is never broken by having to look down to read the lower portion of the page. Sheets are transferred silently from right to left as used, and never become visible distractions for the listeners. The effect given is that of articulate, completely extemporaneous speech, delivered with close attention to the audience.

Some of what the audience sees and hears is illusion, made possible by the idiosyncratic speaking guide described above—a guide that, in truth, serves to disguise a poor memory and poor eyesight. In a like fashion, you must devise a guide that will best serve your unique strengths and limitations as a speaker. The purpose is not to enhance your reputation for oral presentation beyond what you deserve. The purpose is to serve each audience—by making it easy for them to understand what you have to say.

Another strategy that many speakers use is to place key words and phrases on slides or overhead transparencies. This can be very effective for several reasons. It allows you full freedom to move around, and the display of key words helps the audience remember your main points. This strategy, however, has two potential drawbacks. One is irksome and the other is disastrous. Having the words on the screen tempts the speaker to look at the screen instead of the audience. The second potential problem is that the slide or overhead projector can break down, leaving you with no guide at all. A paper copy of your slides or transparencies, with a few extra notes, allows you the freedom to use either slides or notes and should prevent any serious disaster.

In addition to some form of speaking guide, you may wish to prepare aids that will support your oral presentation. There are several reasons for electing to do so. Not the least of these is the fact that any audience of more than a few individuals will contain some people who learn best (or only) when they can inspect a concrete example. The more complex the object or relationship, the more they are disadvantaged by purely verbal imagery. Photographs, models, tables, figures, graphs, outlines, data specimens, diagrams, and demonstrations are just a few of the supporting illustrations that can give your words concrete representation.

There are other important reasons to consider the use of graphic aids. Economy of communication is one. While not all pictures can replace a thousand words, some certainly can. Other graphics, such as diagrams or keyword outlines, help the audience keep track of sequence and relationship in otherwise convoluted explanations. A good example is a flow chart that helps you take your audience through your methodology. Finally, some illustrations provide focus and heighten impact, as in an audiotape segment or transcript excerpt from an interview.

In deciding whether to make use of such aids, subject each possibility to this basic question: "Will the prop really help people (or at least some people) to understand what I am saying?" If you can't honestly conclude that introducing the supplement to your presentation will cause better or quicker learning, don't use it. Each use of an aid consumes valuable time. Each requires the transfer of audience attention from one object to another, with consequent risk of leaving someone behind. Each, therefore, involves a trade-off to be weighed with great care. Be sure your audience gets back more than it has to give.

One simple aid is almost always appropriate. An outline of what you plan to talk about (and do), laid out in sequence, is appreciated by most listeners. Keep it to a single sheet, include no details, and indicate beginning and ending times. Knowing what is to come (and being able to tick off major segments as they are completed) is a reassuring convenience. It also is the first sign of careful planning and concern for the listeners.

Visual aids such as slides, transparencies, newsprint diagrams, and chalkboard illustrations should be *used*—not simply displayed. Present them, explain their significance, allow the audience a brief moment to digest or ask questions, and then remove the aid from sight, firmly directing attention to the next element of the presentation. Leaving aids visible invites continued inspection or simple distraction (as with the case of projectors running without a slide or transparency in place).

There is a hard rule about quality for visual aids, one never to be violated. *If you use it, everyone should be able to see it!* Large print, high magnification, sharp contrast, and reduction of content to bare essentials are basic qualifications for any illustration. Further, every aid has to be judged relative to the limitations of the environment in which you will be speaking. If it can't be seen by everyone, in every part of the room, don't use it. Under most circumstances, this disqualifies newsprint, chalkboards, and even overhead projectors for any but small group presentations. In such cases, slide projectors or handout sheets are the better choice.

Some presentation formats appropriately utilize a continuous stream of graphic aids, as in large-scale lectures. Those special instances aside, the rule again is that less usually will be more. Even with high quality graphics there is the risk that overuse of aids will dilute the focus of what you are saying and begin to intrude between you and the audience. Select only the aids that will advance your cause, use them deliberately for that purpose, then never let them remain as distractors. As a general rule, with you to point out what is salient, a well constructed aid should yield its main message in a few seconds, and should do so for everyone in the room. This means that for your audience, illustrations should feel like a natural continuation of the presentation, rather than an interruption.

PRACTICE AND REVISION

Explaining any research study, or its results, is a difficult task. To the extent that you genuinely care about communicating with an audience, it will be natural and proper to do the job well. If the quality of presentation enhances or restricts the possibility of achieving your goal, practice makes sense. To do so also signals respect for a significant form of craft knowledge in the world of scholarship, a craft that will serve your work—even if you are just explaining a proposal to the members of a small committee.

There are three main varieties of practice: silent reading, solitary speaking, and trial runs before a live audience. Silent reading gives familiarity to the guide, and gradually allows memory to free attention from the bondage of literal reading. It does not, however, give a correct estimate of time required (silent reading always is faster than reading aloud) or give any clue as to how what you say will sound in the ears of an audience.

In contrast, solitary speaking gives both a better estimate of timing and an opportunity to listen to the sounds and sequences of your presentation. You will discover that the syntaxes and rhythms of written text are not those of normal speech, and adjustments will be required if you are to avoid the stilted and unnatural sound of reading aloud. The most common adjustments are simplification of content (often by painful excisions), longer pauses, and more frequent use of words that provide transition between topics.

The use of a mirror, a lectern, and a tape recorder can markedly increase the value of solitary practice, particularly if you now include actual use of graphic aids. This kind of practice accelerates both the fine tuning needed to give confidence, and acquisition of automaticity in performing mechanical tasks—such as managing your note cards. The latter is vital because it allows you to spend more and more time looking into the mirror that is standing in for a live audience.

Finally, practice before a real audience allows you to move toward personalization, the ability to speak with the relaxed informality of serious conversations in everyday social interaction. We say "move toward" because there are some conventions that govern formal presentations that are absent in ordinary conversation. Just the matter of how long one person speaks, who controls the topic, and who is free to interrupt, mark the rules of formal presentation as different. The intent to instruct (and influence) also is different, not in kind, but in the degree of conscious purpose. Those distinctions (and others) notwithstanding, the audience always is made more comfortable and attentive by adopting the tone and cadence of "talking with" rather than "talking at." To achieve that kind of grace, nothing equals live practice.

Friends, relatives, peers, and professors can be drafted for the purpose of live practice. The only absolute qualification is a desire to help you prepare. Of course, the presence of anyone with sufficient background to raise questions about content can elevate the trial to a new level. Questions and comments allow you to revise defective explanations or, at the least, to anticipate reactions and to determine whether the questions raised reveal problems in the proposed study that you must address or whether the questions reflect only an inadequate explanation. Further, now you can practice using aids in ways that truly support rather than interrupt, and now you will discover how much longer everything is going to take than you had first imagined.

Even though not everyone in the audience may be able to help you with the details of the study, all are competent to give feedback about your delivery. Once they understand that critique of practice is helpful (albeit sometimes disconcerting) and not destructive, anyone can notice and report distractors such as the ubiquitous "ok?" or "aaah" that so often intrude without the speaker's awareness. Gestures or postures that erode audience attention such as rubbing the nose, gripping the lectern with white knuckles, staring fixedly above the heads of listeners, swaying from side to side, making eye contact only with individuals on the left, and fiddling with a pointer, are so common as to be almost predictable in novice speakers. Good friends will tell you all about them.

When live practice and feedback yield substantial revisions, second and third trials may be needed. A good practice sequence to follow is solitary speaking followed by three presentations to (a) two or three good friends, (b) your advisor, and finally (c) a small group of people who have some competence in research—all prior to the official presentation of your proposal. The limit often is the availability (and goodwill) of your colleagues. While there may be some theoretical risk of over-practice, it is unlikely to be a serious concern. As with any other task, work at it until you get it right, and then get on with the job.

PREPARING THE ENVIRONMENT

The rule about the environment, the space where you will actually present, is simple. *"Know it, and manipulate it!"* This means that you should inspect the room and arrange it (so far as possible) to suit your purpose. Where particular people sit and the general configuration of seating (as around a table or in a room with freely movable chairs) are first-order concerns. The presence of a lectern, location of light switches, the availability of doors to shut out distracting noise, and the location of power outlets (if in doubt, always bring an extension cord) are all essential information.

If there is a wall-mounted projection screen you intend to use, always pull it down for inspection. More than one unwary novice has discovered an obscene message scrawled there for all to contemplate as the introduction to their first slide! In larger venues, sound systems, projector stands, and lectern lights are never to be taken for granted.

If you are planning to employ one or more assistants to help with demonstrations or the operation of equipment, have them come with you. Where they will sit, how well they can see you, and their familiarity with the environment are matters for your concern.

If you plan to use hand-outs, having a packet already in place as people enter the room avoids the confusion of later distribution and signals a business-like atmosphere. If you include a program outline, it can be placed on top with names marked so that advisors or special visitors can have precedence in seating. It always is good to have the most important listeners located where you can keep the closest possible contact with them during your presentation.

The more you can reduce unexpected intrusions and the more you can make the environment comfortable for the audience, the more closely they will attend what you have to say. Take the time to inspect the field of action. If there is not much you can do to adjust it in your favor, at the least let it hold no surprises.

ORAL PRESENTATION

There are two things most novice speakers do not know (or find difficult to remember). Virtually everyone is nervous before a public presentation. That is normal and, once you learn how to turn that excitement to your advantage, healthy. A second point is that under almost all imaginable circumstances, every one in the audience wants you to do well. Even more, most of them are quite prepared to overlook all sorts of minor slips as part of giving you a full and fair hearing. How many times have you sat in the audience and wished the speaker would give a terrible presentation? The answer should afford some comfort for your next effort.

Having something at stake beyond just the challenge of performing well, as in a proposal review or dissertation defense, does add greater pressure to a presentation. In that regard, you will note that we have not said reassuringly, "Don't worry about it." Anyone in that situation will have at least some honest cause for concern. What we do want to point out is that with solid preparation, the possibility of a truly bad presentation is vanishingly small. Formal evaluation of what you have to say is out of our hands—and at the moment you begin, out of yours as well! There is nothing left to do but concentrate on a good clear presentation and let the rest take care of itself.

Take a deep breath, acknowledge the audience (large or small) with a friendly word or gesture of greeting, and then start at a slow, even pace. In the opening sentences, make a special point of trying to match your speaking voice to your normal conversational tone. Many speakers report that the sound of their own voice provides recurrent feedback. If they are able to sound relaxed and confident, they begin gradually to really feel that way. Likewise, if your voice, posture, and movements signal exceptional tension, your audience will be concerned and begin to reflect the tension back. Start easy, breathe, look at people, and just talk to them.

We did not say "smile," as part of our advice because nothing is worse than the frozen rictus of a false smile. Forget your face and concentrate on how your listeners are responding to your words. If you can do that, smiles will come when they are a natural part of the process.

Particularly in the opening minutes, remember to pause when you have made an important point. Do then the kinds of things we all do in conversation; nod to stress a point, and raise your eyebrows to ask your audience if they understand. Punctuate with a simple gesture, or just wait for a moment as we do when encouraging a listener to contemplate the significance of what we have said.

Later on in your presentation you will want to consider the need for stimulus variation. Changing the display is one of the key factors in sustaining attention, and the need for it grows as the presentation lengthens. Throughout the presentation you might change your speaking location, briefly introduce a graphic display, or simply alter your tone and speed of delivery. Any small change can break the dull grip of too much of one thing.

If possible, you should have someone tape record your presentation. It is unlikely to be the last you give, and although being perfect is not a reasonable expectation, getting better is. Be sure, of course, to use long-playing tape to avoid the distraction of having to flip a cassette in mid-course. In addition to making sure you can profit by listening to your own performance, purchase some further insurance by asking several friends to watch for and record the things you will not be able to hear on a tape. Nonverbal signals, for example, are a powerful part of every communication. Knowing about what your body language is saying, good and bad, is part of learning to do effective presentations.

As you close, three things are almost universally appropriate. First, revisit with your audience the essential points that you wish them to retain. Second, provide a graceful transition by reminding the audience about what will happen next, whether that be a break, a period of questions and discussion, return of control to a moderator, or termination of the meeting. Third, and finally, any audience deserves the courtesy of your thanks. While you are struggling to master the difficult craft of presenting research, a patient and forgiving audience will have earned a good deal more. Remember that, when you are next on the other side of the lectern.

MANAGING INTERACTION

Whether you serve as your own moderator or have someone else to preside over a period of questions and discussion, a little advance planning will make it go more smoothly. If you can tape the discussion that follows your presentation, be sure to do so. Valuable points of comment or advice that seem vivid in the excitement of interaction with the audience may be lost to recall. Few people find it possible to take notes and talk at the same time.

If the audience contains both people charged with some official function (such as reviewing your proposal) and others who are visitors or supporters, make a point of setting the ground rules at the outset. It is good to let everyone who has attended have an opportunity to comment or question, but give priority of first opportunity to those who require it. If you are managing the flow of discussion, be sure to spread interaction around. Some people are not skilled in taking turns, and others need encouragement if their comments are to be heard.

In fielding questions the first rule is: *Get it straight!* Be sure you understand what is being asked before attempting to answer. Repeating or rephrasing complex or unclear questions serves the dual purpose of detecting miscommunication and reassuring the questioner that you do understand what he or she wants to know. Repeating every inquiry, of course, is tedious and to be avoided.

When you just do not know the answer, say so. When you just can't understand the question, say so—but also ask if it can be taken up later when there is more time for clarification. If you know something that may be helpful but you suspect it is not exactly what has been requested, ask permission to alter the question as a way of advancing the discussion. If the question is clear enough but you think it is inappropriate to the occasion, acknowledge it politely and suggest that you would be glad to take it up after the meeting is concluded.

If you are pressed for an agreement that, in good conscience, you cannot give, try acknowledging the existence of alternative or competing views. If that does not close the point, ask to defer the matter until there is sufficient time for deeper examination of the argument. Normally, by this time someone will have interceded to redirect the discussion. If help is not forthcoming, there is little to do except to hold your ground, perhaps asking for comment by others in the audience.

Finally, keep an eye on the clock. Just as the presentation proper should end on time, any follow-up discussion should be limited by prior announcement, mutual agreement of those present, or just plain common sense.

THE AFTERMATH

Within several days, make a point of obtaining and processing all the available feedback from your presentation. Listen to the tape, review notes taken by friends, and solicit feedback on both content and delivery. Some people will do this with greater skill than others, and some will feel more comfortable in providing an honest critique. Predictably, there will be conflicting opinions on some points. What one finds helpful, another may not. Rather than attempt to respond by planning some change to accommodate every comment, listen for patterns. Where concerns overlap lies the point at which effort for redesign or further practice will yield improvement.

Finally, encourage people to indicate what they liked and found helpful in your presentation. This is not so that you can revel in their praise but because you may not be aware of what was most effective. If you can learn what worked, strength can be built on strength.

8

Money for Research
How to Ask for Help

Grant applications, as a generic class of documents, are formal appeals for the award of support, usually in the form of money, for undertakings in which the grantor has special interest. In the strict sense, a grant is an award of funds without a fully defined set of terms and conditions for use, while a contract is a work order from the grantor in which procedures, costs, and funding period have been established in explicit terms. Thus, the majority of what are commonly called grant proposals are applications for award of a contract—not a grant.

Further complication is added by the fact that grants may be sought for projects in which the objective is to provide a needed service, or for research studies in which the objective is to produce knowledge, with any service provided being purely incidental. Specialized guides are available for proposals that seek funds for the development of programmatic services. Some of these, such as the texts by Coley and Scheinberg (1990) and Bauer (1988), will be of interest to all novices in the grantsmanship game. The present guide is directed specifically to proposals involving research rather than service to a client population.

The grant request contains two component parts: (a) the application for funding, and (b) the proposal that explains in detail what activities the funds—if granted—will support. Ordinarily, no distinction is made between the application and the proposal, the terms being used nearly interchangeably. Nevertheless, in any application for the support of inquiry, embedded amidst budgets, vitae, descriptions of facilities, and plans for dissemination of results, is a research proposal. To that extent, then, the preparation of a grant application requires the same skills as the preparation of any plan for research.

The differences between the research proposal embedded in the grant application and the dissertation or thesis proposals described earlier in this text rest primarily in the need to (a) conform to the grantor's format, that may be specified in considerable detail; (b) present the study in a way that will have maximum appeal to the granting agency; and (c) master skills required to complete other parts of the application that are not directly part of the research plan itself. In all other respects, a sound research proposal is a sound research proposal, whether mailed to Washington in a grant application or placed on an advisor's desk in the sixth semester of doctoral study.

Deciding Where to Start:
Choosing the Right Source

THE TRACK RECORD:
ARE YOU READY FOR A GRANT?

Most research projects require financial support, either for equipment, personnel to assist in data collection and management, or for publication and dissemination costs. Because internal sources of support within higher education have declined while research costs have escalated, acquiring external funding for research has become the essential first step for almost all studies. Once under way, a major function for many investigators is to acquire additional funds needed to complete the project.

Departmental budgets, which formerly had small amounts of money allocated to research projects, now are stretched desperately thin just to ensure that classes are taught. Few departments can supply researchers with even minimal funds. Thus a major portion of "research activity" is dedicated to funding the project, and this is no different for beginning researchers. In fact, learning to write proposals for research funding has become an important part of the doctoral education experience. Graduate students who have the opportunity to work in well-funded research projects usually share some of the writing responsibilities so that they can learn the process.

The acquisition of funds must be preceded by a written proposal, so preparation of grant applications has become a skill that often is as important as inquiry skills themselves. Each government agency and independent foundation has a specific form to be completed and a unique process through which the proposal must be evaluated. If the proposer of a research project is skilled, diligent, persistent, patient, and possessed of at least a reasonable share of luck, funds can be obtained. The ratio of proposals presently being funded to those being rejected, however, is very low. Fewer than 30% of first-time applicants to the National Institutes of Health are successful, so it is obvious that the task of writing and submitting a proposal cannot be approached in a cavalier manner.

In deciding where to seek support, our first advice is to engage in some serious self-contemplation. Review committees want to feel comfortable in awarding a grant of financial support to an applicant. The committee wants to be assured not only that the proposed study is excellent, but that the researcher is competent to perform excellent work. The best evidence for competence is a series of publications on the topic to be researched. This has come to be known as a track record in the area of the proposed study. What record of accomplishment will you present to attract and reassure those who review your proposal?

An investigator who proposes a research project and includes in the application reprints of research reports or pilot studies that verify the reliability of the technique proposed or support the directional hypotheses to be employed, is more likely to satisfy the review committee that his or her skills are adequate to perform the study. In contrast, when the grant applicant is a complete neophyte, or has not completed a study in the specific area of the proposal, the committee will be forced to depend on less direct evidence of competence and, in the end, mostly on faith and intuition. It is understandable that committees more often avoid investments based mainly on faith and select instead proposals from individuals with a solid track record. Because a strong track record is so important, successful young grant recipients usually are those who have worked through their doctorate in a very active research program and who also have had postdoctoral appointments. In both the doctoral and postdoctoral programs these new researchers have had ample opportunities to publish with seasoned mentors.

Factors other than track record are weighed by review committees (most notably the quality of the research topic and proposal), and novice researchers or veteran investigators entering new areas do sometimes receive grant support. First-time grant proposals do not automatically encounter a hopeless Catch-22 that demands a display of previous research by the author. The fact remains, however, that previous performance weighs heavily among those factors that determine success.

The track record has been emphasized here, not to discourage the beginner, but to lend support to a suggestion that the authors of this guide have found particularly useful. A good way to build a track record is to begin with limited aspirations and seek limited funding from local sources, particularly from the institution in which the researcher works.

Almost all universities and colleges have faculty and student research funds available. Most major institutions also have federal funds that are provided in block grants to support work in particular disciplines. Such internal sources ordinarily require only a modest proposal document that is not as lengthy or complex as those required by external agencies. A good strategy for eventually obtaining a larger government or foundation grant is to acquire two or three small ($1,000-$5,000) grants, conduct the investigations, submit the results for publication, and subsequently use those reports as the track record supporting a proposal for more extensive funding. This provides you with start-up funds to do the first studies and also indicates to agency reviewers that your work already has been critically and positively reviewed, not only by an editorial board, but by a university funding review committee.

The use of local grant sources also should emphasize how important it is to have envisioned a systematic research program rather than a single study. Each research project can build on the previous one, providing more and more evidence that your ideas are worthy of major funding. In programmatic research it is logical sequence, not the accumulated number of studies, that will impress reviewers. Clearly, a fundable proposal could never be supported by a host of experiments aimlessly conducted on a hodgepodge of tenuously related topics.

AGENCIES AND FOUNDATIONS: LOCATING THE MONEY TREE

The first step in preparing a successful proposal is knowing where to apply. Finding the funding source that provides the highest probability for successful application often is a time-consuming process. Given the time that will be expended in preparation of the proposal, however, it is a relatively small investment that can return significant dividends.

If you are so fortunate as to have access to someone who maintains a grant library or monitors information sources concerning agencies and foundations and who can assist you with identifying a preliminary list of potential sources, your search problem is solved. Many universities house such a library, and increasingly these services are computerized. Many senior professors who have large research programs not only maintain all updated information about sources of funding in their particular area, but know and maintain regular communication with key individuals in granting agencies. Such contacts are invaluable for their knowledge about priorities (and changes in priorities) within the funding agency.

It may be beneficial for a novice to collaborate with a senior researcher on several studies before attempting a proposal on his or her own. A familiar name on a proposal can be very helpful because reviewers have confidence in known quantities and often confer that same confidence on collaborators. Not everyone is in the happy position of associations with a senior researcher or research staff. Many young scholars must undertake on their own the unfamiliar task of locating the money tree.

In this process, the first rule is to throw a wide net and keep an open mind about what might constitute a possible source. Do not expect to find an agency with interests exactly matched to your particular research idea. With some creative adaptation it often is possible to adjust the focus of a study sufficiently to interest a funding agency without distorting the primary intent of the investigation. For instance, a proposal involving the role of motor or play behavior in child development might be of interest to sources as widely disparate as the Center for Research for Mothers and Children in the National Institute of Child Health and Human Development, or an early childhood project within the Office of Educational Research and Improvement, all depending on how the study is presented. For this

reason, a flexible point of view is helpful in assembling the initial
list of potential funding sources.

The search can begin with any of several standard reference works.
A comprehensive listing of assistance available from the federal
government is contained in the *Catalog of Federal Domestic Assistance (CFDA)*. Published annually and updated twice each year,
CFDA is an invaluable tool in locating agencies with appropriate
interests, as well as general information about support programs
within those agencies. Some states publish a catalog that provides
similar information for programs of state assistance.

The most useful tool for identifying nongovernmental sources of
support is *The Foundation Directory* (published by the Foundation
Center). This directory categorizes nearly 3,000 of the largest foundations and includes both application information and the number
and kind of grants available from each source. Also in the private
sector, the Foundation Center operates through its annual publications (*Foundation Grants Index* and *Source Book Profiles*), its regional reference centers, and its computerized information service
to provide extensive coverage of nongovernmental sources. The
center is particularly useful for identifying smaller, local organizations with interest in the support of research.

Many sources in governmental agencies, private foundations, industry and professional organizations are listed in the *Federal Register*, the *Annual Register of Grant Support* (published by R. R.
Bowker's Data Publishing Group), the *Directory of Research Grants*
(published by Oryx Press), and the *Grants Register* (Williams, 1992).
Although it covers sources included in *CFDA* and the *Directory*, the
Grants Register provides much additional information and wider
coverage. Included are such esoteric areas as federal equipment use
programs and foreign exchange opportunities for research personnel.
Directories that list grant opportunities for other areas include the
Directory of Grants in the Humanities (Oryx, 1992), *National Directory of Grants and Aid to Individuals in the Arts, International*
(Millsaps, 1983), *Funding for Anthropological Research* (Cantrell &
Wallen, 1986), and *Grants and Fellowships of Interest to Historians*
(American Historical Association, 1981/1982).

The researcher is likely to use these larger and expensive compendia in the library or at a research center. Once a more specific list of
potential sources has been developed, however, it often is possible
to obtain publications from specific agencies that are free or more

moderately priced. Most state and federal agencies publish material that describes their research support programs and application procedures. Examples are the National Institutes of Health's *Guide for Grants and Contracts* and the National Science Foundation's *Bulletin*. A government document that may be useful to many is the *NIH Public Advisory Groups*, for in this document the Study Section membership lists (those who will review grants in different areas) are provided. It is important to know who will be evaluating your proposal. If you have read the papers of those most likely to review your proposal, you will have a clearer understanding of their perspective on the topic.

Several computer search services are available to the grant seeker. In addition to the retrieval system maintained by the Foundation Center, federal sources are catalogued in the data base of the National Technical Information Service, and both federal and private sources may be searched through the Smithsonian Scientific Information Exchange. Once the research topic can be described with reasonable precision, the modest fees required for computer search and retrieval can circumvent many hours of laborious library work. More important, computer systems provide information about grant sources that is more up-to-date than that provided by annual publications. The most economical way to approach this in terms of time and money is to consult your reference librarian or university grant and contract office. Fortunately, some universities now are providing computerized grant identification services that will allow you to receive grant alerts based on a profile that you provide.

Another source of information is to notice which funding agencies are supporting research that is published or presented at national or regional conferences. The granting agency or foundation always is listed at the bottom of the first page of a research article. Similarly, at the bottom of abstracts printed in conference programs the research grant number and funding sources are given. These can tell an observant reader not only what agencies fund research on a particular topic, but specific interest and funding trends for particular sources. In fact, information in abstracts often is the most current information of this type available.

A number of commercial publications and services have sprung up in recent years to meet the need for help in searching out sources for research support. Some of these provide valuable information about approaching foundations, new agency priorities, formulating more competitive proposals, and the legislative processes that precede new governmental programs. Used as a supplement to direct contact with funding agencies, information from such publications as *Grantsmanship Center News* (published by the Grantsmanship Center), *Grants Magazine* (Plenum Press), and *Foundation News* (from the Council on Foundations, Inc.) can help in both correctly targeting proposals and in improving their quality. The familiar series from Peterson's Guides includes an extensive directory of grants available to graduate students that, although now somewhat outdated, should prove to be a standard reference for those seeking support for theses and dissertations (Leskes, 1986). Finally, a potential source of long-term funding is the development of contractual partnerships with business and industry. If you want to pursue this possibility we recommend reading *Get Funded!* (Schumacher, 1992) before you start.

HOW PROPOSALS ARE REVIEWED:
AN EXAMPLE FROM NIH

Each funding agency has its own review process, often laid out in the detail of an explicit set of procedures. It is useful for proposal authors to have some general understanding of what may be encountered in the review process. As an example, the process for submitting a proposal to an institute of the National Institutes of Health (NIH) will be described here. Later in the chapter we provide general information on foundation review procedures. An overview of the NIH procedure is found in Figure 8.1. Although some aspects of the procedure may vary slightly for different years, the major elements in the review process will be similar for most large government agencies.

The first step in obtaining funds from NIH is to obtain the Public Health Service Grant Application, PHS 398 (Revised September, 1991; Approved through June 30, 1994), which provides guidelines, instruction sheets, and application forms. With this, as with other government documents related to the disbursement of funds, be certain that the most recent edition is obtained because frequent and sometimes subtle changes are made in the application format.

In a typical university or college, an application must go through a multitude of steps on its way to NIH, so the target for a final draft should be set one month prior to the NIH submission deadline. At the least, proposal documents will require signatures of officers at a variety of administrative levels. It is not uncommon for the proposal

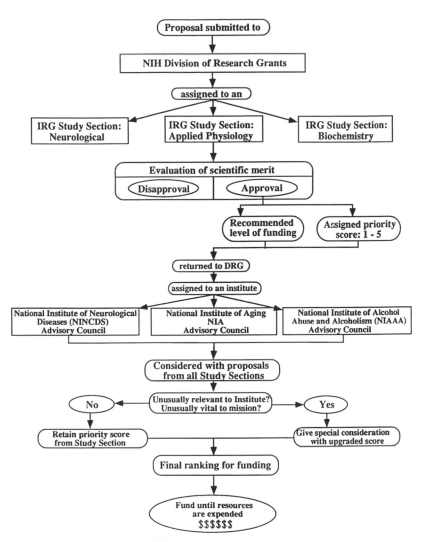

Figure 8.1 Overview of NIH Grant Proposal Review Process

to require signatures from the department chair, dean, computer center director, Institutional Review Board chair, business manager, and vice president or provost. For projects involving a substantial commitment of money, the requirement for review and sign-off may extend to the office of the president or, in the case of a public institution, to the chief executive officer of the state system. All of these are offices from which prompt response is unlikely. Proposals from two or more cooperating institutions will likely require these same signatures from all administrators of each participating university.

Once the proposal is ready for submission, it is sent to the Division of Research Grants (DRG). As noted earlier, the procedure for review after submission to DRG is presented diagrammatically in Figure 8.1. After being received by DRG the proposal is assigned to an initial review group (IRG), called a study section, three of which are symbolically represented in the fourth level of the figure. Each NIH study section is composed of 10 to 15 peer reviewers chosen by and reporting directly to the DRG. The proposal will be assigned to two or three of those reviewers, who will be designated as the primary reviewers for the proposal. They critique the proposal very carefully and make recommendations to the other study section members who probably have not read your proposal as thoroughly. On the basis of these recommendations, the study section members will evaluate the proposal and vote to approve or reject the application.

It is wise for the applicant to examine the membership of study sections that appear likely to be assigned proposals of the type contemplated. This may reveal the general orientation of the group and whether any members of the section are published scholars in the particular area of the proposed study. In the latter case, the investigator will want to take special care that the proposal adequately accounts for the work of such members.

Sometimes, especially if the proposal has a large budget, members of the study section will determine that a site visit is necessary. Either some or all of the members will visit the principal investigator's campus for the purpose of seeing the laboratories or sites where the intended research will be conducted. The purpose of this visit is to convince study section members that the investigator is competent, that the facilities and equipment are indeed adequate, and that all the support personnel are in fact available. In addition, the members of the site visit team have an opportunity to question the investigator directly about specific issues in the proposal. Site visits usually occur if members of the study section feel that the proposal presents a good idea but that some aspect of it is troublesome. Perhaps the investigator has developed a new measurement technique, the description of which has not fully convinced one or two of the reviewers. Perhaps the investigator plans to measure hundreds of individuals who are over the age of 65, and the committee members wish to discuss sampling problems, availability of subjects, and transportation costs.

Investigators should take the decision for a site visit as a positive sign, because the study section would not invest the time and money in a site visit unless the research idea had been judged to be a good one. Nevertheless, the site visit must be planned in careful detail, all important personnel involved alerted, and preparations made for demonstrations of the key techniques that the site visit team may wish to see. Additionally, the team may wish to hear a brief synopsis of the proposed research project. Because several months will have lapsed since the proposal was submitted, the study section members will especially want to see additional pilot data or other evidence of a continued interest. The investigator should plan the presentation with great care. This presentation, possibly using slides or videotape, will be similar to that made by graduate students at the committee review of their proposed study. The major difference is that this presentation may also include budget and personnel costs.

If the majority of the study section votes for approval of the proposal, it will be designated "approved but not funded." If rejected, a summary will be made of the primary criticisms. Each member of the study section adds a scientific merit *priority score* to his or her ballot, varying from 1.0 (highest) to 5.0 (lowest). The priority score is the average of the individual study section members' ratings times 100, so that the priority scores range from the best (100) to the poorest (500). Each proposal also has a percentile rank, which is the relative position or rank of its priority score among the scores assigned by that particular study section at its previous funding rounds. The priority score and percentile rank are attached to the critique of the proposal and accompany the proposal in its journey to the next level of review.

At this point the application will be forwarded to the institute that DRG has determined to be most appropriate to the nature of the proposed study. The applicant may suggest a specific institute that should be interested. Under ordinary circumstances, the proposal, if approved, will be sent there. Sometimes an investigator may be responding to what is known as a request for proposals (RFP), that is a published request inviting proposals for a particular type of research. In this case, the author places the letters "RFP" on the cover sheet with the name of the institute that solicited the proposal.

When the proposal arrives at the institute to which the DRG has assigned it, the advisory council of that institute reviews it. The proposal's percentile rank, the primary index of relative scientific merit, is placed in a single list of the percentile ranks of all applications that have been approved for funding by the study section over the previous funding rounds. Kelly and Shipp (1991) provide a detailed discussion of rankings and success rates for this process.

The advisory council usually concurs in the recommendations made by the study sections. The council, however, also has to balance its funding decisions with other factors, such as the implications of the research topic for the institute's goals, the similarity of the proposed research with other proposals or with existing funded research programs, and the total level of funding available. In some cases, members of the council will recommend that particular proposals be given special consideration for funding, or they may determine that an application is of questionable relevance to the institute's mission and recommend that it be assigned elsewhere. A reassignment, of course, would require several more weeks to process. This point emphasizes how important it is for the applicant to do everything possible to write the proposal with a specific orientation and to direct it to an institute that would find it attractive.

At the final step, when consideration is given to funding, the approved applications are listed in order of their percentile ranks, as modified by the advisory council and grants are approved in that order as far as funds permit. Because the proposals are funded on the basis of relative rank and different institutes have different levels of funding, a percentile rank of 18 may be funded in one institute but not in another. Thus a researcher who has submitted a proposal to an institute with lower levels of funding than others may be disappointed to learn that his or her proposal was "approved but not funded," whereas the same percentile rank was funded in another institute. Such are the vagaries of life in the world of grantsmanship!

If the proposal is approved and funded, notification is sent to the investigator and the sponsoring institution. On occasion, the study section will recommend a reduction in budget, or the advisory council of the institute may suggest such an alteration. In these cases, an officer of the institute will inform the investigator and provide an explanation. Such recommendations may or may not be negotiable. If the institute is willing to discuss proposed reductions, the investigator will have to confront inquiries about the necessity of specific budget items. Having a clear rationale for each expenditure is the best method for preventing serious erosion of the budget in such bargaining.

WORKING WITH FOUNDATIONS

Because every foundation has different procedures for working with grant proposals, we cannot provide a single set of specific instructions, as was possible with the NIH example above. We can, however, provide advice about working with foundation staff and offer some suggestions that will improve your chances for a successful application.

The charter of each foundation establishes a mission that is particular to that organization. Some are constrained only to fund programs providing benefit in the community (for example, grants to support development of legal services for the poor) and do not fund research. Other foundations have been created specifically for the purpose of supporting research in particular areas (for example, mental health or education). Still others fund both public programs and research. Foundations in this latter category often are more likely to support studies that deal with problems closely associated with the service aspect of the their mission.

Accordingly, when investigating a foundation as a possible source of funding, try to learn first about its mission. If the interests of the foundation appear to have some relationship with your research agenda, the next steps are to obtain a sense of the priorities articulated by its leaders and information about the kinds of studies that have been approved for funding over recent years. If there have been successful proposals in areas that are related to your research interests, it will be particularly helpful if they can be obtained for review. Finally, it is essential that you acquire a copy of the guidelines for grant applications.

The initial contacts with foundation personnel are particularly important. Courtesy with everyone is a rule, whether the executive director, board member, or receptionist—and remembering that their time is valuable is the first way to show respect. If it becomes apparent that the agenda of the foundation does not provide a sufficiently close fit with your present ideas, make a point of thanking staff for their time, and withdraw politely. You may wish to return at a future date.

In the highly competitive grant marketplace, trying to force a square proposal into a round foundation is likely to be a poor use of time and effort. If, however, preliminary contacts with staff do suggest that there is some potential for mutual interest, you may wish to extend the discussion with staff before developing and submitting a proposal.

Most foundations welcome opportunity to have staff discuss possible proposals with prospective applicants. Exploring areas of shared interest, as well as providing some preliminary screening of potential applicants, are functions that are in the best interest of the organization. Foundation staff can alert you to deadlines, describe application procedures, indicate areas of investigation for which the foundation currently has particular concern, explain how the review process works, and identify the individuals within the organization who hold final authority for grant decisions.

As with government agencies, some foundations have grant application packets that provide comprehensive information about the required format for all proposals. Others will accept proposals in a variety of formats. Likewise, some foundations make funding decisions only at a specified point (or points) during the year, while others make decisions on applications as they are received. It is your responsibility to obtain whatever regulations exist for the proposal process—and follow them. If the instructions specify that the pages of your proposal be hole-punched, do it (if you really want the money)!

Assuming your proposal reaches the foundation office on time and in the proper form, it will be reviewed. This process may be structured in any of several ways.

1. A single staff member reviews the application and makes a decision based on the technical merits of the proposal, his or her perception of your ability to carry out the research, and on how the study relates to the priorities of the foundation. This is the least common form of review, although it still may be encountered in a few organizations.

2. One or more staff members review the application and provide comments on some (or all) of the points noted above. The foundation's board of directors (or a special committee of the board) then uses that information as the basis for making final funding decisions. This process may be as formal as the one described for NIH reviews—complete with rankings—or may be much less formal, with nothing more elaborate than a committee discussion about which proposal will produce the most benefit for the foundation's money.

3. Comments produced by staff review procedures are supplemented by recruiting the critiques of outside specialists with expertise in the area of the proposal. All comments are then forwarded to the next level of the review and decision process.

In the event that a proposal is not funded, it is to your advantage to obtain feedback from the review committee or foundation staff. Not only can you learn how to improve your proposals, you may wish to approach the foundation with another application in the future. The more you learn about their review process, and which aspects of the proposal are pivotal in determining acceptance or rejection, the more likely you are to succeed on a subsequent try. In any case, it is important to be businesslike and respectful even in the face of a rejection. As one veteran foundation executive told us, "No one likes whiners." Positive interactions with foundation staff are the basis for future receptivity.

PARTNERSHIPS WITH BUSINESS: AN ALTERNATIVE SOURCE OF FUNDING

Funding for research sometimes can be obtained from business or industry, although this is primarily available to university faculty members who hold relatively permanent appointments. Graduate students, post-doctoral scholars, and untenured junior faculty are rarely considered.

The commercial sector needs research findings from a wide array of academic disciplines. Businesses of all kinds can profit from information that improves their operation in such diverse areas as "planning, finance, facilities, accounting, operations, marketing, sales, customer service, human resource management, training and education, retention of personnel, public and community relations, and so on" (Schumacher, 1992, p. 43). Faculty scholars in almost any discipline may be able to convince corporate executives that their research merits support if they bring creative ideas and are willing to persevere in the effort to obtain a hearing.

Most large businesses have research and development units assigned primarily to the tasks of applied investigations, although some devote a portion of their resources to basic research. In either case, some of the research work may be subcontracted to sources outside the organization. This, of course, is a primary point of entry for the development of business/university partnerships.

It is not surprising that businesses are unlikely to be interested in funding short-term projects. Because of their specialized research needs, business organizations often must provide funding for technical support services, facilities, equipment, and even staff. Investments of that kind are reasonable only when a partnership can be sustained over a substantial period of time. Businesses must look to the bottom line of profitability, and that goal is best served when funding can purchase a reliable source of continuing research capability.

Research support from commercial enterprises is a two-edged sword. Not only does it hold potential for support that is substantial in quantity, but additional funding is much easier to obtain once the relationship is established. The disadvantage, however, is that support must go up or down with company fortunes. When profits go down, management changes, or priorities shift, the company can lose interest, and funds may quickly dry up.

The process of shaking the corporate money tree may be very different from that required for government agencies or foundations. Access here often is achieved through contacts with personnel in the organization—frequently with researchers, technicians, or research managers. Usually it is necessary to have someone inside the organization to advocate for your proposal and assist in moving your ideas for a partnership through the channels of corporate management.

In her informative book *Get Funded!*, which is reviewed in Appendix A, Schumacher (1992, pp. 95-108) suggests a variety of ways through which you can identify and cultivate company employees who may be interested in sponsoring your proposal for a research partnership. Some of these are paraphrased in the brief list below.

1. Keep in touch with former students and colleagues who have found employment in business or industry.
2. Enlist the help of alumni who may have contacts in the corporate world.
3. Make use of university staff who have corporate relations as a responsibility.
4. Attend on-campus presentations by corporate representatives.
5. Talk to company recruiters when they come to your campus.
6. Make contact with representatives from the business sector who serve on any of your institution's various advisory committees.

7. Make contact with business organizations through your state's economic development agencies.

8. Use cooperative education programs and field placements to locate some of your students in companies with which you may have shared research interests.

9. Search out possible avenues of contact through the School of Business or Management at your institution.

10. Make contact with corporate researchers who publish in your field.

BUSINESS AND CORPORATE FOUNDATIONS

Most business foundations differ sharply from philanthropic foundations. The availability of research funding from such institutions often is not completely insulated from the profitability of the corporate parent and rises and falls accordingly. Frequently, the nature and purpose of the foundation is closely tied to the interests of its business sponsor, although it is common for the mission statement to be written in such general terms that it is difficult to discern the true priorities (and biases) of the organization.

Grants from business foundations often are made preferentially to particular institutions of higher education. This may be on the basis of some historic relationship, such as the undergraduate education of a corporate founder or the existence of familial ties between company and institution managers. For that reason, applications or letters of inquiry sent without the advantage of sponsorship may provoke little interest from the foundation's management. As in the case of direct contacts with business organizations, it is best to locate an inside advocate who can sponsor your proposal for serious attention.

THE REJECTION OF A GRANT PROPOSAL: WHY DOES IT HAPPEN?

Whether you submit a grant application to a governmental agency, a philanthropic foundation, or a business-affiliated organization, it is virtually inevitable that your proposal will be considered in competition with other proposals. Such grant competitions are mediated through review processes that, whatever unique form they may take, ultimately must involve human readers. This fact produces an implacable rule. *What is not noticed is not funded!*

Amidst the sometimes formidable stack of proposals, the document that does not catch the eye—and thus the reward of closer attention and consideration—cannot compete on the formal criteria associated with quality of design and congruence with the grantor's priorities. For that reason, in the next chapter we will give close attention to the abstract and introduction that must project whatever attractive elements are contained in the research question and proposed methodology.

Beyond the problem of failing to attract attention, the reasons given for rejection may be phrased in diplomatic terms—but they boil down to a surprisingly small set of simple and all too familiar defects. Because in purely statistical terms the probability of rejection for any given proposal is high, beginners in the grant application business have good reason to note the common causes of "submitted, but not funded" with considerable care.

As shown in Table 8.1, reasons for rejection fall into four general categories: mechanical, methodological, personnel, and cost-benefit.

Having made the point that most rejections are the consequence of proposals that are unsound—often in simple and obvious ways—it is important to note that perfectly sound proposals sometimes are rejected. Research of considerable merit may remain unsupported for no reason that can be associated with the quality of the proposal. Because that unhappy circumstance is a possibility, rejection must not be taken, by itself, as evidence of a fundamental defect.

At any point in time, a proposal simply may not appeal to a reviewer who must make a choice among equally strong contenders. Under such circumstances, subjective factors must determine decisions, often leaving no wholly logical explanation for the action. The following section, dealing with resubmission, was prepared with the unfortunate authors of such proposals in mind.

REJECTION, FEEDBACK, AND RESUBMISSION

A rejection, especially of the first grant proposal submitted for review, should not be unexpected. It is a commonplace of the academic life—especially for the novice. Just as it takes practice to learn how to perform any complex task truly well, it takes practice to write

TABLE 8.1 Common Reasons Grant Proposals are Rejected

Mechanical Reasons

1. Deadline for submission was not met.
2. Guidelines for proposal content, format, and length were not followed *exactly*.
3. The proposal was not *absolutely* *clear* in describing one or several elements of the study.
4. The proposal was not *absolutely complete* in describing one or several elements of the study.
5. The author(s) took highly partisan positions on issues and thus became vulnerable to the prejudices of the reviewers.
6. The quality of writing was poor—for example, sweeping and grandiose claims, convoluted reasoning, excessive repetition, or unreasonable length.
7. The proposal document contained an unreasonable number of mechanical defects that reflected carelessness and the author's unwillingness to attend to detail. The risk that the same attitude might attend execution of the proposed study was not acceptable to the reviewers.

Methodological Reasons

8. The proposed question, design, and method were completely traditional, with nothing that could strike a reviewer as unusual, intriguing, or clever.
9. The proposed method of study was unsuited to the purpose of the research.

Personnel Reasons

10. As revealed in the review of literature, the author(s) simply did not know the territory.
11. The proposed study appeared to be beyond the capacity of the author(s) in terms of training, experience, and available resources.

Cost-Benefit Reasons

12. The proposed study was not an agency priority for *this* year.
13. The budget was unrealistic in terms of estimated requirements for equipment, supplies, and personnel.
14. The cost of the proposed project appeared to be greater than any possible benefit to be derived from its completion.

successful proposals. So long as the applicant has an opportunity to profit from evaluative feedback, each attempt should produce significant improvement.

Most review systems contain some provision for feedback as part of the rejection process. Often in the form of a summary review of the proposal, this statement will list the main criticisms and may even suggest changes. The applicant should consider each point. If resubmission is contemplated, the new draft should address as many criticisms as possible through revisions, clarifications, and strengthened rationales. When the interval of time between the original submission and the notification of results has allowed collection of new pilot data, or acquisition of additional support from new publications, these should be added.

The easiest critique to respond to is one that raises questions about design or methodology. There the decision is simple. Either provide better substantiation for the choices made, or change them. The review, however, may center not on what was proposed, but on the way the proposal was written. In some instances, the absence of any substantial comment about the research question or methodology provides the indirect suggestion of a failure to communicate clearly. In other cases, the reviewers may have understood the proposal perfectly but had reservations about a nontechnical issue such as the ratio of costs to potential benefits. In the former, rewriting for clarity is the needed response. In the latter, the only recourse is to either strengthen the rational for the importance of the study or to find ways to cut the budget.

Once responses to criticisms have been devised, the rejected proposal may be resubmitted. An accompanying letter should note that the document is a resubmission, and request return to the original reviewers. When this can be accomplished, it both makes use of familiarity and avoids a new set of criticisms based on a fresh set of perceptions (and biases). Proposals can be resubmitted several times provided feedback encourages revision and there is no suggestion from the grantor that the topic of study is inappropriate.

A telephone conversation or meeting with the individual who coordinated the review process often can clear up ambiguities in the feedback provided with rejection. Such assistance is particularly useful when it is not clear whether the primary cause for rejection lay with the research question, or with the substance of design and method. In some instances, a staff member at the agency or foundation will give the applicant an estimate of the probability for success in a resubmission. A willingness to listen attentively, and politely, can serve to invite suggestions for improvement.

After the first shock, a rejection should not inhibit the urge to find support for a worthy study. With critical feedback in hand, a stronger proposal can be drafted. Doubtless it is better to have approval and the desired funding. An unsuccessful effort when properly understood, however, can yet yield something of value—the opportunity to learn how to do it better. That is a grant of assistance that will pay, and pay, and pay.

PLANNING AND PREPARATION: TAKING THE LONG VIEW

As the competition for grants has grown more rigorous over the years, the amount of detail involved, the advanced planning required, and the complexity of the proposal process itself have dramatically increased. Shaking the money tree is not the straight-forward process it was when funds were more plentiful—and applicants fewer. Once, 1 or 2 weeks were the norm for the time invested in a proposal of modest scope. The same document now may take several months of preparation. Nevertheless, if your goal is to make productive scholarship a part of your career, there is no choice. Particularly if you want to prosper in a university setting, grant writing will be an essential skill for survival.

When the proper steps are taken in a logical sequence, and adequate time is allotted to complete each step, the worst one can say about proposal writing is that it is exacting and sometimes tiring work. The best one can say is that it is challenging, and even stimulating. This is particularly likely to be the case when investigators in complementary areas of expertise collaborate in the process of developing the research plan. The interaction that occurs among colleagues during formulation of research questions and study design can be educational—and a powerful motivation for sustained effort. When a grant application has been completed, the proposal critiqued by expert reviewers, and the project approved for funding, there is more than just the satisfaction of success. There is the excitement of doing what the money can pay for—a good study.

9

Preparation of the Grant Proposal

Once the funding agency is selected, the first step is to obtain its published guidelines for submitting proposals. These guidelines must be followed meticulously. As a convenient illustration, we will discuss here some of the purposes and the considerations to be dealt with in writing the sections required in the "Application for Public Health Service Grant." A Public Health Service (PHS) manual (PHS 398) provides details and recommends information to include in each section of the application for several different types of PHS awards. In addition, information is provided about the PHS peer review process. Many other federal agencies and foundations require proposal designs that are similar to those used by the PHS.

ABOUT ABSTRACTS

The word *abstract* normally designates a brief summary of a larger document. Most published research reports are accompanied by such an abstract. Written in the simple past tense, abstracts of this sort are histories of work already accomplished. In contrast, the abstract of a grant proposal is written in the future tense and summarizes work that will be done. When, as sometimes is the case, the abstract is prepared before the full proposal has been developed, it more properly should be called a *prospectus* or *preproposal*, but such niceties of language are seldom observed.

Abstracts or preproposals are prepared early in the proposal development process to serve several purposes. First, an abstract may focus the thinking of individuals developing the proposal by establishing a clear and explicit goal to which all subscribe. Second, a concise prospectus can be used for internal purposes to obtain preliminary administrative approval or to solicit support and cooperation from other units. Third, many agencies now require submission of a "letter of intent," which, in essence, is a one- or two-page abstract of the proposed study. These letters are screened by a panel of judges who rank them on preestablished criteria. Authors of the best abstracts are invited to submit full proposals for the second phase of consideration. Under such conditions everything rests on the abstract, and no argument is required to convince the proposer that only the best effort will serve. Finally, whatever its function, an abstract prepared prior to development of the full proposal must be revised to maintain perfect congruence with the evolution of that document. Abstracts that do not match the proposal may receive short shrift from reviewers.

Whether or not a letter of intent is required, the abstract that is submitted with the full proposal bears a disproportionate share of responsibility for success or failure. Often limited to a single page, these few paragraphs are what the reviewer will read first. When the bottom of that page has been reached the reviewer must have a clear impression of the study's objective, method, and justification. If the proposal is to have a fair chance to succeed, however, another impression must have been communicated—that the study contains something of special interest, something that will sustain the reader's attention through the pages that follow. Thus the abstract must accomplish the dual tasks of providing a concise picture of the study while also highlighting its unique characteristics.

Although different funding agencies require different lengths and types of abstract, in almost all cases there is no space for throwaways. Each word and sentence must convey a precise message to the reader. If a point is not essential to an understanding of the study, it is better left to the main body of the proposal. Because the abstract is a one-way, one-shot communication, absolute clarity is essential. No matter how well a point may be explained in the body of the proposal, if the reader is confused by the language of the abstract, the game may have been lost.

For both of the reasons noted above, economy and clarity, the watchword for writing the abstract is *plain language.* Avoid any special constructs that require definition. Don't coin new words in the abstract. Avoid slogans, clichés, and polemical style. Keep adjectives to a minimum and omit flowery descriptions. Finally, remember that the sure sign of an amateur is to apply banalities such as creative, bold, or innovative to one's own ideas. Reviewers, unlike graduate advisors, cannot ask what "that phrase" means at the next conference, may not take the time needed to puzzle through a convoluted sentence, and certainly will not bother to figure out what probably is intended by an imprecise description.

While one can assume that reviewers are both literate and familiar with the research process in broad terms, for the purpose of the abstract it is unwise to assume more. Writing beyond the technical competence of the reviewer can be fatal. The best rule is to imagine that you are explaining your study to an intelligent layperson. By eliminating specialized language and reducing esoteric constructs to their essential components, the abstract can be made intelligible to individuals with a wide range of scientific backgrounds—without appearing to write down to any reader.

The typical format required for a proposal abstract includes the following major elements:

General Purpose
Specific Goals
Research Design
Methods
Significance (Contribution and Rationale)

Some agencies may also request that the applicant organization (institution), estimated cost (total funds requested), and the beginning and ending dates be included. It is important to read the instructions and include only what is requested, as the space requirements always are limiting in terms of communicating your ideas.

The specific goal section should begin with a statement of what will be accomplished, presented in the format of a research question or testable hypothesis. For example, "The objective of this study is to determine whether the use of foam cushion inserts in athletic shoes will affect the incidence of heel injuries in runners. Frequency and type of injuries over a 6-month period will be compared for two groups of 100 subjects of varied age, weight, ability, and sex, one group using shoes with cushion inserts, and the other using uncushioned shoes."

One of the hardest things to do is to reduce objectives and methods to just a few sentences. This difficulty probably contributes to several common errors found in the abstract section of the proposal.

Confusion of objectives with procedures. Taking a survey may be a procedure to be employed in the study, but it is not an objective of the study.

Confusion of objectives with the problem. The conditions that make the study important, either in terms of practical application or contribution to knowledge, are better discussed in the section on significance. In the occasional case in which some appreciation of significance is required before it is possible to understand the objective, the best course of action is to create a short subsection titled "The Problem" as a lead into statement of the objective.

Attempting to specify more than one or two major objectives for the study. Save all sub-objectives for the body of the proposal. Do everything possible to help the reviewer focus on what is essential.

Failure to be explicit. The best insurance is to start with a conventional phrase that forces you to write about your intention. "The objective of this study is to. . . . "

The clarity and precision with which your objectives are presented may control how carefully the reviewer attends to the subsequent section on procedures, but it is axiomatic that *agencies fund procedures, not objectives.* How research is performed determines its quality, and it is here that the competence of the reviewer as a research specialist in the area of your proposal will be brought to bear. If the reviewer finishes the one or two paragraphs of this section with a clear, uncluttered idea of what will be done, a full appreciation of how those actions will accomplish the objectives, and a positive impression of what is intriguing or particularly powerful about your approach, your proposal will receive a full hearing.

The significance of the proposed study should be identified in modest but precise terms. Nothing can serve so quickly to make a reviewer suspicious of the merits of a study as to encounter some Chamber of Commerce enthusiasm in the abstract. In plain language, indicate how achieving your objective would be of value to someone, could improve some service, would fill a gap in an evolving body of knowledge, or would permit the correct formulation of a subsequent question. It also is appropriate, and often effective, to indicate a specific example of how a finding from the study might provide human benefit, even at some point subsequent in time or technical development. It is best, however, not to drown the drama of a simple example in needless embellishment. Finally, when deciding which potential consequence should receive emphasis in supporting the significance of the study, it is useful to examine the existing interests and commitments of the funding agency. When the proposed study takes some of its importance from a potential for contribution to ongoing projects of the grantor, there is a powerful argument for special attention to the application.

As the abstract is developed, revised, and given its final review prior to submission, it will be helpful to remember one of the somber facts that has emerged in this age of endemic grantsmanship. Some heavily burdened review committees are so large that it has become necessary to delegate to a subcommittee the task of giving full proposals a complete reading. The remaining reviewers thus may not see more of a given proposal than the cover sheet, the abstract, the author's vita, and, perhaps, the budget. That prospect should be sufficient to encourage attention to producing the best possible abstract.

COMMUNICATING THE SIGNIFICANCE
OF THE PROPOSED RESEARCH

Most funding agencies require a section in the proposal that has a title such as "Significance of the Proposed Research." Funding agencies are accountable either to the public or to their benefactors for the expenditure of their funds. Try to read your proposal from the *funding agency's perspective.* What will they think is important? What aspect of your proposal will attract their attention and interest? Reviewers seek the applicant's best forecast as to the usefulness and importance of the results of the proposed project. This prediction assists the review committee in determining the cost-benefit ratio of the proposed study. The significance of the investigation might be explained in terms of synthesizing information from several research areas or by showing how the findings might be applied to human services. It could be impressive to point out that the findings might enable development of other types of research that previously had been impossible. The section needn't be long, but it should be carefully reasoned and should address concerns specific to the mission of the funding agency.

STAFFING AND CONSULTANT NEEDS

The staff needed for the research project should be carefully planned and kept as small as possible while maintaining services essential to conducting the study. The staff budget generally is what drives up the cost of a research project more than any other expense. Along with staff salaries, fringe benefits (medical insurance, retirement) and raises for each year of the grant often must be included. The beginner at this game quickly finds that the costs of a project escalate rapidly as more personnel are involved. When a neophyte is attempting a first grant application, the proposal for staffing should be constructed with a frugality tempered only by feasibility.

The staff requirements should be explained in detail, and if a staff member's function dwindles in the second or third year, then that member should be phased out. Reviewers will note a conscientious effort on the part of the applicant to execute the project at a minimal cost. Positions to be funded for the full term of the study with only global explanation of responsibilities and no indication of compelling necessity also will attract attention—all of it negative.

Rumor has it that applicants should pad their budget with some excess and unneeded staff so that the reviewers will have something to cut. This is a foolish notion, because it results in the applicant having items in the budget that are not well justified, which ultimately gives the impression of a casually constructed proposal.

Consultants, too, should be requested sparingly and only when absolutely needed. When they are required, the need should be explicitly stated. If a particular consultant is needed, the applicant should explain exactly why and a letter of agreement from that consultant should be included in the appendix.

THE TIME FRAME

Almost every proposal submitted to government agencies is for funding of a 3- to 5-year project. The application and review process is so time-consuming that the applicant, the institution, and most agencies find the investment of such energy and time best returned if the award is for a substantial period. A time frame, therefore, that states explicitly when specific parts of the project will be completed, has several useful functions.

The first and most obvious use of a projected time sequence is that it keeps the investigator and all personnel on schedule throughout a long period. When all members of the research team have a copy of the time frame, and when it is posted in offices, work rooms, and laboratories, where every member of the team will have daily exposure to its terms, the effect is to encourage steady application of effort.

A second function of the time frame is to forecast for project personnel, reviewers, and the funding agency the probable contents of each progress report that must be filed (usually annually or biannually over the term of the funding period). Every reader of the time frame can clearly see what events will transpire prior to each progress report and, consequently, will expect a full and punctual accounting. This serves also to discourage investigators from procrastinating and later finding themselves having to accomplish an enormous amount in the month or two that precedes a progress report.

A third function that the time frame serves is to document the need for three or five years of funding for the project. If the reviewers can see in the time frame that every month is filled with work to be done, then it is clear that a project of the length proposed is necessary.

Fourth, if the time frame is well described, it will enhance the reviewer's understanding of the entire project and will further document the applicant's organizational skills. A well-conceived time frame, in which each part of the project is estimated in terms of its onset and duration, goes a long way toward convincing the reader that the applicant knows the area, the methodologies to be used, and all other aspects of the project. If it is well written, it also will buffer several possible criticisms—that the project cannot be completed in the amount of time proposed, that it does not require funding for the full period of time requested, or that the investigator doesn't understand the topic well enough to know how long certain procedures will take.

The time frame should include the schedule for hiring personnel, ordering equipment and supplies, putting equipment and facilities into operation, meeting with personnel from other institutes or agencies, acquiring subjects for the investigation, data accumulation, data analysis, and report write-up. In preparing the time frame, the applicant should try to think through and record every step that will be taken in the project. Then how long each step will take must be estimated. The more people who are involved in a step, the longer it probably will take. The applicant may even find, after working out the time schedule, that the project will take longer than anticipated, and the funding period must be extended. If such extension makes the project too expensive, it may be necessary to consider a more economical design. For all of these reasons, the time frame should be carefully worked out before the budget is made final.

The proposal writer also should have a personal time frame that includes the amount of time necessary to get the proposal through all levels of the approval process. This part of the time frame, although not submitted with the final proposal, should aid the writer in understanding the full commitment to the research that will be necessary.

SUPPORT SERVICES

Any large project will require an extensive array of support services from the university and any other agency or unit of the community that is involved with the project. Insofar as possible, the need for support services should be anticipated, both by providing money for them in the budget and by ensuring that what must be purchased exists and can be delivered. If a computer graphics person is needed, one should be located to ensure that such a person is available. Specialized computer services may be required from the computer center, or unusual transportation capacity may be needed, such as the need to move video equipment into the community. These types of research support must be located and confirmed as part of preparation for the proposed study.

All space needs such as laboratories, offices, or work areas for technicians should be anticipated. If the research project is going to tax any unit of the university, the people involved should be consulted prior to the final draft of the proposal. Examples include proposed projects in which a large number of telephone calls will be imposed on the departmental switchboard, frequent mass mailings that will be planned for the postal pickup, or dozens of students who are to wait in lines in a hallway immediately outside classrooms. The applicant should try to anticipate any hardship that the project may create for anyone. This will prevent, insofar as possible, logistic problems that create ill will among support service staff and frustration on the part of the researcher.

When support from other sources is critical to the research project, the researcher should obtain a written agreement from the appropriate officials specifying that the needed service will be available. This letter of agreement may be included in the appendix of the proposal. For example, if a specific school classroom is essential to the project, a letter reserving that facility for the specified period of time should be obtained. It would be an unpleasant surprise, for instance, to begin use of another researcher's environmentally controlled laboratory for a year-long study, and then discover it will not be available for the final two months of the project. Every precaution must be taken to prevent such disastrous accidents.

VITAE: PRESENTING YOURSELF

It would be easy to underestimate the importance of this section in a grant application. For many readers, vitae represent one more instance of the paperwork syndrome that infects higher education. Personal resumés are required, accumulated, and ignored in a host of bureaucratic functions. In consequence, unlike people in the business world, academics often pay relatively little attention to the construction and maintenance of attractive and utilitarian vitae. Like McGee's closet, they simply are allowed to accumulate the residues of scholarly and professional life without much thought to order, economy, or impact.

Two common misapprehensions prevail about the vitae section of a grant proposal: (a) that they are not read by reviewers, and (b) that as a *pro forma* section, vitae have little influence on the success of a proposal. Both notions are untrue. Vitae are read. Many reviewers read vitae before they read the body of the proposal. Not only do vitae influence the judgments of reviewers, they are the one part of the proposal in which the applicant can be aggressive by taking the argument for competence directly to the reviewer's attention.

The resumés of individuals to be associated with the proposed study are the primary vehicles for arguing that the interests, training, and experience of the investigator(s) make support of the study reasonable. The techniques for mounting this offensive are not difficult to imagine.

1. If a format is provided, follow it exactly by revising, reformatting, and reprinting every resumé. If a format is not provided, invent one that will best serve the strategies noted below.

2. Keep vitae reasonably short by being selective about content. Reviewers will be looking for the obvious items and these should be given prominence:

   a. Publications in the area of the study

   b. Publications in areas related to the study

   c. Receipt of previous grants in the area of the proposal

   d. Receipt of research grants in any area

   e. Involvement in a similar study whether funded or not

   f. Evidence of relevant training completed (e.g., postdoctoral study in the area)

   g. Unpublished papers or conference presentations in the area of the study

   h. Completed pilot studies in the area of the proposal.

   Take care to give emphasis to current items. Items older than five years should not be included unless they continue to be cited in current work or they help to establish a track record that is directly related to the study. Don't burden the reviewer with irrelevant clutter.

3. Use a uniform format that is divided into subsections with prominent headings. The idea is that the format should make it impossible for a hurried reader to miss material that supports the competence of the investigator. Only research publications should be listed, but if there are few, cite relevant research presentations or abstracts to supplement. Be certain, however, that the research publications are listed first, and that abstracts and presentations are categorized as such. It is not wise to list all of these in a mixture, leaving the reviewer to assume that you do not know the difference between an abstract and a publication, or that you are trying to give the impression of a great deal of scholarly productivity by intermingling these three types of activity.

4. Use short sections of highlighted text to provide detail about the exact nature of previous research experiences relevant to conduct of the

proposed study. You are not limited just to the citation of dates, project titles and publications. Tell the reviewers exactly what they need to know in a form that makes the task as easy as possible.

Where a team of investigators is to be involved, it will not always be easy to prepare an effective vitae section. Individualism in personal matters is a common trait among productive scholars, and the vitae is correctly regarded as a personal matter. Nevertheless, this is a place where flexibility and some cooperative effort will improve the chances that all participants will enhance their vitae—by winning a grant to support their scholarship.

DISSEMINATION OF RESULTS

The final step that transforms the personal act of inquiry into research is dissemination of a report into the public domain. Peers must review procedures if results are to be treated as reliable knowledge, and if knowledge is to be useful, it must reach those who can make application. For those two reasons, many funding sources stipulate that plans for dissemination of results must be included as part of the proposal.

The rules here are reasonably simple.

1. Tell which results will be reported.
2. Indicate which audiences you intend to reach.
3. Specify how you plan to disseminate the final report.
4. Be specific, citing particular conferences, development projects, local, state or federal agencies, publications, or colleagues working on related research projects.
5. Think carefully about how to reach appropriate audiences and go beyond the requisite printed report and ubiquitous paper at a national conference. Consider such strategies as summaries directed to interested scholars in other institutions, use of computer-based retrieval services, and releases through news media.

Typically, costs for dissemination can be built into the budget. Expenditures for everything from travel to conferences, to the printing and mailing of reports are legitimate. Be sure, however, to base each item on careful estimates of actual costs. For example, obtain actual quotations for proposed air travel in support of dissemination.

THE BUDGET

Although not a part of the plan for research, the budget is a central element in a grant application. It will be examined in detail by almost all members of a typical review committee, even those who may not be involved in evaluating the adequacy of design and methodology. Most application formats require that the budget be presented in brief form with no more than a page or two of appended explanation. Experience suggests that such explanation should be provided, even if it is not specifically required.

Personnel for which funds are requested must be essential to the study. The most effective way to demonstrate such need is to specify responsibilities for each position. If project personnel must have special certification or advanced degrees, it is important to tell why a less qualified person could not be used. Enough information should be provided to support the level of commitment required in each position, whether for full-time or fractional employment.

Supplies and equipment must be documented with care. Review committees will appreciate efforts to give exact and realistic estimates of supplies needed, rather than the use of speculative round numbers. For instance, if videotape is to be used, rather than simply requesting $1,125 for the purchase of tapes, the applicant should explain that 15 minutes will be required for 100 subjects on three occasions without possibility of reusing tapes. That will require one tape per four subjects, or 75 tapes at $15 each, or a budget item of $1,125.

If funds for the purchase of large equipment are requested, the budget justification section might explain what attempts have been made to obtain the items by other means and why alternative plans such as rental or sharing won't suffice. Generally, funding agencies are not well disposed to requests for extensive equipment purchases, particularly large and expensive items. The position of many agencies is that the university or college should supply all of the basic and less specialized equipment, as well as most large items that represent expensive and permanent investments in research capability. Young researchers may be dismayed to discover that their university takes the opposite position, holding that the investigator should obtain all expensive equipment through extramural funding, but that is the way things often work in a complex society.

Funding agency officers understandably would rather award money to applicants who already have the necessary equipment. In that manner, the agency's funds go directly into research activities rather than into building the capacity to perform research. The only counter to this logic is to make the best possible case for why the applicant's facility is ideally, if not uniquely, positioned for the conduct of the particular study—given the addition of the needed equipment. Another helpful strategy here is to point out any substantial ways the applicant's institution is contributing to the proposed study in terms of equipment, facilities, or personnel assigned to the project. Agency and foundation personnel like to feel that research projects, especially large ones, are a joint university/agency enterprise, and they tend to resent any implication that they constitute a goose that lays golden eggs.

Budget lines for ancillary items such as analysis of data, preparation of manuscript, and communication with consultants may be permitted under the rules for application, but should be explained with great care. Consultants, for example, must be justified in detail. In the golden days of research when grants were plentiful, consultants sometimes were included in proposals simply because they were good professional friends who had an interest in the study. Today, a consultant must be demonstrably necessary to completion of the study. Even when such need exists, caution is required in preparing the explanation. If the consultant is needed because the investigator has not mastered a technique that is central to execution of the study, a reviewer may wonder why the grant should be awarded to someone who is deficient in skills commonly used by workers in the area.

Travel costs also require careful explanation. Only travel that is necessary to complete the research and, perhaps, to disseminate the findings should be included in the budget. If travel to specific conferences for the purpose of presenting reports from the study are included, the nature of the audience should be indicated and the relevance of the conference to the study demonstrated. More important, the relevance of the conference attendees to the interests of the funding agency should be specified.

Another major item in a proposed budget will be indirect costs (overhead) that the funding agency will pay directly to the institution. At this time such costs vary widely and are negotiated by the agency and the university or college. Many large institutions have a standing policy on overhead for all grant contracts. Indirect charges presumably reimburse the university for the cost of building maintenance, processing of paper work, utilities, and so on—all items that would have to be purchased by the grantor if the study were conducted at a facility owned by the agency. Other budget items dictated by the institution are insurance, retirement, and medical benefits for project personnel.

It is wise to take an early draft of the budget to the university officer in charge of grant negotiations and obtain assistance on all items not directly dictated by the nature of the research process itself. After several projected budgets have been written, the mysteries associated with indirect costs and employee benefits may become understandable to the researcher, but a substantial amount of grief can be avoided on the first effort if competent help is solicited and advice faithfully followed.

As a corollary to budget making, if a significant amount of support is to be provided by the institution in the form of new inputs of equipment, facilities, supplies, or personnel, the researcher must be sure to obtain formal approval from appropriate officers before proceeding too far into development of the proposal. In many institutions, agreement of the chairperson, dean, and a vice president (at minimum) is required for such expenditures. It is best to have the needed commitments in hand well in advance of the point at which the proposal will be submitted for review.

It may be useful to demonstrate that respected scholars with expertise in the area of the proposed research regard the project as worthy and the investigator(s) as competent. For this purpose, letters containing such endorsements may be included in the proposal (usually in an appendix).

LETTERS OF ENDORSEMENT AND CONFIRMATION

A second type of letter includes those that confirm the cooperation, support, or participation of organizations or individuals essential to the study. If, for example, schools and teachers or students are to be involved in any way, it is essential to have evidence that the appropriate authorities have reviewed the proposal and are prepared to participate if the grant is awarded. Similar brief notes may be required from the directors of service units such as the computer center, university health services, or laboratory facilities in other departments.

The documentation provided in such cases need not be elaborate or extend beyond what seems essential. The goal is simple. The applicant must provide some assurance that the staff, facilities, support service, and subject populations envisioned in the proposal will, in fact, be available.

USING PLANNING MODELS AND FLOWCHARTS

Preparation of a grant proposal often involves dealing with a number of individuals in administrative units external to the author's home base. Institutional review and approval, soliciting peer reviews, obtaining letters of support, accumulating budget information, gathering commitments from personnel, assembling vitae, and obtaining multiple signatures all serve to complicate the process. A set of subdeadlines emerges that must be met in serial order. For these reasons, even a relatively straightforward grant proposal may quickly exceed managerial habits that are entirely adequate for the limited scope of theses or dissertations.

In response to the complicated network of steps that are demanded in developing many grant proposals, a number of management models, flowcharts, checklists, and step-by-step guides have been devised to assist the author (see Appendix A). Some of these, such as the PERT (Program Evaluation and Review Technique) system (Borg & Gall, 1989), lend themselves primarily to larger research or development undertakings.

The best option for the novice who is attempting to stay organized may be to devise a do-it-yourself flowchart, complete with assigned responsibilities and deadlines. Once a problem has been defined and an appropriate funding agency has been identified, the following items can be supplemented as required by local circumstance and displayed with boxes and arrows to form a flowchart of sequenced events with appropriate time frame warnings. This is, in effect, your own personal time frame, that precedes the one you submit with the grant proposal. Table 9.1 includes the elements that most proposal writers should include when planning their time frame.

The novice will do well to remember the corollary of Murphy's Law that states, "Everything takes longer than you expect." Where one must depend on the voluntary cooperation of busy individuals

TABLE 9.1 Items to Include in the Time Frame

Important Dates	Prepare abstract or prospectus and submit letter of intent
First response to the request for proposals	Contact units for support or collaboration
Deadline for preproposal or letter of intent	Obtain initial administrative approval
Deadline for submission to Human Subject Review Committee	Complete review of the literature
	Determine study design
Deadlines for obtaining administrative signatures	Prepare first draft of proposal
	Prepare abstract of proposal
Chairperson	Initiate human subjects review
Dean	Initiate internal peer review
Office of Sponsored Research	Prepare budget
Director of Computer Services	Revise proposal based on feedback
Deadline for submission to typist	Collect vitae
Deadline for submission of proposal	Obtain letters of endorsement
Award announcement date	Obtain written assurances from support sources
	Complete institutional forms
Major Development Steps	Type final document
Obtain guidelines	Obtain administrative signatures
Contact program officer at funding agency	Duplicate proposal
Select primary authors of proposal	Submit proposal

in other parts of the university, several weeks of cushion are wise when establishing any set of target deadlines. This particularly is true of the typing and collation of the proposal. Even when produced on a word processor, the typing alone may take several weeks. Invariably, it will take longer than you anticipate. Because a proposal is a large project often involving 50 to 100 typed pages, all of which must have no errors at all, it will take the office staff away from other duties for unacceptable periods of time if typing is left to the last minute. Further, each draft must be checked and double-checked. The end result is a process that makes Murphy's corollary look positively optimistic.

SUMMARY

If you have read this far, we hope you are not immobilized by the thought of undertaking the tasks described. Difficult and demanding as proposal writing can be, the rewards are clear and attractive—a well-planned study and money to make it go. In addition, each time a proposal is written the process becomes easier. Many of the proposal sections, when written on a word processor, simply can be updated and reused in subsequent documents. For example, each time a proposal is submitted, the basic description of a university research facility simply is updated and reprinted. The same process can occur with a particular methodology used in a line of research. Once the description has been written, it need only be updated and then recycled. Grant gathering, like any other intellectual skill, improves with practice. You may never find yourself regarding the process as enjoyable, but the challenges are always fresh and the sense of satisfaction in completing a good presentation can be a significant reward. Better still, of course, is obtaining the money!

PART II

Specimen Proposals

Introduction

The specimen proposals presented here were selected with several intentions. First, we wanted to display proposals using different designs and paradigms for research. Second, we wanted the proposals to involve research topics drawn from different areas. Third, we wanted to illustrate typical proposals for both theses and dissertations as well as for grant funding. All four proposals presented in this guide have accomplished the goals of their respective authors—successful acceptance by a graduate committee or, in the case of the grant proposal, the award of funding for research.

The reader may wish to examine more than one of these proposals. Since different designs and styles are used, each proposal illustrates a different way to implement our suggestions. You may gain valuable ideas for proposal writing from reading the proposals in which the research designs are different from the one you plan to use. In the specimen proposal presented first, we have provided an experimental laboratory study focusing on adult subjects of different ages. This proposal has been edited so each section corresponds to a task presented in Chapter 1. We provide comments to help you focus attention on the important aspects of each task. The second proposal presented is a dissertation proposal employing qualitative methodology to examine women returning to a community college after an extended absence from schooling. The third example presented in this part of the book employs a quasi-experimental design for a study to be conducted in the field setting of elementary school classrooms. The final proposal involves the field test of a work site intervention to reduce smoking.

Each of the proposals in this guide has been edited for the present use and is accompanied by our comments. The documents were not selected for perfection but for general excellence and demonstrated success. Also, because some of the proposals were prepared several years ago, the content information should not be construed to represent current knowledge in the field. Our accompanying analyses are not intended to be critical of the authors. It is easy to play the role of "Monday morning quarterback" with ample time and little of the pressure associated with preparing a proposal. It also is likely that each of the authors, having implemented the proposed study, would now make some changes in the original document. Hindsight always is 20/20. Our comments, then, are intended to draw the reader's attention to parts that we feel are particularly well executed, to raise needed questions, and to make apparent alternative courses of action.

Proposal 1: Experimental Design

The Effects of Age, Modality, Complexity of Response, and Practice on Reaction Time

Introduction

In the introduction, the author moves from an artificial introduction to a specific focus on the important constructs for this
proposal. In the first paragraph, a brief vignette from history
effectively captures the reader's attention. In the second paragraph, the author further piques the reader's interest by suggesting that recent findings are challenging 75 years of dogma
concerning the topic. The next three paragraphs introduce primary constructs, the mechanisms that may control motor responses with aging. In paragraphs six and seven, the author
introduces special aspects of design that will be incorporated
into the study. The introduction is concluded by a sentence that
summarizes the major topics of the previous paragraphs and
leads into the rationale to follow. Note that the introduction

AUTHOR'S NOTE: This proposal was prepared in 1985 by Lance Osborne as part of the
thesis research requirement in the Department of Kinesiology and Health Education at The
University of Texas at Austin. The thesis was supervised by Waneen Wyrick Spirduso.

immediately acquaints the reader with the topic and leaves
extensive detail for later sections of the proposal.

Eighty-six years ago, visitors to an international health exhibition
had the opportunity, after paying a small fee, to "try their powers."
Men and women of various ages, from the teens to the seventies,
were timed to see how quickly they could press a key in response to
a light [their reaction time, (RT)]. The results of this "study" (Galton,
1899) reflected exactly what one might intuitively expect: The older
subjects were slower than the younger ones. In the years since, the
research techniques have steadily grown more rigorous and the
paradigms have varied considerably, yet the findings continue to
support the notion that as individuals grow older they become slower.

The long history of reports indicating that older individuals are
generally slower than young ones in reaction time suggests that
any exception would be quite a surprise. Yet in the last 10 years,
data supporting an exception to the age-related slowing of response speed have surfaced. Nebes (1978), Salthouse and
Somberg (1982), and Thomas, Waugh, and Fozard (1978), using
simple reaction-time paradigms incorporating vocal responses,
found no significant differences between the response latencies
of old and young subjects. These findings have raised the questions, "Is the motor act of vocalization really immune to the
age-related decrement in response speed typically found for other
types of motor responses, and if so, why?"

Because of its potential to resist aging, vocalization may be a
very important phenomenon to study in order to understand more
clearly the mechanisms responsible for age-related slowing. The
control of limb movement is independent of the motor control of
speech, even though the same central nervous system structures
are involved in its planning and control (De Renzi, Mottle, &
Nichelli, 1980; Heilman et al., 1973). A better understanding of how
age differentially affects control of manual or vocal responses to an
external stimulus also might elucidate the extent to which the two
motor systems share similar information processing mechanisms.

In the search for the mechanism(s) to which age-related changes
might be attributed, certain peripheral changes can be safely eliminated. First, although an age-related muscle atrophy occurs throughout most of the body, the duration of muscle contraction does not
contribute a very high proportion of the total delay from stimulus

to the onset of the movement. Delay in this component of the response would not result in a large delay in simple reaction time (Clarkson, 1978; Weiss, 1965). Thus the lack of age-related atrophy in muscles involved in vocalization cannot account for the apparent lack of decrement in vocal response speed. Second, since the peripheral nerve conduction velocity is slower in older individuals, and the path from the brain to the finger is longer than the path from the brain to throat structures, it might be inferred that the effect of age would be less with speech motor acts. However, it has been shown that, although foot and finger movements are slower than jaw reaction times, the difference in response speed between old and young is similar for each of these responses despite the difference in peripheral nerve conduction velocity (Hugin, Norris, & Shock, 1960).

These two motor modalities, manual and vocal, differ in their levels of complexity, and because complexity presents a greater challenge to older people, this might be an explanation for the age differences that are seen. The general slowing of response speed with age may, however, be related to a change that is more generalizable to one or more stages of information processing, such as the programming of motor responses (Haaland & Bracy, 1982). Vocal responses to a stimulus involve motor control of a multiple-joint action. These actions are more flexibly controlled due to motor equivalence/compensatory patterns than manual responses, which are constrained by the necessity to operate around one or two joints. This constraint makes the movement more complex because it has fewer degrees of freedom (Abbs et al., 1984).

Haaland and Bracy (1982) suggest that by methodologically varying both manual and vocal skills along the dimension of motoric complexity, more may be learned about differences that exist among motor systems in the aging person. To isolate the effects of response complexity on response programming, it is important that conditions are held constant across the two earlier stages of information processing: the stimulus identification stage and the response selection stage (Kerr, 1978).

Finally, most investigators reporting age differences in performance of psychomotor tasks have failed to provide enough practice at those tasks. To obtain a valid measure of any differences, should they exist, requires the control (through substantial practice) of confounding factors such as task unfamiliarity or high anxiety. Vocal responses are much more highly practiced than manual responses such as depression of a key, and it may be that the differential activation of manual and vocal responses is a key factor in different rates of aging in these two systems. Practice will be used in this experiment in an effort to reduce the novelty of the tasks and to equate the stability of vocal and manual reaction times. In addition, the effects of practice on age differences in performance for all of the reaction time tasks will be examined. The analysis of practice effects, should they exist, and the manipulation of both response mode and complexity, may clarify knowledge concerning the interactions of age, response mode and complexity.

Purpose

In the statement of purpose, the four experimental factors of the study are introduced: age, mode of response, complexity, and practice. The general question of interest in the study (see Chapter 3 for a discussion of the difference between a question and a purpose) is implicit in the purpose stated in the first sentence (Do *age* differences exist in response *speed* in two *different motor* systems?). In the second sentence, the factor of complexity is added. A secondary purpose, to control for practice effects, is described in the last sentence. Each of the purposes grows out of the introduction, and the statement here prepares the reader for the rationale that follows.

In this investigation, an age difference in response speed will be tested in comparable vocal and manual tasks. Two motor systems (vocal and manual) will be varied in terms of response programming complexity (simple and complex) in parallel fashion in both motor systems. The level of complexity in this study will be varied according to whether the response requires a limited or relatively larger number of coordinated muscles in the response. To ensure that the question raised pertains to manual or vocal capacities and not to learning, the tests will be administered over a period of three days.

Rationale

In this rationale, the theoretical logic of the relationships assumed and postulated are clarified. Following a simple pattern of argument (see Chapter 4), *if* (a) old individuals respond slower than young individuals with their hands, *and* (b) motor task complexity exaggerates age differences, *but* (c) old respond as quickly as young with their voice, *then* (d) old manual response is slower because it is more complex. The final statement shows how the clarification of these relationships will provide information that not only accurately describes the source of differences between the reaction latencies of the young and old, but also contributes insights as to the nature and mechanisms of motor control.

The central control of manual reaction responses is slower in older individuals, particularly those responses that may be more complex than others (Welford, 1982). Vocal reaction responses, however, appear to be spared by aging. Inasmuch as the manual and vocal motor systems are independent, and older individuals are relatively more affected by complexity, the failure to find age differences in vocal reaction time paradigms might be attributed to the fact that vocal and manual tasks differ not only on the dimension of the motor system used, but on complexity as well. The results of this study should provide information that will determine whether aging affects a central motor processing stage that is general to all motor systems, or whether the prime aging effect is specific to a particular motor system.

Hypotheses

Note that the hypotheses are specific to a particular relationship that is being tested statistically. For example, in hypothesis 1 the relationship between the type of motor response and the speed of response is tested by the analysis of variance main effect for motor system. This is a very clear and unambiguous test.

When the literature provides the investigator with information suggesting the direction of differences (in this example several of the cited reports suggest that the manual responses will be longer than the vocal), the directional hypothesis provides a more powerful test. No similar information is available to suggest whether complexity of response would interact with a specific type of motor system; thus hypothesis 3 is written in the null form. The reader may wish to submit each of these hypotheses to the tests suggested in Chapter 1: Is the hypothesis unambiguous? Does it express a relationship? Is the appropriate statistical test implied?

In order to fulfill the purposes of this study, several hypotheses are formulated. These hypotheses are expressed directionally where the results from past experiments suggest directionality. When direction is unpredictable, they are written in the null form.

Hypothesis 1. The mean reaction time for manual responses is significantly slower than that for vocal responses.

Hypothesis 2. The mean reaction time for simple responses is significantly less than that for complex responses.

Hypothesis 3. The difference between mean reaction time for response type (simple or complex) is not significantly interactive with mode of response (manual or vocal).

Hypothesis 4. The mean reaction time of young subjects is significantly faster than that of old subjects.

Hypothesis 5. The mean reaction time of old subjects is not significantly different from that of young subjects when using vocal responses.

Hypothesis 6. The mean reaction time of old subjects is significantly greater than that of young subjects when using manual responses.

Hypothesis 7. The difference between the mean reaction time of the old subjects and of the young subjects using the simple response type is not significantly different from the difference using the complex response type (regardless of response mode).

Hypothesis 8. The mean reaction time for old subjects is not significantly different from that for young subjects using simple-voice responses.

Hypothesis 9. The mean reaction time for old subjects is not significantly different from that for young subjects using complex-voice responses.

Hypothesis 10. The mean reaction time for old subjects is significantly greater than that for young subjects when using simple-manual responses.

Hypothesis 11. The mean reaction time for old subjects is significantly greater than that for young subjects when using complex-manual responses.

Hypothesis 12. The mean reaction time, averaged over all conditions, is significantly decreased (improved) from day one to day two.

Hypothesis 13. The mean reaction time, averaged over all conditions, is significantly decreased (improved) from day two to day three.

Hypothesis 14. The decrease (improvement), with practice, in mean reaction time for the old subjects is not significantly different from that for the young subjects.

Delimitations

The delimitations expressed below specify that inferences from this study may only be made to the sex, age, and educational level of the sample used. Other restrictions are related to the specific type of response investigated and the amount of practice provided. Those who would replicate the proposed study are cautioned that results will pertain only to samples matching the description given. By describing the delimitations, the author also is promising the committee that, when the analyses are complete and the results are known, inferences will not be made that extend beyond what is appropriate.

Because of the age grouping and sex of the subjects chosen for this study, it is not possible to generalize the results to females or to other age levels. The results also cannot be completely generalized from this university-drawn sample to the general population. Any conclusions concerning motor-system-specific, dependent age differences will have to be limited to the two response modes (finger and voice) used in this experiment; these results cannot be generalized to other modes of response. Conclusions concerning the response-complexity issue must be limited to the degree and types of complexity provided in the responses in this experiment; the results cannot be generalized to

other levels of complexity. Because the amount of practice provided in this experiment was limited to three days, the results
cannot be generalized to include the performance of tasks where
more than three days of practice are provided.

Limitations

Inasmuch as older people are more variable in their responses,
the results from this study would be more reliable if older individuals could be administered many trials over several days, dependent on when the subjects' performances plateaued. Also, direct
measurement of important control variables, such as blood pressure, are always better than self-reported or indirect assessments.
However, although advanced age contributes to greater variability,
it also is a limiting factor in terms of the intensity and duration of
testing. Some tests simply cannot be performed on elderly adults,
nor can tests be repeated for long periods of time. The elderly, and
their medical advisors, won't stand for it. The author has determined that information to be gained from self-reported indirect
measures is nevertheless valuable and will contribute a reliable
answer to the questions proposed.

Older individuals tire quickly and become disenchanted with
testing after several blocks of trials. They have reached the age
where they may not be motivated and certainly do not feel compelled to tolerate a long, arduous battery of testing for many
consecutive days. Devoting extended periods of time to being
tested is inconvenient and difficult for most subjects; consequently, the time required for practice and testing in this study will
be only three days. Pilot work has provided evidence to suggest
that reaction times are close to baseline levels by three days. The
screening of subjects for health problems such as high blood
pressure or the use of response-slowing drugs will be limited to
self-report. Formal methods of screening are costly, inconvenient,
and unavailable to the investigator. However, by excluding all
subjects with self-reported medications and health problems,
errors that might occur should be minimized and should be an
error on the conservative side.

Definitions

Below, the author has provided definitions for those terms that are system language words used within the domain of motor control research. Most of the words to be defined (e.g., response programming) are words that either singly or in phrases have an invariant meaning for researchers in this field. In the case of the term "complexity," the investigator operationally assigns an invariant meaning to a common language word. This makes it available for systematic use throughout the proposal. Note that source citations are provided where possible.

Complexity. In this study, movement response is operationally defined as more complex if the response latency is significantly slower. The motor responses were selected because of (a) differences in the relative nature and number of coordinated muscles involved in producing the immediate response and, (b) significant differences in the response latencies observed in pilot work.

Fractionated Reaction Time. Reaction time can be partitioned into "central" and "peripheral" components by using electromyography (EMG) to record the electrical activity from the muscles (Weiss, 1965). During a portion of the RT, the EMG is silent, indicating that the signal to move has not yet reached the muscle. Later in the RT, electrical activity is recorded from the activated muscle, but no movement occurs for a time. The interval from the stimulus signal to the first EMG activity is termed *premotor RT* and is thought to represent time spent in central processes; while the interval from the first sign of change in EMG to actual movement is termed *motor time* (MT) and represents processes associated with the muscles and their actions in initiation of the response (Schmidt, 1982, p. 75).

Response Programming. Response programming occurs in the final stage of the information processing model. Once a stimulus has been identified and the proper response has been selected, the response programming stage is responsible for the preparation of the motor apparatus and the initiation of the action (see Schmidt, 1982, p. 93, Figure 4.3).

Variable Error. The variable error used in this study is a measure of inconsistency in responding. It is the variability of a

subject's response latencies about the subject's own mean response latency (Schmidt, 1982, p. 66).

Review of Literature

This review of literature section provides the background for
the selection of hypotheses and method. Note that in paragraph
three an overview of the review section is provided. This is an
important step in helping the reader understand what is to
follow. The review may or may not have a short introduction (as
provided here in the first two paragraphs) before the overview
paragraph. In Chapter 4 we provide an extended discussion of
how to prepare a literature review. As you read this, however,
notice how the author often summarizes the literature in conceptual categories rather than undertaking a study-by-study
discussion. Summaries provided at the end of the two longer
sections help the reader identify the important generalizations
to be made.

Throughout its history, the behavioral study of aging has revealed at least one consistent finding: that older adults are slower
than young adults in response speed. Reportedly, this phenomenon
can be observed regardless of the mode of response (Birren &
Botwinick, 1955; Welford, 1977) and regardless of the type of stimuli
(Talland, 1965; Welford, 1977) involved in the response task.

Efforts to isolate possible mechanisms responsible for this
age-related slowing have been largely successful only in reveal-
ing mechanisms that are probably not causes: the slowing is not
the result solely of sensory diminution (Botwinick, 1972, 1978),
not muscle atrophy (Weiss, 1965), nor a reduction of nerve
conduction velocity (Hugin, Norris, & Shock, 1960). Possible
compound effects of all of these changes have not been tested.
Through default, most investigators agree that an alteration in the
central nervous system is presently the best candidate for the
mechanism responsible for the age-related slowing (Botwinick &
Thompson, 1966; Clarkson, 1978; Weiss, 1965). In addition, lack
of sufficient practice with a particular task has been suggested as
a possible cause for at least some of the age differences observed

(Grant, Storandt, & Botwinick, 1978; Murrell, 1970; Salthouse & Somberg, 1982a).

In this study the focus will be on age-related changes in RT in performing simple and complex tasks. The review of literature section has three subsections related to this topic: (a) response-specific aging effects; (b) motor responses and an information processing model; and (c) vocal reaction time paradigms (without age as a factor).

RESPONSE-SPECIFIC AGING EFFECTS

Vocal Responses

Surprisingly, an exception to this general slowing in older individuals has been reported. In studies of simple reaction time using vocal responses, Nebes (1978), Thomas, Waugh, and Fozard (1978), and Salthouse and Somberg (1982) found no significant age differences. These findings were somewhat incidental: they were reported in investigations in which other response tasks were of central interest, or where the vocal RT measures were used as controls. These results were obtained only from simple response tasks and when (except in Salthouse & Somberg, 1982) a limited amount of practice was provided. Nebes (1978) is the only investigator among these who discussed a possible explanation for the vocal RT findings. He suggested that perhaps the neural substrate for speech is less susceptible than that of manual movements to the loss of brain cells which has been shown to occur with increasing age. However, Nebes (1978) added that explanations along those lines must remain speculative.

Voice Onset Time

Another recent study in speech research was conducted to determine the effect of aging on voice onset time (VOT). VOT was defined as a delay in the onset of vocal fold vibration for the vowel that follows release of the consonant; this reflects supralaryngeal and laryngeal coordination speed. Neiman, Klich, and Shuey (1983) measured VOT from spectrograms for 10 women between 20 and 30 years old and 10 women between 70 and 80 years old.

Their findings, contrary to their expectations, revealed that VOT was generally the same in older and younger subjects. The only explanation that was offered was that changes due to aging may have little effect on glottal adjustments and/or articulatory adjustments used to control VOT.

Summary

Together, the results from these various studies lend support to the notion that the act of vocalization, unlike other behavioral acts, may be affected differently or not at all by age. Furthermore, the mechanism that is responsible apparently involves the central control processes. Haaland and Bracy (1982) have proposed that the general slowing of response speed with age may be related to the response programming stage in an information processing model. The motor programming of manual and vocal responses, rather than using a centralized, general control mechanism, may be specific to the motor system used. Motor response specificity has been demonstrated with simple reaction time (Nebes, 1978; Thomas et al., 1978). Thus, different mechanisms of response programming for different modalities might respond differently to aging.

MOTOR RESPONSES AND AN INFORMATION PROCESSING MODEL

Stages of Information Processing

At least three stages have been proposed that intervene between the presentation of a stimulus and the evocation of a response. First, the subject must identify the stimulus and acknowledge that it has occurred. This is commonly known as the stimulus-identification stage. Second, after a stimulus is identified the subject must decide what response to make. This occurs in the response-selection stage. Finally, after the response has been selected, the system must be readied for the correct action and must initiate that action. This final stage is frequently called the response-initiation (Kerr, 1978) or response-programming stage (Schmidt, 1982). It is the final stage that, when isolated, may reflect response-specific programming changes with aging.

The author provided in Figure 1 a box diagram of a currently accepted model of information processing. In the interest of space we have deleted the diagram, but it was a clever technique as it allowed the author to organize the description of each stage of the model, and commonly used methods of identifying the stage, around the boxes in the figure.

Kerr (1978) outlines the appropriate steps for focusing on the response programming stage:

The time for encoding and identifying stimuli and for associating stimuli with task-appropriate responses must remain constant across conditions so that differences in initiation time can be identified with movement programming stages rather than processes that occur before programming (e.g., remembering that red means right). The most straightforward approach standardizes the number of task alternatives across conditions. Other variables known to affect reaction time (e.g., signal intensity, warning interval duration) must also be controlled. Only when one is comfortable with the assumption that initial processing times remain equal across conditions should differences in initiation time be attributed to programming stages. (p. 64)

Response Programming and Response Complexity

While information about the first two stages of processing was obtained very early in the history of motor behavior research, information about the response programming stage was, until recently, undeveloped. It was not until the early studies by Henry and Rogers, that thinking about a response-programming stage began. In 1960, Henry and Rogers studied the nature of the movement to be made in a simple-RT paradigm, in which subjects knew on any given trial which response was to be made. The three responses ranged from the simplest (merely lifting the finger from a key) to the most complex, which involved lifting the finger from a key, moving forward and upward to strike one ball with the back of the hand, moving forward and downward to push a button, and then forward and upward again to strike a second ball. For each level of complexity, the stimulus and response alternatives were the same; therefore, the processing time in the stimulus-identification and response-selection stages should have been constant. These levels of increasing complexity involved additional *accuracy* requirements and increased movement *duration,* and for each level there was a significant increase in the reaction time. Since the publication of the Henry and Rogers study many investigators have found similar results (see Kerr, 1978, or Klapp, 1977, 1980, for reviews). In one modification of the original paradigm, Sternberg, Monsell, Knoll, and Wright (1978) found that RT was directly related to the number of elements in a sequence of action by studying response speeds for spoken words and typed letters. In a review of several of these studies, Schmidt (1982, p. 112) observed that: "Regardless of the variations in method and movements, the effect of movement complexity on RT has been interpreted as relating to the time necessary to prepare the movement during the response-programming stage of RT." Like that of Henry and Rogers (1960), and the others that followed, this investigation involved the isolation of changes that occurred in the response-programming stage due to changes in the complexity of the motor response; but, in the effort to find the locus of aging differences between vocal and manual tasks, the manipulations of complexity were along somewhat different lines.

Complexity Differences Between Manual and Vocal Tasks

Even at its simplest level, the act of vocalization involves the coordinated effort of several muscles in the respiratory system, while a manual act, such as pressing a button with the index finger, requires the flexion of two adjacent, co-agonist muscles. Perhaps the aging differences found between vocal and manual response speeds are not based on the obvious motor system differences, but are instead the result of differences in the motoric complexity of the two skills. Other investigators have suggested theories along these lines.

Abbs, Gracco, and Cole (1984) have suggested that movements constrained around a single joint may present a more difficult programming/control problem to the nervous system than their apparently "more complex" multijoint counterparts (i.e., speech). Based on speech perturbation studies of their own, and consideration of other recent experiments on speech and manual movement coordination, Abbs et al. (1984) summarize some of their findings:

Multiple degrees of freedom in natural motor behaviors may facilitate rather than burden the processes of motor learning and neural control. . . . The learning and neural programming of skilled motor behaviors would be significantly more demanding if the criterion for successful performance is restricted to a single stereotyped pattern of muscle contraction and movement (p. 227).

Summary

These observations, when coupled with those of Haaland and Bracy (1982) suggest the possibility of a response-specific programming difference involved between vocal and manual activities that lends itself to a greater or lesser aging affect; and that perhaps that difference, rather than being just modality-specific, is a function of the differential complexity in *initiating* the two acts. Motor response specifically can be tested directly, but specific programming differences such as these are more difficult to isolate. Haaland and Bracy (1982) suggest that investigators who directly manipulate the complexity of (only) the motor response would be more directly determining whether motor programming capabilities change with aging. This would require circumventing the earlier stages of information processing in order to isolate any response programming differences which, as discussed in the previous section, is not a novel idea (for a review, see Kerr, 1978; Klapp, 1977, 1980; Schmidt, 1982, chap. 4; Sternberg et al., 1978); but, in this investigation, the accuracy and duration of the response movements were not factors. In fact, after the initial response, there was no additional movement; it was simply the number of coordinated muscles involved in the direct initiation of the response that provided the levels of complexity. It was assumed that if the response-programming stage was properly isolated, and latency differences (between the levels of complexity in this study) were observed, that those latency differences would be the result of different processing speeds in the response-programming stage. If age differences interacted with these complexity differences, it would support the notion that the modality differences were actually the result of differences in complexity.

VOCAL RT PARADIGMS
(WITHOUT AGE AS A FACTOR)

Other researchers studying speech have focused on vocal reaction time, but not age effects. However, several of these studies described results and methodologies that were helpful in pursuing the present investigation. Izdebski and Shipp (1978) measured the difference between voluntary vocal and digital (finger) response speeds in young adults using simple RT methodology. The vocal RT's were studied as a function of sex, stimulus type (auditory and somesthetic), and subject lung volume. Among these variables, only lung volume produced significant differences, suggesting a need to standardize lung volume in any future vocal reaction time paradigms. More relevant to this investigation, Izdebski and Shipp (1978), Nebes (1978), Thomas et al. (1978), and Salthouse and Somberg (1982) found that the average digital RT's were significantly shorter than the times for vocal reactions; a finding that may be a result of the measurement used in the vocal tasks. Results from pilot work for this investigation indicated that hidden, highly variable latencies may characterize reaction times that are measured with a vocally triggered relay such as that used by these investigators. Latency measurements made directly from voice patterns reproduced on a storage oscilloscope are more reliable and accurate.

SUMMARY

If the results from previous studies involving vocal response are valid, it may be inferred that the act of vocalization is an exception to the general slowing of response speed observed in the aged: that age-related slowing is response-specific. It is important that such an exception be validated through replication; taking care to avoid possible confounding with insufficient practice and unreliable measurements. Furthermore, it may be possible—by manipulating certain variables and isolating the response-programming stage—to search for the mechanism(s) responsible for such an exception. Once possible mechanisms are isolated, theories that explain a response-specific age difference can be generated and tested more readily.

Method

The method section that is presented here begins with an overview paragraph and a diagram of the steps in collecting the data. For most proposals an overview paragraph should come first and, if supplemented with an appropriate diagram, few readers will have difficulty in understanding how the parts of the method section mesh into the overall plan. All the major components of method are identified by side headings. The author makes good use of pilot data in this section and, appropriately, puts complex detail into an appendix.

In this study, age differences in reaction time will be examined in the performance of simple and complex manual and vocal tasks. The reaction time of a group of older (60 years and over) and younger men (18-30 years old) will be tested on three days on four tasks: (1) a manual task that is simple; (2) a manual task that is complex; (3) a vocal task that is simple; and, (4) a vocal task that is complex. A diagrammatic overview is presented in Figure 2.

SUBJECTS

The subjects will be 40 males obtained from a university population. Sampling males of different ages from this population will provide some university-related homogeneity in the variation in cognitive abilities and types ordinarily found in the general population. Results from previous studies involving reaction time indicate a need to control for variations in cognitive ability and type. Twenty of the subjects, composing the older group, will be volunteers from the faculty population and will be 60 years of age or older. Since many of these individuals will be close to or beyond the age of retirement, only those who remain actively involved with the university (retired faculty organization, alumni association,

PILOT TEST

RECRUIT SUBJECTS

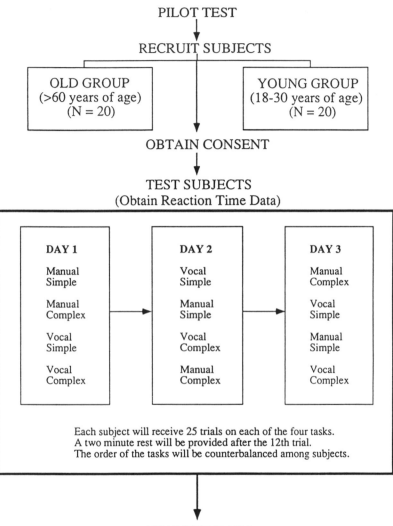

OLD GROUP		YOUNG GROUP
(>60 years of age)		(18-30 years of age)
(N = 20)		(N = 20)

OBTAIN CONSENT

TEST SUBJECTS
(Obtain Reaction Time Data)

DAY 1	**DAY 2**	**DAY 3**
Manual Simple	Vocal Simple	Manual Complex
Manual Complex	Manual Simple	Vocal Simple
Vocal Simple	Vocal Complex	Manual Simple
Vocal Complex	Manual Complex	Vocal Complex

Each subject will receive 25 trials on each of the four tasks.
A two minute rest will be provided after the 12th trial.
The order of the tasks will be counterbalanced among subjects.

ANALYZE DATA

Proposal 1: Figure 2. Overview of Research Design

part- or full-time lecturer, instructor, or researcher) will be included
in the study. The remaining twenty subjects, composing the young
group, will be volunteers from the student population and will

range from 18 to 30 years of age. All subjects will be screened to ensure that they are non-smokers and not currently taking any medication that might alter response speed. All subjects will be right handed, in good health and, according to self-report, without any neurological disorder.

DESIGN

Reaction times of the two age groups (old and young) will be compared with regard to the complexity of the reaction task (simple or more complex, hereafter called *complexity*), the response modality (vocal or manual), and the number of days of practice (1-3 days). The design will be a between (age) and within (complexity, mode, and practice) model analyzed by a 2 x 2 x 2 x 3 factorial analysis of variance (ANOVA).

APPARATUS

Measurement of simple manual reaction time will be accomplished using an index-finger-activated microswitch connected to a Standard Electric Time digital timer (Model ABC-11) (see Appendix A for an instrumentation diagram). The timer has a manufacturer reported accuracy of +/-.00016 seconds. Measurement of the complex manual reaction time will be accomplished using index-finger- and thumb-activated microswitches connected in series to the same timer. The speech acoustic signals from vocal reactions will be recorded through an Ebel XY89A microphone, on a Packer Dck 1234 tape deck at a speed of .75 inches per second. The signals will be reproduced on the same tape deck and channeled into a Brand Name Storage Oscilloscope (Model XXYY) to produce voice patterns from which reaction times will be obtained (see Appendix B for an instrumentation diagram).

The red stimulus light for all reaction time tasks will be a 120 VAC neon lamp, measuring two centimeters across, and set in a flat-black background. The occurrence of a warning bell will be manually controlled via a French millisecond timer (Model 00033). The same timer will control the activation of the stimulus light. The inter-trial interval of five seconds will be controlled by a French interval timer (Model 00112). Both the millisecond and interval timer have a manufacturer reported accuracy rating of 0.1%+/–1 LSD and a repeatability measure of 0.1%+/–1 LSD.

PILOT TESTING OF INSTRUMENTATION

Manual Instrumentation

Because RTs on several different instruments will be compared, it is important to establish that differences observed will not be attributed to instrument-related mechanical or biomechanical differences rather than central processing differences. In the manual tasks, RTs on one microswitch were to be compared in a pilot study with RTs on two additional microswitches, set in series. If these switches were mechanically different or caused biomechanical inconsistencies that would bring about latency differences, it would confound interpretations of the manual results.

Since this investigation will center on changes in latency due to changes in the central processes (only), it has to be established that the speed in the peripheral components of RT (motor time, pressure, throw times, and spring tensions of the switches) is constant across each task (see Figure 3). The construct validity of this investigation would be suspect if any differences in this peripheral component existed from task to task, for example, if RT on the simple task was significantly shorter than that for the complex task the results would be confounded if the motor time for the simple task also was significantly shorter.

Equipment was not available to test the throw times and spring tensions of the switches *mechanically,* nor the muscle-exerted pressure, but (behavioral) RT tests were conducted with each individual switch: a well-practiced subject, who had just completed three days of testing, completed 10 warm-up trials and 25 test trials of RT with each *individual* switch (see Table C-1, Appendix C).

In addition, in a separate test, the EMG of the muscles involved in the responses was recorded during several trials on both the simple and complex apparatus. The motor time for these trials was compared and analyzed for differences between tasks (Table C-2, Appendix C). The behavioral RT test revealed very little difference between the means from each switch. However, in the

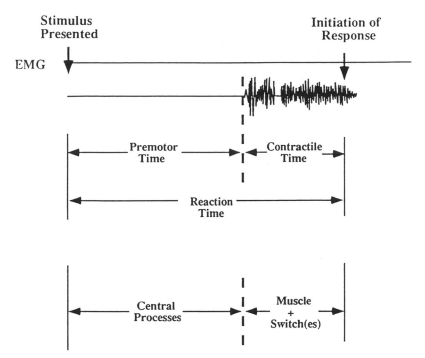

Proposal 1: Figure 3. Reaction Time Events

NOTE: Critical events involved in the reaction time paradigm. The trace is a hypothetical EMG record.
SOURCE: Adapted from Schmidt, 1982, p. 75.

EMG testing, the motor time made up a larger proportion of the total RT in the simple task (index finger only) than in the complex task (finger/thumb). Therefore, because in this experiment the RT on the simple task was significantly shorter than the RT on a complex task, the difference seen was probably a conservative estimate of the real differences that existed.

Vocal Instrumentation

In order to make valid comparisons between vocal RT (measured from the onset of a voice pattern on an oscilloscope) and manual RT, which was recorded directly from a digital timer, it was important to make certain that measures of RT on the digital timer would be the same if measured on the oscilloscope. Therefore, RT for several trials of the manual tasks were simultaneously viewed on the timer and on the oscilloscope (see Figure 4), and absolutely no differences were observed between the RT recorded on the two instruments.

In the vocal tasks, it also was important to establish that no inherent latency differences existed between the instrumentation for the two different consonants, e.g., that the vocal fold vibration necessary for producing the "zz" sound occurred simultaneously with the onset of the voice pattern, and not before or after (thus shortening or extending the apparent latency). To make this particular comparison the production of the consonant sounds was recorded simultaneously at the vocal cords and at the mouth. Vocal fold vibrations were recorded via a phonometer (a device for measuring the intensity of sounds) and the onset of the voice pattern was, via the microphone previously described, viewed on the same phonometric readout (see Appendix D for instrumentation diagram). As expected, no vocal fold vibrations occurred in the production of the "ss" sound, and in addition, there were no latency differences between the onset of the voice pattern and the onset of vocal fold vibration in the production of the "zz" sound.

PROCEDURES

General

Each subject will be administered a consent form (Appendix E) to read and sign. He will be seated at a table where the microphone, manual apparatus, and stimulus lights are positioned. Before trials for either vocal or manual reaction time begin, each subject will receive standardized instructions (Appendix F) for that task. The order (Appendix G) in which the two response types (vocal and manual) and in which either a simple or complex version of the two tasks will be administered will be counter-balanced across all subjects. Each subject will complete 25 trials of both the simple and complex versions of the manual and vocal tasks on three consecutive days. Based on pilot data, 25 trials will be enough to provide sufficient practice and a sufficiently large

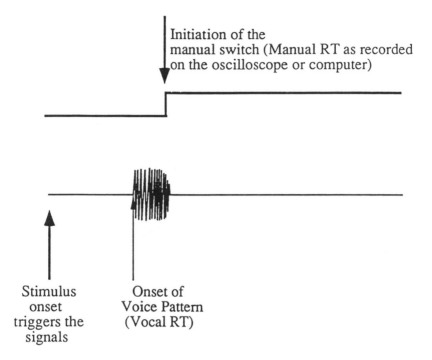

Initiation of the
manual switch (Manual RT as recorded
on the oscilloscope or computer)

Stimulus
onset
triggers the
signals

Onset of
Voice Pattern
(Vocal RT)

Proposal 1: Figure 4.   Schematic Diagram of Manual and Vocal
Response Signals as Seen on a Storage Oscilloscope

sample, but not so many as to fatigue the subjects. In the pilot
study, a two-minute rest was given after the first 12 trials of each
task on all three days of testing, a procedure that will be continued
in the proposed study.

Manual reaction time

In the simple version of the manual task, upon hearing a
warning buzzer, the subject will direct his attention to the stimulus
light. After a randomly assigned warning interval (2, 3, or 4
seconds), the stimulus light will be activated. The subject will
press the microswitch with the index finger as quickly as possible
upon seeing the stimulus light activated. In the complex version,

the procedure will be the same except that, upon seeing the stimulus light activated, the subject will engage the index-finger microswitch and the thumb microswitch on the complex reaction-time apparatus (see Appendix H for a diagram of the manual tasks; see Appendix I for the muscles involved in the production of the manual tasks).

Vocal reaction time

In the vocal RT tasks, the protocol will be similar. A warning buzzer will sound to direct the subject's attention to the stimulus light, prompting him to place his tongue in a neutral position against the lower teeth, and, after a randomly assigned interval (2, 3, or 4 seconds), the stimulus light will be activated. The subject will be constantly monitored by the experimenter to ensure that his mouth is the proper distance from the microphone. In the simple version, upon seeing the light activated, the subject will say the consonant, "ss" (producing a hissing sound) into the microphone as quickly as possible. In the complex version, upon seeing the light activated, the subject will say the consonant, "zz" (producing a buzzing sound, as in the beginning of the word xylophone) into the microphone as quickly as possible. The initial enunciation of the consonant will form the onset of the voice pattern from which reaction times will be measured. Pilot data were not obtained for these particular sounds, but for a variety of others. The results reflected a low level of within subject variability for the various vocal sounds tested (see Table J-1, Appendix J). These sounds—"ss" and "zz"—were chosen because the muscle activity involved in the production of each is relatively simple, and because the enunciation of each yields clear and reliable voice patterns (Figure 4) from which to measure RT. The pilot data provided a basis for complete confidence that no significant difference in variability will occur between (and therefore confound) the measures from the vocal and manual tasks (see Table J-1, Appendix J).

ANALYSIS

The mean RT and standard deviation for each set of trials will be computed. Scores that are two standard deviations above or below the mean will be discarded and new means and standard deviations computed. These data will be averaged across subjects in each age group for each of the 3 days: a 2 x 2 x 2 x 3 (age: young/old x modality: vocal/manual x complexity: simple/complex x practice: days 1, 2, and 3). ANOVA factorial analysis with repeated measures on the last three factors then will be computed. Tukey's-HSD post hoc comparisons will be made between means in the interactions.

In the proposal the author used appendices to include the following:

Appendix A. Instrumentation Diagram for the Manual Apparatus
Appendix B. Instrumentation Diagram for the Vocal Apparatus
Appendix C. Pilot Testing of Instrumentation
Appendix D. Instrumentation Diagram for the Testing of the Vocal Tasks
Appendix E. Subject Consent Form
Appendix F. Task Instructions
Appendix G. Testing Order
Appendix H. Switch Diagram
Appendix I. Muscles Used in the Manual Tasks
Appendix J. Pilot Data

Appendix J, Pilot Data, contained descriptive data for each group, subgroup, and interaction, sample analysis of variance tables, and figures plotting the pilot data. As indicated in Chapter 4, sample tables are a valuable and often neglected component of the proposal. When included, they may reveal problems that are not easily identified from a reading of the text.

Proposal 2: Qualitative Study

*Returning Women Students
in the Community College*

NOTE TO THE READER

The proposal that follows involves use of the qualitative paradigm for research. If you are unfamiliar with this kind of inquiry, reading Chapter 5 will help in understanding the unique planning problems that must be confronted. If you are familiar only with experimental and quasiexperimental designs, Chapter 5 will explain what may seem to be unusual or inappropriate ways of handling some elements in the proposal.

Not only may this be your first encounter with some of the methods used here, but the author's assumptions about such basic matters as the nature of reality, the definition of truth, and the meaning of reliability, generalizability, and replicability, may seem sharply different from those ordinarily made. The test of a

AUTHOR'S NOTE: The original of this proposal was prepared by Mary Bray Schatzkammer under the direction of Professor Earl Siedman, in partial fulfillment of the requirements for the Ed.D. in the Division of Instructional Leadership of the School of Education at the University of Massachusetts, Amherst. The ensuing dissertation was completed and accepted by the Graduate School on May 15, 1986.

qualitative proposal, for example, is not whether it is so carefully explicit and thorough as to allow replication with similar findings. Details of research focus, method, and analysis often are not established in the proposal because they only can be fully determined once the investigation is in process. Further, if replication were attempted (most qualitative specialists would argue that it is impossible), the production of identical findings would constitute more of a surprise than an expected outcome.

There must, of course, be rules of thought and procedure, which ensure that qualitative designs represent systematic inquiry. Research must always be distinct from reportage, reflective observation, or connoisseurship. The research traditions of qualitative study are sufficiently different from the more familiar canons of quantitative science to require some investment of study before attempting to read a proposal or study report.

It is in those very differences, however, that the special powers of the qualitative paradigm reside. In the following proposal, the author examines the problems encountered by women returning to college after absence from formal schooling. The research question, however, does not focus only on a reconstruction of what happened to them. The author asks as well, "What did it feel like to be there?"

A method of inquiry designed to help us discover and share the experience of other individuals produces consequences for both the investigator and the reader. No longer the detached, dispassionate outside observers, they are led toward the center of things—toward life as it is lived. That is a different vantage point for understanding the world, one which can yield results of exceptional utility as well as dramatic persuasiveness.

The title clearly identifies the subjects (women students), the setting (community college), and a key variable in the study (returning to school). It has the virtues of being both brief and easy to read. As in-depth phenomenological interviewing is a relatively infrequent and recently developed tool for qualitative research, the method of investigation also might have been named in the title. What was lost in brevity might be more than returned in improved retrieval. At this particular time in the history of educational research, with so much interest in new paradigms for inquiry, both graduate students and established scholars will be using key words for both research paradigms (such as "qualitative") and particular methods (such as "in-depth interviewing") as the basis for retrieving studies of interest from database systems (such as *Dissertation Abstracts International*).

Introduction

QUESTIONS AND OVERVIEW

In the dissertation, I will explore, through in-depth interviews, the meaning of the experience of older women students who return to school after some years of absence from traditional education and who choose a community college as their first point of reentry. What is it like to be a returning woman student? What are the aspirations, expectations, and concerns of returning women students? How does the community college experience fit into the context of their everyday lives? Given where they have been and where they hope to be, what meaning does the community college experience have for them? In a time when women are returning to school in record numbers, when the press for equal rights for women is a dominant political issue, and when, among institutions of higher education, the community college proclaims most strongly an egalitarian mission—do these returning women students find their educational experience adequate and equitable?

The opening sentence is a model of its kind. No reader will have the slightest doubt about what is to be studied. Even though relatively long and complex in structure, it reads smoothly. Removing the phrase "from traditional education" might tighten it a bit, but the author may have had reason to remind readers that informal, non-school education had continued for these women. The word "meaning" can be troublesome for many readers, but the rhetorical questions that follow leave little doubt about what is intended.

The first paragraph is longer than the ideal opener. In the art of gentle introduction, anything longer than 10 lines runs the risk of daunting the wary reader. The paragraph might be divided by detaching the closing sentence, which introduces the concept of equity, and combining it with the opening sentence of the next paragraph. With a few added words to connect the theme of equity with the previous questions about personal meaning, the two paragraphs thus organized would yield a slightly more inviting format for the first page.

Because of the importance to women today of issues of self-definition, independence, power, and opportunity, or racism, class-ism, and ageism (as well as sexism), equity[1] is a central concept among perspectives from which the results of this study will be viewed. The literature of the following disciplines will be examined for their contribution to understanding further these issues as they are related to the problem of older women seeking education in the community college: (a) demographics—of aging, gender, and education; (b) history—of the women's movement, and of the community college; (c) life-span developmental psychology; (d) feminist sociological research.

Assuming the first paragraph is left intact, note how the theme of equity forms a bridge between the last sentence of the first paragraph and the opening sentence of the second paragraph. The closer and more evident such ties are made, the easier it is to read and understand any document. Each paragraph must have its own independent, major thought, but the more these thoughts can be made to flow in an apparent sequence of logic, the more clearly the reader can comprehend the writer's reasoning. When-ever the context permits you to do so, it is desirable to end each paragraph by pointing forward to the next thought and to start the next paragraph with a glance back at the previous thought.

The reference to note 1 leads to a note section at the end of the main text. This particular note provides a brief definition and discussion of the word "equity" (and associated terms such as *equality* and *equal opportunity*) for readers who might not be familiar with the specialized term. As adequate treatment would require a full page of double-spaced text, and as no "Definitions" section is used in this proposal, placing the discussion in a note is the appropriate choice. Those who need help have it available, and those who do not can ignore the superscript.

The qualitative research process will be used to investigate the experience of returning women in community colleges. In this study the primary methods used will be analyses of transcripts of in-depth, phenomenological interviews of a sample of returning women at community colleges in three states. Selection of participants will be based on fairness to the population of returning women students in their colleges: the interview sample will include a range of ages, ethnicities, class backgrounds, work experience, family histories, and college program choices (liberal arts and vocational programs) in colleges that are urban, suburban, and rural.

> The word "fairness" is troublesome here. Usually it is intended to suggest that the selection will be done so as to produce a representative sample. The substantial demands of in-depth interviewing, the size of the data mass produced, and the complexity of any analysis likely to be used all suggest that achieving a truly representative sample would be singularly difficult for a doctoral candidate. It seems more likely that the author intends only to be sure that some important variables are represented among the selected participants. In which case, approximation of the true population of returning women is moot, and the whole matter of fairness is better left unmentioned. What the reader will really want to know is *how* subjects with the desired characteristics will be selected. A few words on that topic would mean more here than any promise about fair sampling.

In the following sections of this proposal the rationale for and the plan for conducting this study will be outlined more fully. Sections will include: (a) importance of the study; (b) extent of the study; (c) methodology (bias, assumptions and epistemological support, selection of participants, the interview process, interpretation and analysis, profile construction); (d) conclusions and implications; and (e) appendices (forms, tables, notes, bibliography).

> Advisors vary considerably in their enthusiasm for such brief overviews of organization (and any previewing of content that may be included). Some find it appropriate only here, at the close of the introduction. Others like to find such previews at

the end of every major section. Certainly, with an adequate table of contents and the correct use of headings and subheadings, these are a convenience and not a necessity. The use here seems appropriate and may have some of the same utility as an advance organizer in any instructional process.

Importance of the Study

This study is important today because of (a) demographic factors that influence school populations at all educational levels; (b) the confluence of two historic movements: the struggle of oppressed groups (including women) for "equal rights," and the widening stream of offerings in higher education (most apparent in the community college); (c) the potential conflict situation in the community college: wide-open doors and concomitant pressures to close them—the tension between "come-one-come-all" and having "standards," between growth and taxes; and (d) the paucity of studies that look at the stories of the women who go through those doors.

The above paragraph is anything but elegant. Yet it transmits a great deal of information to the reader in a short space. Some sympathy for the task of reading, however, would lead to a search for ways to simplify things. At the least we could remove the quotes from around "equal rights" (which probably were there for reasons that could be appreciated only by specialists in the area). The third item could be rewritten so as to merge some of the clauses (as for example, "wide-open doors welcoming everyone, and concomitant pressure to close the doors so as to maintain academic standards . . ."). Finally, the conflict between expansion of higher education and growth in the tax burden appears to dangle at the end of item 3. It would be easier for the reader to find it numbered as a separate item.

What is missing from the opening paragraphs of this section is some preliminary indication, however brief, of the unique contribution that a successfully completed qualitative study might provide. It *is* helpful to list all of the converging factors that make problematic the return of older women to higher education. That, however, argues more for the importance of the question than for the study itself. Thirty pages later, at the close of the proposal, the author points out the great utility to community college administrators, faculty, and counselors of the results that should emerge from this study. That is the point that seems most directly appropriate to a discussion under the heading "Importance of the Study."

The author next proceeds to present supporting evidence for each area identified as bearing on the importance of the study. Facts, statistics, and significant reference sources are woven into a running commentary that argues for the meaningfulness of the topic. We have omitted most of that discussion (about 5 pages) and pick up the text as the author finishes comments about the growing tensions that surround the purposes and operation of community colleges.

These continuing tensions have deeply affected the work and morale of community college faculty (Seidman, 1983). How do they affect the education of returning women students? Considering the number of older women returning to colleges of all kinds, but particularly to community colleges, and considering the astonishing growth of community colleges, it is surprising that more studies are not in existence in which these phenomena are examined from the point of view of the woman student. There is indeed a large promotional and critical literature about women students in the community college, which consists mainly of descriptions of and recommendations for programs. Among topics addressed are women's centers and access to occupational education. The general tone of these reports may be described by the titles of some of them: *Community College Women: A Golden Opportunity* (Eliason, 1977); *Second Wind: Program for Returning Women Students* (Carter, 1978); "Serving New Populations" (Walsh, 1979). (See also Brawer, 1977; Dibner, 1976; Eaton, 1981; Mezirow et al., 1978; O'Neill, 1977.)

There is, however, little research on this subject in which interviewing is an important element of the methodology. Two useful studies, which include interviews and which demonstrate the need for further research of this kind, are Tittle and Denker's *Returning Women Students in Higher Education* (1980) and the

Project on the Status and Education of Women series (1981, 1982). Data in these studies indicate that older women who turn to the community college usually do so because it is closer to home, less forbidding than the 4-year college or university, immediately helpful and welcoming, and less expensive (sometimes free). It offers programs that appear to lead quickly to higher earnings, and special counseling and women's centers are advertised and available. In addition, 2 years seem more manageable than 4 when a family must be nurtured. Community colleges also require minimal admissions red tape or entrance requirements (except high school graduation or high school equivalence). Some barriers to reentry reported by women are: financial need; image of college as only for white middle-class women, the elite, and the privileged; concern for the college's relevance to them; fear of being the "only one"; lack of home and community support; and needs for child care and transportation. Tittle and Denker's (1980) "vignettes" of ten students are based on a strict interview schedule derived from Levinson's (1978) theory of male adult development, although half of the students were women. Problems for returning women are briefly summarized as anxiety about ability, indecision about careers, conflicts related to school and home, paucity of needed information, the "alien language of academe," and unsatisfactory counseling services. The crucial questions were: Am I intelligent enough? How will I compare with 18-year-olds? Will my husband be resentful? Will my children suffer? Do I have the right to make demands for my self-improvement?

A paragraph of this length (over 30 lines in the original) is unreasonable. A comfortable break could have been made at the point where the topic shifts from reasons for selecting community college to the subject of barriers to reentry.

Note how the author merges results from three documents under four topical headings: choice of college, barriers, problems, and questions. This avoids the cumbersome task of treating each publication as a separate source, and adds a useful conceptual framework for thinking about the research topic. This kind of writing can make a review of the literature both readable and truly useful.

The sentence dealing with the subjects used in Tittle and Denker's study seems out of place in this otherwise exemplary summary. In might have been placed at the front adjacent to the introduction of the sources, or it might have been omitted as not contributing anything essential to the reader's understanding.

Much important information about the returning woman in the environment of the community college is available in the studies cited. Significant and useful as this information is, a sense of the concrete day-to-day life of the students as they go about their work is absent. Absent, too, is a sense of the inner life of women as they choose their classes and interact with faculty and with other students, a sense of how their college life affects, and is affected by, their work outside the college and their family life, and what these interactions mean to them as women, as workers, and as human beings in this institution that promises them so much. The value of in-depth interview studies of aspects of women's experience—women's work, motherhood, being middle-aged—is demonstrated in British and American feminist research (McGrindle & Rowbotham, 1977; Oakley, 1976; Rivers et al., 1979; Rubin, 1979). A similar approach could be important for illuminating educational experience.

More detail on the methodology of the in-depth phenomenological interview that I propose to use in this study will be discussed in the section on methodology below. I should like to turn first to what I consider the necessary extent or spread of this investigation and to defining its limits.

The author acknowledges the importance of work previously done in the area, but makes clear what is missing. This accomplished, the next step is to argue for the utility of the proposed methodology in providing what has been missed. Notice how smoothly each of those steps is accomplished in the penultimate paragraph.

In the final paragraph the use of "I" rather than the familiar convention of third person ("the investigator") commonly used in quantitative studies seems unsurprising and comfortable in this context. As explained in Chapter 5, the person of the investigator is a proper and necessary part of the inquiry process in the qualitative paradigm. Any attempt to seem distanced from method would sound out of place.

At the close, the author acknowledges the growing need of the reader to learn more about the proposed method. By making this point explicit, the reader is encouraged to remain engaged through the additional step of establishing the limits of the study. That kind of sensitivity to the reader's experience helps to sustain a bond of joint enterprise with the writer.

Extent of the Study

Though the central focus of this study will be the investigation of the experience of returning women students in the community college, certain broad questions about women and education must remain as framework and backdrop. A brief overview in this proposal will replace an in-depth discussion in the dissertation, of the literature of five related areas of inquiry: (a) demographics of aging, gender, and education; (b) the history of the community college as an "open-door" institution; (c) life-span developmental psychology of women; (d) history of the women's movement; and (e) feminist sociological research.

A decision has been made to include in the dissertation report a substantial section of discussion, which provides a framework for interpretation of the data. This will differ from the usual "Review of the Literature" that supports definition of the question and justifies the choice of methods and mode of analysis. As indicated in Chapter 4, the functions of the latter must be served in the proposal and use of the literature tightly restricted to those purposes. The review that is previewed here will serve a different function, one particular to this type of study.

At this point, the reader already will suspect that the center heading above is something of a misnomer. The extent of the study as a whole will not be the subject here. The degree to which the study report will be expanded to include an extensive discussion designed to frame the analysis and presentation of data is the true target. A heading that more accurately reflects that fact would prevent any misunderstanding by the reader.

The first and second of these "backdrop" areas—demographics and the community college—already have been provided sufficient coverage in the rationale above (Importance of the Study). The last three areas are closely interconnected, but are separated here for purposes of a brief discussion.

In order to enrich the essential background for this study—the psychological, social, historical, and political aspects of women's education—I have undertaken the task of examining certain literature by and about women. The necessary minimum for this task appears to include an exploration of what is known about the life-span development of women in relation to learning and schooling, what the record says about the history of women's struggle for equity in education, how and why feminist research has developed, particularly in sociology, and the extent of its effect on individual women who attempt to continue their schooling and work.

The middle years are a "largely unexplored phase of the life cycle," say Brim and Abeles (1975). For the purposes of this study of women students, most of whom are in their "middle years" (30 to 50), some exploration into what is known about this phase of the human life cycle is called for. When the mean age of students in the community college is 27, with the range broadened to include 80-year-olds (Chickering, 1980), our learnings from the study of child and adolescent development no longer serve.

As a result of influence exerted by such factors as the women's movement and the higher proportion of older persons in western countries, a new literature has become available. Though in no way approaching the richness of research and writing on early human development, work on later life development has expanded greatly in recent years (Baltes, 1978; Birren & Woodruff, 1973; Eisdorfer & Lawton, 1973; Erikson, 1980; Jarvik, 1978; Lowenthal, 1975; Mass & Kuyper, 1974; Neugarten, 1968).

In this new literature there clearly is more research on the aging process in general than on the aging of women. The life-span development of men has had more attention in the past than that of women (Kohlberg, 1969; Levinson, 1978); recent studies have concentrated on women (Barnett & Baruch, 1979; Fuller & Martin, 1980; Rubin, 1979; Wetzel, 1982). Other studies reveal differences between men and women at different life stages in their responses to issues of morality, justice, and life choices (Erikson, 1980; Gilligan, 1982). Important differences seem to exist in the way chronological age defines stages in women's and men's lives (Barnett & Baruch, 1978). Problems such as this are related to the subject of equity and returning women students in some important ways. This is particularly true of the relationship between aging and learning (Baltes, 1978; Botwinick, 1978; Diamond, 1978). Though most longitudinal studies show no loss in intellectual capacity with age, and in some cases a continual rise even though the eighth decade, the returning woman student often has a sense of uncertainty about diminished capacities. Experiences described in interviews of women (McGrindle & Rowbotham, 1977; Seidman, 1983; Tittle and Denker, 1980) demonstrate how their school lives are often affected negatively by cultural stereotypes that become assimilated in their own self-images. Women who are both female and old are victims of a "double standard of aging" (Bell, 1975; Sontag, 1980).

The study of aging and of life-span development is relatively new in the history of the social sciences, but the struggle for recognition of women as persons other than wives or mothers has gone on for a much longer time. With regard to the classic works I shall not discuss here, it is sufficient to say that it is impossible to understand what is happening for women today without a comprehensive reading of the women's studies literature, from Wollstonecraft (1792), Mill (1869), Gillman (1915), Woolf (1929, 1938), and Klein (1949) to the newest wave that began with Simone de Beauvoir's *Second Sex* (first published in 1952), continued with Friedan's *Feminine Mystique* (1963), and gained momentum with the work of many women writers—poets, novelists, social scientists, and journalists: Ellman (1968); Firestone (1970); Flexner (1970); Rossi (1973, 1976); Lerner (1977); Olsen (1978); Morgan (1982)—to name only a very few. A passage from Tillie Olsen's *Silences* (1978), "One Out of Twelve," captures the meaning behind much of the women's movement literature:

Linked with the old, resurrected classics on women, this movement in three years has accumulated a vast new mass of testimony, of new comprehensions, as to what it is to be female. Inequities, restrictions, penalties, denials, leechings, have been painstakingly and painfully documented; damaging differences in circumstances and treatment from that of males attested to; and limitations, harms, a sense of wrong voiced. (p. 41)

Later in this same work, Olsen describes "the differing past of women that should be part of every human consciousness." Among these pasts, she writes, are the imposed conditions of unclean, taboo; being, not doing; bound feet; corsets; powerlessness; fear of aging; fear of expressing capacities; marriage, slavery, dissembling, manipulating, appeasing—"the vices of slaves."

> The discussion at this point has become slightly more polemical than is appropriate in a research proposal. To say that "it is impossible to understand what is happening for women today without a comprehensive reading of the women's study literature" may be true in the abstract, but may leave the reader feeling a bit beleaguered. The point is to reassure the reader that the author *will* make this body of literature understandable and through that will make accessible some sense of what is happening to women today. The purpose of a proposal is to explain and justify a plan for investigation, not to convert or overwhelm the uninitiated.

Much women's literature has concentrated on the problem of equity in education for women. Some authors have traced the tortured story of women's gradual progress from being—some of them—the "daughters of educated men" (Woolf, 1938) to being admitted with reluctance into the select company within institutions of higher education (Deem, 1978; Greene et al., 1983; Sexton, 1976; Spender & Sarah, 1980).

Though we have seen that the *numbers* of women in college have finally come close to being equal to men—and in community colleges surpassing them—the question of equity in schooling is still murky: are women actually being treated fairly and equitably, with all that implies, as students? An example of a problematic area is that of relative numbers of female faculty compared with those of male faculty. Is the question of equity for the older woman student related to the problem of equity for women faculty in community colleges, as well as in other colleges?

Reports by women academics over the last 25 years indicate the slow progress that has been made in the establishment of women's positions in colleges and universities, both as faculty members and in administration (Bernard, 1964; Newcomer, 1959; Price, 1981). The combination of rapidly increasing numbers of women students and the very slow increase of women faculty is a theme that has been referred to in the work of Seidman (1983). Faculty are often aware, students less so, of the contradictions inherent in the fact of a minority of women faculty serving as models and mentors for a student body that is becoming more female than male—largely due to the increasing numbers of older women students.

Feminist research is already a source of new ideas on equity in academic institutions. Although theoretical work on women, and usually by women, as originators of a different style of observing the world—psychological and sociological research from a woman's point of view—appears to be still in its infancy, women social scientists in England and the United States have begun to develop their own research styles in the investigation of social and psychological questions and to attempt to free themselves from the patterns and constraints of what they now see as flawed research based on assumptions of the dominant male culture (Bunch & Pollack, 1983; Gilligan, 1982; Lerner, 1980; Oakley, 1972; Roberts, 1983).

I propose to continue the search for the feminist scholar's approach in literature that is related to women and aging, learning and schooling. With the rapid changes and shifting factions in the widening women's movement and the spreading interchange among women researchers in several countries (Roberts, 1981), it will be important to follow closely the "literature" of news stories and current journals, as well as publications of organizations like the Feminist Press and its counterparts in Great Britain, France, and elsewhere. Though this study is limited to returning women students in this country, it is clear that the press for equity among women is not limited to one institution in one country. How and why this movement has come about is one of the basic questions underlying this research.

Here the author is writing about a personal commitment that extends beyond the proposed study. The reader may well begin to feel put upon. A graduate student's dispositions about future scholarship are of vital interest to mentors, but are not the proper subject of discussion in the proposal. Remember the purpose of the document and stick to it.

One difficulty with the qualitative method of research is identifying and maintaining limits, when in some ways there appear to be none. It is true that to examine *all* the literature in the fields I have suggested are relevant is an impossibility, considering constraints of time and energy, as well as appropriateness. I have set certain boundaries, but may pull the edges in even closer: for example, limiting my review of life-span development material to that related to women and learning in the middle years, limiting attention to women's movement history to the most notable writings of the last fifteen years, and examining only recent feminist sociological work that pertains to education of women—rather than the whole gamut of feminist research. The literature on community colleges is extensive but not all applicable to this study; and the demographics of aging, gender, and education are well-defined and manageable.

> The tentativeness here would be disturbing to some advisors. If these are reasonable limitations, why not make them a stipulated part of the contract? The practical answer to that question may be that much of this reading has yet to be done. That is perfectly reasonable at this stage, but a firmer hand in setting limits would be helpful. Reasonable changes usually can be negotiated if it is discovered that they are required.

The limits of qualitative versus quantitative studies—and vice-versa—are well known (Smith, 1983). In this study I am giving up the possible advantages of the clean simplicity of an experimental study that cannot be appropriate for what I want to know (see *Methodology,* below). In exchange, I am plunging into research that will present me with a "vast matrix of interlocking message material" (Bateson, 1979) that must be transcribed, studied, coded, translated, interpreted, and analyzed with the methods of the field researcher (Johnson, 1975; Lofland, 1971; Rubin, 1979). Anthropologist Jules Henry (1965) has said that "science is the relentless examination of the commonplace." The self-reports of the commonplace, everyday life of women "of a certain age," in this period of ferment searching for equity through education, and of their reflections on their experience, is the material for my search. The next section on the methodology I have chosen will further clarify and define the limits of this inquiry.

> Although intended here as a transition pointing toward the section to follow, the paragraph above presents the reader with a jarring shift. The topic of contrasting qualitative and quantitative paradigms is important and complex, but is inappropriate at the conclusion of this section. It deserves a better introduction, and certainly one that does not use the "as everybody knows" ploy. Here the author loses some of that fine, gentle touch that to this point has made the reader feel a collaborator rather than a target. In addition, the author reveals considerable naiveté in describing experimental methods as automatically "clean and simple." Reminding the reader of the purpose served by the section just completed, perhaps indicating appreciation for the rather lengthy deferral of questions about methodology, might make a happier transition.

Methodology

In this section I shall describe briefly: the epistemological basis for choosing in-depth interviewing as the instrument of investigation of the experience of another person, the selection of participants to be interviewed, the interview process, "profile" composing, and options for interpretation and analysis of the material. As a first step, I should like to make a statement concerning bias, in the form of a short history of the development of my interests and values as they are related to the subject of this research.

POINT OF VIEW

My mind is not indeed a blank slate on the research questions of this proposal. In fact, my interests, values and close acquaintance with the research problem are the source of motivation for this study.

As noted in Chapter 5, in qualitative research it is customary to confront the issue of objectivity and personal bias in a direct manner. In the pages that follow the author describes those aspects of personal background that would bear on how the research problem is viewed, and that might be expected to influence interpretation of the data. The purpose is not to divest sources of bias, but to clarify them for both author and reader.

In addition to personal and educational background, the author discusses interest in feminism and equity problems as relevant prior involvements. Particular attention is paid to what was learned from a previous National Institute of Education-financed study of the work of community college teachers. This material has been omitted here and we pick up the text with the paragraph that closes the section.

I start this study, then, with a recognition of a "vested interest" in its outcome. Not for the outcome to take one direction or another—to demonstrate, for example, that there is or is not an equitable situation for returning women in the community college—but with an energy developed from the concerns of my own experience that will sustain the minutiae of the exploration, and with the recognition that all scientific investigation begins with the observer's "biased" curiosity and continues on its way bolstered and nourished by those values. It is not, of course, possible to keep one's research pure, "objective," and untarnished by one's interests or values or presence (Bateson, 1979; Glazer, 1972; Heisenberg, 1958; James, 1912; Johnson, 1975; Matson, 1966; Myrdal, 1969). It is possible and preferable to search for, recognize, and state such bias (Myrdal, 1969) and to be aware, as William James points out, of ideas that seem especially important to us, that "desire introduces them; interest holds them; fitness fixes their order and connection" (James, 1912).

EPISTEMOLOGICAL BASES
FOR CHOOSING IN-DEPTH INTERVIEWING

For investigation of the problem I propose here, I find that a quantitative experimental study cannot tell me what I want to know: the realities of the experience of another human being and how that person thinks and feels about that experience. Knowing that I can never "know"—in the same sense that I "know" my own thoughts and feelings—what another person's experience is "really" like, I want nevertheless to get as close to that knowing as possible. I have, therefore, chosen the in-depth interview as my research instrument. The following is a brief exposition of my assumptions and the philosophic positions that undergird the qualitative approach to this study.

The distinction between "facts" and "values," or between objectivity and subjectivity, cannot be taken for granted, and the observer cannot be conveniently eliminated. William James (1912) makes a strong case for the inseparability of "subject" and "object." If the observer affects, or contributes to, what is observed, there cannot be such an entity as a pure, objective "scientific fact." Social scientist Gregory Bateson goes further: "There is no objective experience; all experience is subjective." The social scientist looks for "the pattern that connects" and "the notion of context, of pattern through time." Describing the data of naturalistic or field research, he says that "what has to be investigated is a vast network or matrix of interlocking message material" (Bateson, 1979). Among other philosophers and scientists whose works have provided pieces of the theoretical structure underlying the methodology of my research are: Mannheim (1936), Polanyi (1962), Rawls (1971), and Sartre (1968).

The last sentence here seems to be tacked on as an afterthought. Following the powerful case created by artful use of quotes from James and Bateson, it is a shame to spoil the flow of ideas that lead so nicely into the next paragraph. These things happen sometimes where the novice panics and, in attempting to cover every possible base at the last minute, inserts references wholesale. If the references really matter, then they should have been included in a way that displays their significance. If in doubt, leave them out.

A significant part of this study on returning women is based on the assumption that it is possible to discover motives and meanings of other persons through our connections with them, through their words as they communicate with us, and through our knowledge of our own words and actions as we see them reflected in others. As we find verification through our own experience and through hearing the repeated experience of others, we come as close as possible to knowledge about other human beings.

Alfred Schutz, in *The Phenomenology of the Social World* (1967) explores these concepts in depth. An assumption of my research that follows especially from my reading of Schutz, and that is basic to this methodology, is: If women talk to me about their lives as students, and about what led to their decision to return to school, and about what the decision and process mean to them in their lives, I shall then know more than I do now about the interconnections of women's experience in this country and at this time with what it is like to be a student in American schools—particularly, in this case, in the latest version of "postsecondary" education—and I shall perhaps then understand more clearly how the returning woman student is situated in the midst of political, social, and economic changes affecting her schooling and indeed affecting her choices, though she may be unaware of these issues.

Above is a perfect example of a sentence that has gone berserk. Thirteen lines long (in the original), it is impossible to read aloud without several pauses for deep breathing, and it is impossible to understand as "an assumption about methodology." Such monsters are best trapped (and then eliminated) by the simple strategy of reading the text aloud to someone else. If you turn blue before wading through the subordinate clauses, or observe that the eyes of the listener glaze over in utter confusion—something must be wrong. Edit, edit, edit, and then edit some more.

SELECTION OF PARTICIPANTS

For the purposes of this study, the returning woman is 25 to 70 years old; her education has been interrupted for a period of at least several years—perhaps three or four but more often 10 to 30, sometimes more—and she has returned to continue her education in a community college. Eighteen to 22 participants will be chosen from community colleges in three states; California, Massachusetts, and New York. The choice of states was made on the basis of per capita expenditures for community colleges in different states: California was strongly supported (third in the United States in per capita expenditure by the state); Massachusetts was 48th, and New York was in the middle—25th (Chambers, 1979). The choice of these three states also offers a wide variety of community colleges in terms of both size and surrounding environment.

Given that most readers will not be disposed to argue the question of exact sample size in a study of this kind, leaving that matter unsettled has all the logic of waving a red flag before a bull. Unless there is some compelling reason, such details should be settled before submitting a proposal. The final number will be arbitrary in any case, and certainly should be open to subsequent negotiation as the events of the study unfold.

As a random sample of the population of returning women community college students, twenty participants is too small a number; moreover, the sample cannot be truly random in an interview study when the subject must consent to be interviewed. Other precautions, then, must be taken in this kind of qualitative study, in which the aim is exploration in depth. In the selection of participants, I have considered a range of ages, ethnicities, class backgrounds, marital and family statuses, children, and fields of study in order to represent fully the population of returning women enrolled in community colleges and to maximize the possibility of looking at a wide spectrum of experience.

In this paragraph the author attempts to explain the selection of participants. The opening sentence is intended to help the reader understand why any expectation for random selection is inappropriate. Whatever the intention may have been in this, there is a serious potential here for misunderstanding. The use of system language words normally associated with quantitative

research seems out of place. More to the point, the whole
discussion really is not required.

Even well-prepared graduate students display occasional
symptoms of defensiveness about qualitative research, lapsing
into defensive explanations of why it is not like other forms of
inquiry. That may or may not have been the case here, but it
would have been far better to go directly to the point—*participants will be selected so as to ensure inclusion of persons with
characteristics that seem important in the context of the study.*
Arguments about random selection and representative samples
are irrelevant to the matter. Given how subjects will be selected,
the phrase "represent fully" now is seen as inaccurate, while
"maximizing the possibility of examining a wide spectrum of
experience" is precisely the point to be made.

Because the issue of equity is central to this proposed research,
and because race, gender, and class are significant elements in
the unequal distribution of educational resources, I believe that it
is important to cast as large a net as possible in the search for
participants of diverse backgrounds. I intend to supplement the
nine interviews from a pilot study (Seidman, 1983) with nine to
thirteen more. (For table of participant characteristics, see Appendix A. Limited space precludes the inclusion in this table of
designations of class and family description, but these characteristics are assessed in the original record.) I am also considering
at this time the possibility of adding a small number of interviews
of older returning men students, as a frame and additional context
for the understanding of the position of women who may have a
different view of their imperatives from that of men. (I have
interviewed four returning men students as part of a previous
study. This group could be a start on this sample.)

The plot thickens. In addition to the problem of an indetermi-
nate number of subjects, the reader now learns that data from a
previous study will be merged with material from new interviews conducted after the approval of the proposal. This makes
the exact nature of the pilot study a matter of some concern. To

complicate things further, in the same paragraph, the possibility of adding a male subsample is raised.

The best advice here is to take things slowly, one at a time—especially things that are likely to attract immediate concern from the reader. Although usually undesirable, merging pilot data with results from a proposed study is not impossible. At the least, questions about the equivalence of method (Will the interview procedures be identical?) must be addressed. As the pilot study appears to have reached publication, the absence of extensive explanation may make some sense. Perhaps it could be assumed that all reviewers had read the report of the earlier study. Whatever the case may have been for this study, in your own proposal be sure to introduce one at a time any points that are likely to be problematic and resolve each before proceeding. The place to settle questions about possible subsamples is in discussion with the advisor(s), not in a proposal document.

How shall participants be located? Seidman (1983) found that location of participants was most successfully accomplished through informal channels, and wherever possible through peers rather than superiors. The uncertainties about motives of teachers and administrators (students, for example, possibly feeling that their success in school might be connected to consent for the interview) could affect the relationship between interviewer and participant, and thus affect the interview material. In my pilot interviews (Siedman, 1983), students were located through other students in student affairs offices, through counselors and friends of friends not connected with the college hierarchy, through relatives, and through other sources that I believed would least obligate the students to any mode of behavior, or prejudice their attitude toward the interviewing process before meeting with the interviewer. In some cases, an interested women's center coordinator was a useful source.

This process naturally produced many more prospects than were actually selected, thus allowing for final selection to be made according to the categories described above and in the table (Appendix A). The process also cannot guarantee "representation" of every category of returning women students; it also will result in including a larger *proportion* of "minority" women than actually attend community colleges. I prefer to err in this direction as my investigation is concerned with equity for all women. To fill in the last empty cells (see spaces for names in the table), I plan to continue the selection through a process similar to that described above. As will be apparent on observation of the table, some of these prospective participants have already been approached, with an eye to locating women whose age, ethnicity, and field of study match the remaining requirements for diversity.

The first 9 students were interviewed in California, Massachusetts, and New York State. I shall select the next 9 to 13 students from the same states, keeping in mind types and sizes of colleges and cities. The distribution so far, of the 9 students, is: California, 3; Massachusetts, 2; New York, 4. Final distribution will include at least 6 from each state.

At this point the reader will suspect that the issues raised by a plan that requires merging data from a prior pilot study with data from a proposed study, is going to receive no further attention. There are a number of supporting arguments that might be made here, some having to do with the nature of qualitative research, and perhaps others made on the grounds of method and circumstance. Given what has been provided in the document to this point, however, our best guess is that few dissertation committees would be satisfied. Whether the rationale offered turns out to be simple or complex, the issue would have to be confronted head-on.

INTERVIEW PROCESS

The process of the in-depth phenomenological interview to be used in this study will follow closely the methodology developed by Seidman (1983) and Sullivan (1982). The process can be described generally as open but focused. I shall not use an "interview schedule" but neither will the interview be as casual as a conversation or open to indefinite length. The procedure is for the participant to review the constitutive factors of her life before coming to the community college, the details of her community college experience, and lastly, to reflect on her past life and present experience and talk about the meaning that this educational experience has for her.

The purpose for this method of research is *meaning-making*. My task will be to listen as the student reflects aloud on past and present experiences and considers them in relation to significance in her life as an older student, woman, family member, worker, and learner.

Each participant will be interviewed three times, each time for the length of a 90-minute tape. (All interviews are audiotaped. I generally use a small inconspicuous tape recorder without a microphone and fitted with batteries in case of difficulty with electrical connections.) Interviews will be spaced at least 2 days apart to allow time for reflection, and, if possible, no longer than a week apart.

The interviews will be held in a place mutually agreeable to participant and interviewer. With the permission of the college library staff, a small room used for audiovisual materials usually provides privacy and reliable electricity. At least one of the three interviews will be held at the participant's home if possible. The important consideration here is equity—reciprocity and sensitivity to the other person's time constraints. I find this aspect of interviewing attested to in feminist research especially: McGrindle and Rowbotham (1977), Oakley (1976), Roberts (1976), and Rubin (1979).

Previous to the first visit, contact will be made by phone, with confirmation by letter, and a date set for the first meeting. I have found it more satisfactory to allow for this initial contact visit before the interview series begins. During this shorter visit, the purpose and nature of the research is explained, the prospective participant fills out a brief information form (see Appendix B) that includes data on age, program, and so on, and makes a decision about whether she is willing to be interviewed. If so, dates are set for the next three meetings. At the first of these, participant and interviewer discuss the written consent form (required for university-based research, but also essential for clarity, prevention of misunderstandings, and simple courtesy) and both sign, indicating mutual agreement (see Appendix C for copy of this form). This process allows time for any final uncertainties to be resolved.

Procedures for such matters as incomplete interviews and subject attrition should be established here. For example, if the third meeting proves impossible for an otherwise valuable interview sequence, what happens to the data? It is best to anticipate such events in advance when the investigator and advisors can agree on appropriate decisions.

Each of the three interviews opens with a focusing question from the interviewer: (a) Could you tell me about your life before you came to the community college? (b) What is it like to be a student at this college? (c) What does this experience mean to you in your life? These questions may be flexible as to wording and may be rephrased when the meaning of the question seems unclear to the participant. After the interview has begun, I ask questions rarely, and then usually for clarification. I may comment occasionally to move the talk to another level, or to check on my understanding. But mainly the words will be those of the participant. Almost always, I have found that participants say, "I can *never* talk for an hour and a half!" And almost always they want to continue when the tape is ended. (The rationale for this interview methodology is explained in greater detail in *The Work of Community College Faculty*, Seidman, 1983).

Interviews will be transcribed verbatim (I shall share the task with a typist) resulting in manuscripts of 60 to 90 single-spaced pages for each participant. Because of the volume of this work, it is possible that some compromise with the totally verbatim transcript might be made: for example, abbreviating interviewer statements (Rubin, 1979) and omitting management details that are unrelated or unimportant to the focus of the interview. I hesitate to do this, however, because of the possible research value of having the total record.

It may be impossible to know the magnitude of the transcription task in advance, but it is not impossible to indicate on what basis a decision to abbreviate will be made. A reader can appreciate the problems of data processing, reduction, and display in a qualitative study, but the indecisiveness displayed in the last sentence is inappropriate to a proposal. For any anticipated problem, tell the reader how you will decide what to do. Given that, the reader often will be perfectly happy to leave the difficult details of in-process decisions to the investigator.

PROFILES

The interviews (in transcript form) that are strong in all three sections (each section will represent a taped session), complete in the sense of not missing significant material (so that there are no puzzling omissions in the story), compelling in the story-telling and meaning-making, will be selected for "profiles." A profile, as developed by Seidman (1983), is composed from the transcript of an interview series. The words of the interviewer are omitted and the participant's story stands alone. The words are entirely those of the participant unless it is necessary, for reasons of clarity, to add a word or phrase, which will then appear in brackets. A team process may be used for constructing the profile. The major steps include:

1. Share the process with at least one other person familiar with community colleges and with the research material and method. Each person reads the transcript individually, underlining the sections, words, or phrases that he or she feels strongly should not be omitted from the final story.
2. Retype, or cut and paste the manuscript, which should now be reduced by one-half or one-third of the original.
3. One person, taking responsibility for the final version of the profile, edits, punctuates, paragraphs, rearranges if necessary for coherence and flow of the story, coding and otherwise disguising identifiable material and proper names, omitting repetitive passages and awkward expressions that might do damage to the dignity of the participant, or that add nothing to the story.
4. The second person reviews the edited version, checking for unclear passages; suggests revisions or omissions for sense and strength of final version.
5. Final version of profile is completed by the person who has assumed the main responsibility for this profile.

A similar procedure can, of course, be followed by one person only. I may find it necessary to complete most profiles without assistance. But a team approach has several advantages that are important: a fresh, unbiased (or differently biased) view of the material, a check on the choice of most meaningful material, another ear and eye for language and editing.

As indicated in Chapter 5, the nature of qualitative research often requires that certain aspects of the data analysis be left open-ended. It is impossible to predict the exact form the data will take or what aspects of the data will present themselves as worthy of attention. Nevertheless, as the author has already accumulated considerable experience with analysis in the pilot study, the reader might expect more decisiveness here. If, for example, profiles for one-third of the pilot subjects were developed through use of a team, then why not set that as a target for the next sample? Finally, having so carefully confronted the problems of bias presented by her own background and personal dispositions, it is puzzling to find that the author mentions no plan to prepare a similar section for the second reader.

The total process is both an intellectual and aesthetic one; the words "construct" and "compose" are both needed in a description of the profile-making process. The important thing to remember is that it is the participant's words we are hearing. The process is something like cutting a diamond to the shape that brings out its best qualities. Profiles thus composed and constructed are compelling communications; they may be compared with the interview work of Terkel (1972) or Coles (1978).

OPTIONS FOR INTERPRETATION AND ANALYSIS

The mechanics of working with the material may require more than one copy of each transcript. In addition to, and along with the profile-making, the analytic process will continue: identifying themes, marking transcript margins, collecting and filing theme material so that it may be easily retrieved.

Here we learn, from an almost offhand comment ("the analytic process will continue . . .") that, in addition to profile
construction, the data will be subject to another operation.
While it is easy to guess that this will consist of extracting
themes, a commonly employed technique in qualitative studies,
the matter is inadequately introduced and left almost as an
afterthought to the profiling process. At the least, reviewers will
want a listing of procedural steps and several illustrations. All
this might have been negotiated more gracefully by inserting a
short paragraph surveying the several methods (or levels) of
analysis before launching into the section on profiles.

No interview process guarantees that the protocols will be full
of references to, or insights on, the basic topics of primary interest
to the researcher, though the in-depth interview makes this more
likely. A question such as, for example, "Were you treated fairly
as an older women student?" might elicit only a brief convergent
response (Lofland, 1981; Schumann, 1982). But the in-depth
interview can provide enough time, an atmosphere of trust, and a
setting that encourages the free flow of reminiscence and reflection so that opportunity is provided for a full story to emerge and
for reflective meaning-making to take place. That story, in its full
and concrete detail, when transcribed becomes the data (material) for analysis and interpretation, which is an ongoing and
"continuing process of recording, refining, and reformulating"
(Rubin, 1979).

Before all the data are collected, it is not possible to say exactly
what final form the analysis shall take. But the process of analysis
begins in part with the first field experience and builds gradually
as the material is collected (Lofland, 1971). One possibility for the
form of the analysis is based on a question of perspective: for
example, are the community college's older returning women
students finding their educational experience equitable? A model
of analysis might be based on the following organization: (a)
grouping of participant interview material according to what was
expected or wanted by the student; (b) analysis of the concrete

details of the college experience—what was actually found; and (c), given (a) and (b), as well as the participant's reflections on both, how does the educational experience in the community college relate to the issue of equity?

Here the author attempts to anticipate a possible basis for analysis. At this point the reader needs both to sense the broad form that analysis will assume and to evaluate the author's capacity to establish potentially fruitful formats for reducing the data and extracting meaning. Given the availability of pilot data, the reader might reasonably expect much more here by way of explanation and illustration.

As well as I can now construct a scaffold for unknown conclusions, I see this analytic and interpretive process as a combination of the meaning that the participant makes of her experience and the meaning that I, as researcher, find in the words of the participant, seen through assisting lenses of other observers and writers in related inquiries. Whatever the final form of the analysis, presentation of results will be, in part, in the words of the participant interviewees (profiles) and in part through interpretation of the thematic material that emerges from the collection of transcripts during the ongoing process of field research and analysis (Johnson, 1975; Lofland, 1971; Rubin, 1979; Seidman, 1983).

Planned Presentation of Results

Results of the study will be summarized in a final chapter of the dissertation. This commentary also will include an assessment of the usefulness and effectiveness of the methodology, implications for educational policy change, and indications for further research.

What the author intends by proposing to assess the "usefulness and effectiveness of the methodology" probably is some thoughtful reflection of how fully the actual events of the study matched the intentions of the proposal, and how difficult certain procedures proved in actual execution, as well as how fruitful the results seem in terms of implications for the world of professional practice. The caution to be raised here, for this and any other proposal, is that the question of whether or not the proposed method is an effective means for addressing the question should have been convincingly settled in this document. To promise retrospective evaluation of method is reasonable, but this is not the place to appear to flinch on the choices you have made. Both you and the reader should be convinced that, given the nature of the question and the constraints of your circumstance, this is the best possible study that could be proposed.

Results from this study will illuminate the realities of everyday life in the community college for one fast-growing group in the nontraditional student population. Implications for the future of women in community colleges, and for the future of educational policies for nontraditional student populations, may be revealed through the words of older women students as they talk about their experience. More important, perhaps, will be the possibility for new connections, insights, and understandings for women who are considering a return to school and for those who are already there, for faculty and counselors whose work brings them into everyday contact with reentry women, and for administrators to whom the returning woman may be just a statistic, albeit a comforting one when enrollments are down and money is scarce. Better understanding of problems of equity in educational institutions—and in the society of which the institution is a reflection—is the ultimate goal of this research.

It is typical to find an author at this point feeling rather optimistic and expansive about the implications of the proposed study. If restrained to only a few paragraphs, most readers will wink at a modest excess of enthusiasm here, even if they suspect that some painful lessons about the limits of inquiry remain to be learned by the novice.

The honest hopes expressed here are what drive the machinery of inquiry. The human need to better understand our world, ourselves, and our institutions, and the human desire to act in more humane and effective ways are the beginning and end for all research.

Note

1. Equity, equality, and equal opportunity: Equal educational opportunity is one of the "rights" sought by women, as by other oppressed groups. I see the movement of women back to college as part of the larger struggle for equal rights of many different groups throughout recorded history. The importance of this movement as part of the women's movement may be fundamental to and primary to other struggles (Engels, 1942; Olsen; 1983). *Equity* is different from *equality* in that it conveys the idea of equal *treatment*. *Equal* means the same, or "just like." *Equal rights* says that the *rights* are the same for everyone involved, and that no one shall be deprived of those rights (the equal rights amendment). *Equity*, if strictly used, is a legal term and has some other meanings somewhat different from the way I use it here. To be treated equitably is to be treated fairly and justly, to be given the rights of all human beings (Rawls, 1971). Fairly and justly do not imply identical treatments, but they do imply a way of thinking that assumes that no human being has greater or more rights than another. Fair and just, or equitable, treatment may require more than equal opportunity. But there must be equal opportunity to permit an equitable situation to occur. The word *"equity"* is being used more frequently, in titles such as The *Women's Educational Equity Act, The Women's Equity Projects*, and the *Women's Equity Action League*.

PROPOSAL 2: APPENDIX 1
Expected Distribution by Stage, Age, College, City, Program (liberal arts or career), Ethnicity, Part- or Full-Time (initials indicate interviews completed)

California	Age	College	City	Program	Ethnicity	PT-FT	Interviewer
1 PM	59	A	J	LA	B	PT	MBS
2 LW	50	A	J	LA	W	FT	MBS
3 MMW	38	A	J	C	H	FT	MBS
4	35	B	K	LA	W	FT	MBS
5	30	B	K	LA	W	FT	DA
6	33	C	L	C	A	PT	MM
Massachusetts	Age	College	City	Program	Ethnicity	PT-FT	Interviewer
1 KB	30	D	M	C	W	FT	MBS
2 LM	70	D	M	LA	W	PT	MBS
3	48	E	N	C	CV	PT	MBS
4	42	E	N	C	W	FT	MBS
5	27	E	N	C	W	FT	MBS
6	30	F	O	C	B	FT	MBS
New York	Age	College	City	Program	Ethnicity	PT-FT	Interviewer
1 LP	25	G	P	LA	W	FT	MBS
2 SL	49	G	P	C	W	FT	MBS
3 HK	49	G	P	C	W	FT	MBS
4 RS	35	H	Q	C	B	FT	MBS
5	28	I	R	LA	A	FT	MBS
6	31	I	R	C	B	FT	MBS

NOTE: Age range = 25-70. Initials under state names are of woman students interviewed in Seidman (1983) study. Other figures are for possible participants; initial contacts have been made. The above is minimum; more interviews are likely.

The table in Appendix 1 violates the first rule of acceptable construction—it cannot stand alone. It is full of undecipherable material. Further, it is more cluttered than should be necessary. Information about the city, for example, seems nonessential so long as distribution among colleges is provided. Instead of subject initials for interviews already obtained, why not a single word (such as "completed")? The question of how many subjects will be interviewed should be addressed in the text, not at the foot of a table in the Appendix.

PROPOSAL 2: APPENDIX 2

PARTICIPANT INFORMATION FORM

NAME _____ DATE _____

ADDRESS _____

TELEPHONE (HOME)_____ (WORK, COLLEGE, ETC.) _____

NAME OF COLLEGE _____

COLLEGE ADDRESS _____

PLEASE CHECK WHERE APPLICABLE:

    LIBERAL ARTS? _____ TRANSFER? _____

    VOCATIONAL OR OCCUPATIONAL PROGRAM? _____

    SPECIAL PROGRAM? _____ OTHER? _____

    (PLEASE DESCRIBE) _____

_____

WHAT IS THE GOAL OF YOUR PRESENT STUDY? _____

_____

PREVIOUS EDUCATIONAL ATTAINMENT (NUMBER OF YEARS IN

SCHOOL, LAST YEAR IN SCHOOL, DIPLOMA, DEGREE, GED, ETC

_____

_____

_____

PREVIOUS WORK EXPERIENCE _____

_____

_____

BIRTH DATE _____

A CONTACT WHERE YOU COULD BE REACHED IN CASE OF

CHANGE OF ADDRESS OR TELEPHONE _____

_____

> This clearly is only a mock-up of the form actually to be filled in by participants. It is possible that the investigator intends to fill this out on the basis of questions asked during the interview. In either case, advisors usually prefer to see any record form in final draft, not as a sketch.

PROPOSAL 2: APPENDIX 3

WRITTEN CONSENT FORM
Returning Women Students in the Community College

To participants in this study:

I am a graduate student at the University of Massachusetts at Amherst. The subject of my doctoral research is: "Returning Women Students in the Community College." I am interviewing women in California, Massachusetts, and New York State, and possibly in some other states, who have returned to study at a community college after an interruption in their education for any one of a number of reasons. You are one of approximately twenty participants.

As a part of this study, you are being asked to participate in three in-depth interviews. The first interview will be focused on your experience before you came to the college, the second on what it is like to be a student in the college, and the third will be concerned with what it means to you to be back in school—as you reflect on your earlier experience and look ahead to the future. As the interviews proceed, I may ask an occasional question for clarification or for further understanding, but mainly my part will be to listen as you recreate your experience within the structure and focus of the three interviews: your previous life, the college experience, and the meaning of that college experience.

My goal is to analyze the materials from your interviews in order to understand better your experience and that of other women who re-enter schools and colleges for their own various reasons. I am interested in the concrete details of your life story, in what led up to your decision to return to school, in what your everyday experience is like now, and what it means to you. As part of the dissertation, I may compose the materials from your interviews as a "profile" in your own words. I may also wish to use some of the interview material for journal articles or presentations to interested groups, or for instructional purposes in my teaching. I may wish to write a book based on the dissertation.

Each interview will be audiotaped and later transcribed by me or by a typist (who will not be connected with your college and who will be committed, as I am, to confidentiality). In all written materials and oral presentations in which I might use materials from your interview, I will not use your name, names of people close to you, or the name of your college or city. Transcripts will be typed with initials for names, and in final form the interview material will use pseudonyms.

You may at any time withdraw from the interview process. You may withdraw your consent to have specific excerpts used, if you notify me at the end of the interview series. If I were to want to use any materials in any way not consistent with what is stated above, I would ask for your additional written consent.

In signing this form, you are also assuring me that you will make no financial claims for the use of the material in your interviews; you are also stating that no medical treatment will be required by you from the University of Massachusetts should any physical injury result from participating in these interviews.

I, _____ have read the above statement and agree to participate as an interviewee under the conditions stated above.

_____

Signature of participant

_____   _____

Signature of interviewer   Date

Note that the informed consent letter does *not* promise anonymity for the participant. Instead it indicates a commitment to
maintain confidentiality and provides details concerning the
steps that will be taken toward that end. That subtle point does
not mean the researcher will be any less diligent in protecting
the privacy of the participant. It simply reflects the wisdom of
not promising something that is not directly under your own
control. Note also that while the right to withdraw from the
study during the interviews, and to deny use of specific excerpts, are explicitly established, the right to withdraw entirely
after a final draft has been reviewed is not specified. In this there
is an attempt not only to protect the rights of the participant, but
also to maintain some reasonable balance with the concerns of
the investigator. It might have been wise to include a statement
that clearly establishes ownership and proposed disposition
procedures for the audiotape and transcript document.

BIBLIOGRAPHY

Note: The following is a working list of literature I have investigated that is
related in some important way to the study of the experience of returning
women students in the community college. Subject areas include life-span
development, the education of women, the community college as institution,
feminist research, and aspects of qualitative research methodologies.

Achenbaum, W. Andrew. *Old Age in the New Land.* Baltimore: Johns Hopkins
    University Press, 1978.
Adam, Barry D. *The Survival of Domination: Inferiorization and Everyday Life.*
    New York: Elsevier, 1978.
Agonito, Rosemary. *History of Ideas on Woman: A Source Book.* New York: G.
    P. Putnam's Sons, 1977.
American Association of Community and Junior Colleges. *Assessing the
    Educationally Related Needs of Adults.* Washington, DC: The Center for
    Community Education, 1979.
American Association of University Women. *But We Will Persist.* Washington,
    DC: Author, 1978.
American Educator's Newspaper of Record. *Demographic Predictions for Next
    Twenty Years.* Vol. 1, No. 29, April 14, 1982.
Andreas, Carol. *Sex and Caste in America.* Englewood Cliffs, NJ: Prentice Hall,
    1971.

Aptheker, Bettina. *Women's Legacy: Essays on Race, Sex, and Class in American History.* Amherst, MA: University of Massachusetts Press, 1982.

Arlin, P. K. "Cognitive Development in Adulthood: A Fifth Stage?" *Developmental Psychology,* 1975, 11: 602-606.

The remainder of the bibliography is not presented here.

Merging a "working list" of background literature with the actual list of references cited in the proposed document would not be acceptable in many graduate schools and should never be done in the case of a grant proposal. Readers may wish to locate a full citation quickly, without sorting through pages of unused items. Some reviewers make it a regular practice to cross-check the reference list against the citations in the text for exact congruence. That would be most difficult with a merged bibliography. A list of references should consist only of items named in the text of the proposal.

A bibliography of other important documents used by the author is perfectly appropriate as an item in the appendices to the proposal. A list of such background literature may serve the purpose of indicating the sophistication and care with which the author has prepared. If lengthy, such a bibliography may be divided into topical areas as suggested by the author's lead note. Should the author be particularly anxious to draw the attention of readers to the bibliography, a note indicating its location and content may be placed in the introductory section of the proposal.

Final Notes to the Reader

Our primary concerns about this proposal have been noted in the interspersed comments. There are several points, however, for which the content of the document, as reproduced here in abbreviated form, did not invite comment. As these deal with matters that are likely to be encountered by graduate students proposing qualitative studies, we will do so in these final notes to the reader.

1. Most advisors find it helpful to have at least a rough sense of how much time the student anticipates for each stage of the study. An economical way to address this is by laying out a time-line with projected dates for completion of each major step. Although such plans must be speculative, the act of creating one insures that the novice investigator has thought realistically about that very practical aspect of what has been proposed.

2. Given the substantial volume of transcript data and the complexity of the proposed analyses, consideration of computer processing would now be a natural expectation for a proposal of this kind. At the time the author was preparing her proposal, software for the specialized purposes of qualitative research was just becoming available and was not yet in common use.

3. Returning the transcribed interviews to participants for their review (a process sometimes called "member checking") is done to invite corrections, clarifications, or comments, and at other times is used as a means of sharing ownership of the research process, or empowering participants with a feeling of control over their own words. The purpose and wisdom of such procedures is the subject of continuing debate among researchers, but on most committees you would expect the possibility to be raised and discussed.

4. The author of this proposal shows persisting concern for her participants and seems very likely to be highly respectful of them during both the interviews and the subsequent analysis. What is absent, however, is any direct discussion of reciprocity. As indicated in Chapter 5, there are no easy solutions to concerns about equity between researcher and participant, but it would be expected that at least the issue be raised in the proposal.

5. The author undertook to read broadly as well as deeply on a variety of topics that, for her, formed the conceptual framework for the study. The breadth of such activity will always be a function of the topic, advisor, candidate, and academic context. Our position in this guide, however, has been that, whatever may be read by the author as background to the study, what is actually used in the proposal should be limited to framing the question and supporting the methodology proposed. This proposal went far beyond that limitation, and we would not wish readers to regard it as a model for what must be accomplished in the review of literature.

Proposal 3: Quasi-Experimental Design

Teaching Children to Question What They Read: An Attempt to Improve Reading Comprehension Through Training in a Cognitive Learning Strategy

This is a particularly interesting proposal as it involves a quasi-experimental treatment in a topic area, the acquisition of reading skills, that is not often studied in such fashion. The strength of the introduction is that it immediately convinces the reader of the seriousness of the topic—the need to be able to read in our society.

AUTHOR"S NOTE: This proposal was prepared by John David MacDonald as part of the dissertation research requirement in the Department of Educational Psychology at The University of Texas at Austin. The dissertation was supervised by Beeman N. Phillips and Claire E. Weinstein. The completed dissertation received the Outstanding Dissertation Award by the Southwest Educational Research Association. Dr. MacDonald currently is a school psychologist with the North Kitsap School District, Poulsbo, Washington, and is an adjunct faculty member at Western Washington University, Bellingham.

Introduction

One of the main tasks assigned to schools is that of training students to be linguistically competent. In an industrialized society and national political culture such as the United States, this requires competence in the written as well as the spoken word. It is, for example, very difficult to administer secret ballots except in writing. In the workplace, instructions to workers, including safety precautions, are in printed form. Reading is a means to gain control over one's life, whether one is reading about an upcoming election or one is choosing where to shop for food economically.

While reading may be a necessity for everyday living, evidence is ample that many people never acquire the skills necessary for reading. Several years ago, Gibson and Levin (1975) suggested that as many as 25% of all school children are more than one year below grade level in reading. In some inner-city schools in New York City, the proportion may be as high as 85% (Fuentes, 1980).

Here the author reveals the purpose of the study. As you will note, later in the proposal a problem and question also are stated.

The purpose of the proposed study, therefore, is to assess the effectiveness of a proposed reading intervention technique, a technique that appears conceptually to be consistent with the recent developments in cognitive learning. Not learning to read has, of course, more than social and economic costs. It has personal costs as well. Never to know the intricacies of John Le Carre's plots, or Joseph Conrad's evocative descriptions, or even the self-awareness that comes from reading about one's own condition, is to be isolated from the national culture, and to some degree, to be a person without a past or a present. Calling the over-60 age group the single largest cohort of functional illiterates, the White House Conference on the Aging (Kasom, 1981) suggested that this population is more at risk for mental health problems due to the isolation, poverty, and boredom that result from being illiterate. But personal satisfaction and participation in national culture are not the only costs of illiteracy.

In the paragraph below, the author makes the critical point that reading is the underpinning for success in all school subjects. This provides a strong rationale for a study in which the major purpose was to identify an effective method with which to improve reading skills. So that the reader will not miss this important rationale, the author both coins and underscores an important word, *keystone*, to describe the construct.

Reading may serve as a "keystone" for other curricular skills, that is, certain skills may be prerequisite to curricular skills in science, social studies, literature, and so on. While some authors complain, perhaps correctly, that the reason for "scientific illiteracy" is the emphasis on basic skills or reading instruction for its own sake, it is difficult to imagine a student obtaining a scientific education while not reading. Because of this *keystone quality*, a lack of reading skills may result in low achievement and premature school dropouts. Curtis, Doss, MacDonald, and Davis (Note 1) found that the best predictor of late dropouts was below-average scholastic grade-point average, and many of the dropouts who were interviewed reported chronic reading problems and that they withdrew because they believed these problems were insurmountable.

Here the author shows that the need for reducing school dropout rates by improving reading performance is relevant to the city in which the study is to be conducted. Thus the problem of developing reading skills is not an abstraction. It is specific to the locale, and new information will have potential for immediate consequences, a point that will not be lost on the university committee or the public officials who must approve the execution of the study in the school system.

Withdrawal from school can have dire economic consequences: In this city, 48% of non-high school graduate males aged 16-21 were unemployed, but only 18.4% of the same age high school graduates were unemployed (Bureau of the Census, 1973). It is not inconceivable that illiteracy is related to unemployment.

The section below is an excellent example of demonstrating the need for the study. It directly answers the query we posed in Chapter 1, "Why bother with the question?" Sometimes the answer to this is woven into the rationale, as shown below. An alternative, which is sometimes required by committees or funding agencies, is to separate the "need for the study" section from the section on rationale. If this were the case, the earlier discussion of the personal costs of not knowing how to read, the potential for mental health risk, and the likelihood of employers shunning nonreaders could be shortened and combined into an effective section on "need for the study."

Employers seem reluctant to hire illiterate workers because they view them as more likely to injure themselves and their fellow workers, and because they view them as more likely to cost the company large sums of money for misreading instructions (Lauterborn, 1981). Of 800 companies Lauterborn surveyed, 35% thought it necessary to supplement their employees' education with basic English and business writing. The increasing sophistication of modern weaponry and support equipment along with the failure of the armed services to attract more highly educated recruits has led the Army to invest $37,000,000 over a four-year period in the research and development of instructional systems in basic skills, English as a second language, life-coping skills, and cognitive learning strategies (Begland, 1981). Thus good reading skills are of more than personal benefit for the reader; they are related to the economic and defense interests of the nation.

While the reading skills of the nation's school children may be viewed by many as distressing, there are some encouraging indications that reading performance is improving and that poor reading is less of a problem. The National Assessment of Educational Progress (Burton & Jones, 1982; National Assessment of Educational Progress, 1976a, 1976b) has reported improving performance on both literal and inferential comprehension items for 9-year-olds, and improvements have surfaced in literal comprehension among 13 and 17 year olds. Differences in reading scores between whites and blacks have declined from a 17 point difference in inferential comprehension in 1970 to a less than 10 point difference in 1980 (Burton & Jones, 1982).

Below is a section that does not speak directly to the question at hand. The volume of specific detail breaks the flow of the introduction. The reader will be struck by the observation that the style of writing is not parallel with the rest of the introduction. It seems clear that the introduction would not suffer if this section were located elsewhere.

In the 1972 assessment, the National Assessment of Educational Progress (NAEP) sponsored a special survey of students' attitudes towards reading and literature. These results are encouraging, if one accepts the validity of student responses to adult interviewers. Of the 13-year-olds interviewed, 43% strongly agreed that it is important to study literature, while an additional 34% somewhat agreed with the statement. In the inner-city schools, 58% strongly agreed with the statement. The majority of 17-year-olds (90%) believed literature should be taught in every school. A majority of the 9-year-olds (84%) and 13-year-olds (78%) reported they read for their own pleasure at least once a week, with 54% of the 9-year-olds and 44% of the 13-year-olds reporting they read for pleasure every day. When asked if they had read a particular type of literature on their own (e.g., short story, novel, poetry, etc.) 98% of the 13-year-olds replied they had read at least one of the types, and 86% gave verifiable titles when asked. For an adult sample, 89% replied they had read at least one genre, while 76% gave verifiable titles (NAEP, 1973).

In general terms, the outlook is hopeful. However, there remain substantial numbers of children and adults for whom reading is troublesome. Unless they receive effective interventions, their economic prospects are grim, they are disenfranchised from the political process, and much of the world's cultural heritage bypasses them. For the 78% of the 1973 13-year-olds who reported reading at least once a week, 6% of them reported never having read for pleasure. In the 1980-81 school year, some 5% to 6% of the students in the city Independent School District's average daily enrollment had reading problems so severe they required classification for special education services under the category of Learning Disabilities (Bass, Note 2). Knowing what to do for these students to help them improve their reading is troublesome for teachers, learning disability specialists and school principals. Yet these individuals are legally mandated with providing an appropriate education for these students, that is, charged with improving these students' reading (McClain, 1981).

Despite a large number of research studies of reading instruction, little is presently known about the relative effectiveness of different methods of teaching reading (Maxwell, 1972; Pflaum, Walberg, Karegiones, & Rasher, 1980). Most children arrive in kindergarten not knowing how to read, and most leave high school as fairly competent readers; thus although we know little about effective reading instruction, most children do learn how to read while in school. It is likely that few students who do not attend school will attain the same reading competence as they would if they attended 12 years of school, although this interpretation of descriptive studies of school nonattendance suffers from selection factors.

Here the author begins establishing a background for the particular approach to be used in this study, that is the identification and measurement of behaviors specific to reading competence.

It seems likely that acquisition of reading competence is directly related to teacher and student behaviors, although at this stage in reading research it is difficult to state precisely what these behaviors are. The attempt to define them to validate their effectiveness as mediators in the acquisition of reading competence should contribute to "cracking the problem of what happens to reading achievement after the second or third grade" (Glaser, 1979, p. 8). Identification of these behaviors may then contribute to a system of intervention practices with regard to reading problems.

The following discussion provides a historical framework through which to understand the significance of the study to be proposed. New techniques to determine teacher and student behaviors relevant to reading acquisition make possible acquisition of heretofore inaccessible information.

The field of reading diagnosis and intervention has been plagued by systems of nonexperimentally-validated constructs regarding the processes involved in reading, resulting in assessment instruments with unacceptably low levels of reliability. In turn, the use of poor assessment instruments has contributed to ineffective intervention procedures (Arter & Jenkins, 1979; Hammil & Larsen, 1974a, 1974b; Hammill, Goodman, & Wiederholt, 1974; Larsen & Hammill, 1975; Minskoff, 1975). However, three developments have improved the likelihood of identifying those teacher and student behaviors involved in the acquisition of competent reading. The first development is the identification of a series of learner behaviors that are directed at constructing meaning from text (Bransford, Barclay, & Franks, 1972; Perfetti & Lesgold, 1977; Rumelhart, 1975), behaviors that are directed at understanding and recall (DiSibio, 1982; Weinstein, 1978; Weinstein, 1982; Weinstein & Underwood, 1983; Wittrock, 1979; Wittrock, Note 3), and the discovery that these behaviors can be learned and can be brought within the cognitive control of the learner (Rothkopf, 1970; Weinstein, Cubberly, Wicker, Underwood, Roney, & Duty, 1981).

The second development is in the application of task analysis to the acquisition of curricular knowledge (Chi & Glaser, 1980; Gage & Briggs, 1974; Glaser, 1976; Resnick, Wang, & Kaplan, 1973). It is now possible to model complex hypothesized reading and knowledge acquisition strategies through the use of task analysis. The third development involves methodologies for determining causal relations (Blalock, 1971; Duncan, 1975; Wolfe, 1980; Wright, 1971) and methodologies for evaluating aptitude treatment interactions (Cronbach & Snow, 1977), which have been called, along with the developments in cognitive learning (Wittrock, Note 3), "the most significant developments of the past 5 to 10 years, developments that may have significant if not greater influence on educational research during the 1980s" (Kerlinger, 1982, p. 120). The study of causal relations is now being applied to the experimental validation of task-analytic models of curricular skill acquisition (Bergan, 1980; Hill & McGaw, 1981). These developments are of great importance for the assessment of learning problems and for the design and implementation of interventions for learning problems.

At this point the author included an extensive review of the literature. A variety of topics were covered including reading comprehension, individual differences, methodology, and analysis. Since we have suggested a shorter, concise review focusing specifically on decisions for the proposed study (see Chapter 4) we have chosen not to include the review of the literature here.

STATEMENT OF THE PROBLEM

A small number of children do not attain functional reading skills and suffer economically, socially, and politically. The consequences for these children necessitate that effective reading remediation strategies be developed and implemented. Remediation strategies need to be derived from theories of what it is that good readers do that enables them to be competent readers. Although such theories are in their infancy, they are now specific enough in their implications that specific intervention strategies may be developed and evaluated.

The author now has identified a problematic area (some students do not attain functional reading skills), but only later on does he actually state the question for the study. The paragraph below is intended both to introduce and support the treatment to be examined. For the reader, it would have been helpful to undertake the two communication tasks separately, and in sequential paragraphs.

One such strategy that has been recommended to reading teachers is having students generate their own questions about the content of the reading material and then having students seek the answers to these questions. This recommendation has appeared in teacher preparation texts (Durkin, 1978), in journals directed to reading teachers (Alexander & Fuller, 1973; Dillworth, 1980; Eeds, 1980; Hopkins, 1979; Olmio, 1975; Seifert, 1980), in journals directed to learning disabilities specialists (Wong, 1979), and in publications directed at psychologists (*Comprehension is the Key,* 1981). Without exception, these authors have presented the technique in a favorable, noncritical light, but little data have been presented in these articles to support this position.

Here the case is made that, although the technique of having children generate their own questions about reading material facilitates reading skills, children must be trained to generate these questions. Here, the proposed study is seen to be firmly grounded in the current understanding of how children learn to read. By identifying the limitations of previous research, the author positions himself to argue for the design features of the proposed study.

Experimental evaluations of this technique have recently appeared (e.g., Andre & Anderson, 1979; Dreher & Gambrell, Note 5; Frase & Schwartz, 1975; Weiner, 1978), which suggest that at least one qualification be made to the recommendations for the use of this technique. This qualification is that children may need to be trained how to generate questions that are targeted on important ideas in order for the technique to be effective.

Unfortunately, previous studies of the efficacy of training students how to use this technique have serious flaws. While the finding that students who generate good questions benefit more from the use of this technique than do students who generate poor questions is a well-established one, these authors (with the exception of those of one study) have failed to demonstrate that improvements in question-asking lead to improvements in reading comprehension and reading recall when using the technique (Andre & Anderson, 1979; Dreher & Gambrell, Note 5; Frase & Schwartz, 1975). This failure appears to have been the result of too brief or inappropriate instructional activities.

The statements below argue the need for an intervention of longer duration with a wider range of student abilities. Again, this establishes the grounds for selecting a particular research format.

The author of the one study in which significant improvements in reading recall following training were shown used a more extensive training program than did other investigations (Weiner, 1978). Weiner's subjects had above-average reading skills, however, as did the subjects in the other training studies. Thus although the recommendation to use this technique has been directed at teachers of below-average readers, the efficacy of training these students to use this technique has never been tested.

Differential treatment response by reading level groups will be an important variable in the proposed study. The following discussion introduces this concept so that the reader will later understand why an analysis by skill level is proposed.

This technique appears promising, based on the theoretical rationale underpinning its design. Empirical trials of the use of the technique, however, indicate that its implementation is problematic. Recently, some progress has been made in preparing average and good readers for its use, but the critical question is how poor readers might be best prepared to benefit from the technique. If the technique cannot be made accessible to poor readers, then teachers attempting to use it may have a detrimental effect on their students' reading skills, if only because time spent learning and implementing the technique may be time spent off-task. Understanding how to make the technique accessible to poor readers is thus of critical importance before further recommendations for the technique can be made.

Below is the actual statement of the question. It expresses two questions succinctly. It could have been stated much earlier. Also, from a research perspective, it would have been more explicit to substitute a nonvalue-laden phrase for the word "better," such as "higher order" or another appropriate term.

Specific hypotheses appear on the following pages, but this study will be directed at answering the following questions: Can students with adequate vocabulary skills for the material they will be reading be trained to generate good questions, and if so, will the improvement in question-asking result in improved reading comprehension and reading recall when students are told to use the technique?

HYPOTHESES

In this study the following hypotheses will be tested:

1. A group of junior-high-school students who are below average in reading and who receive training in generating good questions will ask better questions than will a group of similar students receiving a control training program (when posttest question quality is controlled for pretest question quality).

2. A group of junior-high-school students who are below average in reading and who receive training in generating good questions will perform better on a task of reading recall than will a group of similar students receiving a control training program (when posttest free recall quality is controlled for pretest free recall quality).

3. The amount of improvement (pre to post) in free recall will be directly related to the amount of improvement (pre to post) in question quality.

METHOD

An overview of the research design would have been helpful at the start of this section. This is a complex study in which many measurements will be utilized. A flowchart or brief outline (see our suggestions in Chapter 1) would assist the reader in understanding how each type of measurement contributes to the overall purpose of the study.

The first paragraph in this section provides information about the subjects. Inasmuch as the author has suggested earlier that failure to control for grade and reading ability has been an important confounding factor in previous research involving the proposed treatment, it is especially important to provide details about these factors.

SUBJECTS

Students in reading classes in a rural, central Texas school district will serve as subjects in this study. About half will be students in seventh-grade required reading classes who demonstrate a wide range of reading ability. The other subjects will be students in eighth-grade remedial reading classes; these students represent about the lower third of the district's eighth-graders in terms of reading comprehension scores on the Science Research Associates (SRA) Achievement Series (Thorpe, Lefever, & Naslund, 1973). Subjects will range in age from 12 years to 15 years.

This next section gives details about the specific tests to be used in the study. Six tests will be used: four that were previously available and two that were designed for this study. The author provides details on the purpose and reliability of each test. Note that reliability for the first test has been reported elsewhere. Accordingly, the author provides just the reliability coefficient and a citation. Interested readers can obtain the reference, and the proposal is not cluttered with unnecessary detail. The description of why this subtest was selected is excellent. Readers may wonder, however, why the subtest was administered exactly six months prior to treatment and not at some other time. The timing of test applications is a particularly important factor and should be justified with care.

INSTRUMENTATION

SRA Achievement Series (Thorpe, Lefever, & Naslund, 1973). This test yields both reading comprehension and reading vocabulary subtest scores. Confounding of these subtests occurs, however, because the vocabulary subtest uses the same materials as the comprehension subtest (Fry, 1965; Guthrie, 1972). Therefore, only the comprehension subtest (SRA-C) will be used in this research, while another test will be used to assess pretest vocabulary skills. The SRA-C subtest requires students to answer questions concerning main ideas, supporting details, and inferences from a series of reading passages. It has been reported to have an alternate-form stability coefficient of $r = .83$ (Guthrie, 1972) after a one-year test-retest interval. The SRA-C subtest will be administered to the subjects six months prior to the training program.

Three other tests were presented in a similar fashion: (a) Test of Reading Comprehension-General Vocabulary (TORCGV), (b) Test of Reading Comprehension-Paragraph (TORCPR), and (c) Test of Reading Comprehension-Syntactic Similarities (TORCSS). The fifth test, Question Quality Rating, was created by the author. Because no reference is available for this test, greater detail is provided. The author alerts the reader to why the content was chosen and particular procedures devised for administering the test. Note, however, that the actual test is included in an appendix.

Question Quality Rating. This task was created for use in this research, and it will be used as both a pretest and a posttest measure. The reading passages and instructions to subjects are contained in Appendix A. Two reading passages (A and B) were selected from sixth-grade social studies texts that had not been in previous use in the district. Passage A, 984 words long, is a discussion of the economies of the British North American colonies (Jones, Young, & Boutwell, 1971, pp. 38-43). Passage B, 695 words long, is a narrative about the struggles to control Mexico from colonial times until the twentieth century (Chapin, McHugh, & Gross, 1971, pp. 62-66). These passages were chosen because students were likely to be somewhat familiar with the content (although much of the content would be new), because the style and readability of the passages are similar to text materials students are and will be required to learn from in their school program, and because the passages are complete and long enough to be sensitive to the use of efficient reading strategies while being short enough to allow testing during a single class period.

Subjects read either Passage A or Passage B on the pretest, and the other passage on the posttest; subjects will be randomly assigned to passages. They will be instructed to write down, while reading, "the best questions about the story that [they could] think of . . .[,] questions that [they] could ask someone else [in order to] find out if they had read the story too." Fifteen minutes will be given to complete this task, and they cannot get help from each other. They can request help from the experimenter if they do not understand a specific word; the experimenter will then define the word for all subjects.

The questions that the subjects will generate will be rated on a 1 to 5 equal appearing interval scale with "1" representing a poor question and "5" representing an excellent question. Raters will receive training and practice materials before rating and will be told to base the rating of question quality on the degree to which the question targets important information in the passage and on the degree to which answering the question requires the reader to organize the content of the text. If these two qualities are present to a high degree, raters also are to consider the amount of elaboration required by the question, and the degree to which answering the question taps the higher levels of Bloom's taxonomy, for example, understanding, application, analysis, synthesis, and evaluation. If raters do not understand the question, it will be rated "1," or poor.

> In the paragraph above, the author provides detail on how the raters will score this test. Below he provides a careful description of the raters. In this study the raters serve as a form of instrumentation, and because a good proposal requires that all instrumentation be described fully, the paragraph is needed.

The ten raters are either graduate students in educational psychology ($N = 5$) at the university or advanced undergraduate education students who have completed a course in Tests and Measurements and have been recommended by their instructor as being skilled at evaluating test items. All raters have had courses in Tests and Measurements, five have had courses in Psychometric Theory, and one has taught Tests and Measurements courses. Seven raters were experienced teachers at either the elementary or secondary level with a median of 4.0 years of experience. The questions generated by students and the instructions and training materials given to raters are contained in Appendix B.

In the paragraph below the author presents the reliability for each of the passages in the test. Since individual questions were rated, but means were used in the analysis, the author provides reliability estimates for both.

To determine reliability of the test, pre- and posttest questions for the same passages were combined and question order was randomized. Five raters (similar to those used in the study) rated all questions for Passage A and five rated all questions for Passage B. The mean of the five ratings for a question was used as the estimate of the quality of that question. Interrater agreement by the Spearman-Brown formula (Winer, 1971, pp. 283-287) was estimated to be $r = .84$ for Passage A questions and $r = .73$ for Passage B. Subjects generated between 0 and 9 questions. The quality estimates for all the questions a subject asked were combined and the mean of these was taken to be the estimate of that student's question-asking skills. Reliability of this estimate by the Spearman-Brown formula was estimated to be $r = .96$ for Passage A and $r = .92$ for Passage B.

Throughout the rest of this proposal, the estimates of student questioning skills are referred to by the mnemonics PREQUES and POSQUES, for pretest and posttest question ratings, respectively.

A second test, Free Recall Quality Rating, also was created for this study. The author presented it in much the same way as the test above, and that material has been omitted here. A final item of data will be collected by interviewing students, and that step is presented here. Note that the experimenter will debrief the subjects as a part of the final process of data collection.

Other measures. In addition to the previous measures, the *number of questions* asked on both the pretest (PRENUM) and on the posttest (POSNUM) will be included in the analyses. After the posttest, subjects in the experimental training group will be asked if they have *used the strategy* they had learned about, and will be told to write down their answers on experimenter-supplied paper without writing their names. The experimenter will then explain to the subjects that he or she did not know whether this strategy would work, but in order to find out if it did, their help was needed, because they were the only ones to know if they had really tried to use the strategy.

> The procedure for collecting pretest and posttest data is presented in the next section. The level of heading (not separate from the paragraph) should be changed so that it is the same as "Subjects" and "Instrumentation." Note that the author plans for the contingency that some students may not return the parent permission slip. Since it is unlikely that all students will get permission or remember to bring back the letter, it is wise to address this in the proposal.

Procedure. During the second week of the fall semester, the subjects' regular reading instructor will explain to them the nature of the research project and distribute parent permission forms to be reviewed and signed if desired by the subjects' parents. This form is contained in Appendix C. If any students are not permitted by their parents to participate, these students will work on individual assignments during assessment sessions and participate in the control group training because the control training is part of the regular instructional program.

> The paragraph below performs the function of an overview paragraph. Notice how a simple diagram, as suggested in Chapter 1, would help in grasping the overall pattern of the study.

Subjects next will be administered the Test of Reading Comprehension-General Vocabulary (TORCGV) subtest, the Pretest Question-Asking task (PREQUES) and the Pretest Free Recall task (PRECALL). SRA Reading test scores are available for subjects who had been present the previous spring. Following pretesting, subjects will be randomly assigned to control and experimental groups.

The author provides a concise depiction of the treatment group. Details of the specific instructional objectives for the treatment are presented in Table 1. The figure is logical and easy to read. By presenting this information separately from the text the reader is given the option of reading it for greater detail.

Experimental Group. What occurs during the experimental group training is critical to testing the main hypotheses of this study. The training the students will receive involves four components: (a) instruction and practice in problem solving (as a prerequisite to presenting reading comprehension as a problem-solving task), (b) instruction and practice in question asking, (c) instruction and practice in recognizing text structure, and (d) practice in asking questions while reading. In Table 1 more details are contained about specific instructional objectives of these four components. The instructional manual for this experimental training is contained in Appendix D.

The experimental training will be conducted by the experimenter, and all experimental sessions will take place in the subjects' regular classroom. The experimental training will last nine sessions for a total of 7.5 hours of allotted instructional time. All students must attend seven or more sessions to be included in the final data analysis.

The last sentence above establishes the minimum participation standard required for each subject. Those who do field research, particularly in school settings, are aware of the fact that it is *very* unlikely that all subjects will be present for the entire treatment. As we indicated in Chapter 4, it is better to anticipate and resolve such problems before collecting data than to be faced with difficult decisions after the data have been collected and disagreements between student and committee become potentially disastrous.

Below, the author provides concise information on the control group and posttests. Note that students were debriefed after the posttest and that each student then received the alternative

Text continues on page 269.

PROPOSAL 3: TABLE 1 Specific Instructional Objectives for the Four Components

Problem Solving	Questioning Skills	Text Structure	Applications
1.1 Students will be able to identify a situation as problematic and the reason why it is a problem.	2.1 Given a word or phrase from text, students will be able to identify attributes of that word or phrase.	3.1 Students will be able to identify similarities between reading to learn information and problem-solving.	4.1 When given a text, the topic and first paragraph, students will be able to generate explicit statements of information they want to obtain from the text.
1.2 Students will be able to list the six steps for solving problems.	2.2 Given a word or phrase from text, students will be able to state implied attributes of that word or phrase (e.g., "postpone" implies an event, a person controlling its occurrence, a previous time for the event and a new time).	3.2 Given a short passage of discourse, students will be able to identify the probable intent of the author.	4.2 When given a text, students will generate questions about the text and will search for answers in the passage.
1.3 Given either an example of a school (intellectual) problem or a general social problem, students will be able to identify the steps they will follow in seeking a solution.	2.3 Given a word or phrase from text, students will be able to state what information is missing about implied attributes.	3.3 Given a passage of discourse, students will be able to identify the main ideas and their supporting details, and will be able to outline the passage without omitting, adding, or distorting main ideas.	

2.4 Students will list several types of strategies aimed at obtaining information and will be able to identify several types of questions and the type of information they elicit.

2.5 Students will demonstrate improved skills in asking constraint-seeking questions by reducing the number of questions necessary to win the "twenty questions" game.

2.6 Students will demonstrate improved skills in domain-seeking questions by reducing the number of questions necessary before a correct subordinate class is identified in the "twenty questions" game.

3.4 When given a passage of text and a set of questions about the passage, students will identify where the answers to the questions about the passage, are likely to be found and will successfully find answers to these questions.

Continued

PROPOSAL 3: TABLE 1 Continued

Problem Solving	Questioning Skills	Text Structure	Applications
	2.7 Given a problem to solve, students will be able to rank a series of informative facts as to their value in solving the problem.		
	2.8 Given a problem to solve, students will be able to make a statement about a possible solution and will be able to test the truth value of the statement by obtaining and interpreting appropriate information.		

treatment, even though further data were not collected for the study. The reversing of treatments ensures that all of the subjects have the chance to experience the primary intervention. If in fact the treatment provides significant benefits, the control group has equal access to them, *after* all data essential to the study have been collected.

Control group. The control group will receive instruction and practice in using a dictionary, a thesaurus, and the library. The instruction will be done by the regular reading teacher and will take place either in the library or in an alcove adjacent to the regular classroom. Precautions will be taken to ensure that the control group cannot hear teaching that occurs with the experimental group.

Posttesting. One day after the last training session and three weeks after pretesting, the subjects will be administered the TOR-CPR, the TORCSS, the Posttest Questioning task (POSQUES), and the Posttest Free Recall task (POSCALL). After posttesting, all subjects in the experimental group will be asked if they had used the strategy, about advantages and disadvantages of the technique, and about whether or not they would use the technique again. The nature of the research will again be explained to the subjects and any questions they have about the study will be answered to the best of the experimenter's ability at that time. The following week, treatment conditions will be reversed, with the control group receiving the experimental training, and vice versa.

In the final section of the body of the proposal the focus is on data analysis. The author reports all the techniques to be used for each part of the analysis. More detail would help many readers. It would be particularly helpful if the author had discussed the analysis in light of each hypothesis stated earlier. Including sample tables for the analyses to be performed is a good idea for all studies, particularly when there are as many variables as in this study. An illustration of the path analytic model to be tested, such as the one presented in Chapter 1, should be included here so the model to be tested is apparent.

Data analysis. Reliability estimates for PREQUES, POSQUES, PRECALL, and POSCALL were calculated using a hand calculator with programmable statistics functions. These estimates were doublechecked by the experimenter. All other analyses will be performed using the Statistical Package for the Social Sciences (SPSS) statistics package (Nie, Hull, Jenkins, Steinbrenner, & Bent, 1975) edition 8.3, on the CDC 6000/Cyber 700 computers at the university. Data-checking activities will include running subprogram FREQUENCIES to check on variance distributions and plotting distributions on probability paper. Subprograms FREQUENCIES and CROSSTABS will be used to generate the characteristics of treatment groups. Subprograms REGRESSION and PLOT will be used to run preliminary path analyses and to check that regression assumptions have been met, and subprogram REGRESSION will be used to run the final, restricted model path analysis. Subprogram PLOT will be used to generate figures that illustrate significant aptitude-treatment interactions.

Proposal 4: Funded Grant

A Competition Strategy for
Worksite Smoking Cessation

This is a proposal for a "competitive renewal grant." The investigator is seeking funding to continue a project that already has been supported. Such applications are called "competitive" because the proposal must be evaluated with all other proposals submitted within a given time frame, including both renewals and those that are new. If the study is of particular interest to the funding agency and is technically sound, a competitive renewal application will have the advantage of a "halo effect," that is, the reviewers will recognize that the investigation already has been deemed meritorious enough to have received funding from the grantor.

The competitive renewal, however, faces the additional challenge of providing a rationale for continuation—in some

AUTHOR'S NOTE: The original of this proposal was prepared by Nell H. Gottlieb, Ph.D., while a faculty member at The University of Texas at Austin. Dr. Gottlieb is an Associate Professor in the Department of Kinesiology and Health Education, and the Department of Sociology at UT-Austin. The grant was part of a comprehensive research agenda that focuses on the reduction of behaviors that are linked to cancer and was funded by the American Heart Association-Texas Affiliate.

cases, despite the fact that the goal of the original study has been achieved. The proposal presented here met that challenge and was funded for continued work. One of the particular strengths of this proposal is that it is unusually concise, yet it manages to communicate the details of the proposed study very effectively. This is well illustrated by the abstract below, which conveys a surprisingly complete account of the study in the small space permitted.

SUMMARY OF PROPOSED RESEARCH

This research uses a quasi-experimental design to assess the effectiveness of competition/high social facilitation on the recruitment of employees of a large state human resources organization to participate in a self-help smoking cessation program and on the treatment outcomes of the self-help program. Two pairs of regions will be assigned at random to the experimental condition, an inter-program area competition to increase the percentage of smokers and nonsmoking supporters participating in the cessation program or to the control condition, which employs only the usual marketing of program availability. The program will be offered in conjunction with the Great American Smokeout and with Valentine's Day. Besides testing the effect of social facilitation on program recruitment and smoking cessation using a controlled intervention, we will specify a general model of the process of smoking cessation, which includes cognitive, behavioral, social influence, and social structural variables. Smoking behavior will be measured using a self-report and the physiological markers of saliva thiocyanate and, for quitters only, cotinine. This research will contribute to the knowledge base of social psychological factors related to smoking cessation and will be immediately applicable to the design of more effective worksite-based smoking cessation programs.

The author provides a brief overview of the notion of health interventions in the workplace. This serves as the kind of "gentle introduction" discussed in Chapter 1 of this guide—a preface that will be particularly helpful for reviewers who did not read the proposal for the original study.

AIMS OF THE RESEARCH PROGRAM

The worksite offers unique opportunities for cardiovascular disease risk reduction programs. Organization-wide, on-site interventions are convenient and sanctioned for employee participation and provide increased social support for individual behavior change. Self-help behavior change programs, which do not require employer-subsidized time off the job, offer the potential for cost-effective worksite health promotion.

> Here the author provides a concise description of the intervention. This is given at an early point in the proposal so that the reader can use it as a general frame for considering the details that follow.

We propose to field test two conditions of social facilitation, measuring the impact on the recruitment to and outcome of a self-help worksite smoking cessation intervention, which uses previously evaluated materials. In the high social facilitation condition, a region-wide competition among Texas Department of Human Services (TDHS) program areas to involve the most smokers and smoker-supporters (nonsmokers who assist smokers to quit) will be used to generate enthusiasm and strong social reinforcement for program recruitment, adherence and outcome. In the standard social facilitation condition, smokers will be recruited using the same intensity of marketing but without the competition aspect, to participate in the self-help program. The research will test the impact of the two social facilitation conditions on the proportion of smokers employed at the worksite who volunteer for the program (program penetration) and the proportions of quitters/program participants and quitters/smoking employees at program completion and 6 months following the program. Four regions of TDHS (two competition and two noncompetition) will participate. Two will hold the recruitment drive during the Great American Smoke Out (GASO) and two during a Valentine's Day "Save a Sweetheart" program.

By the end of this paragraph, the reader will know both the nature and length of the intervention, as well as the benefits to be gained—both theoretical and applied.

We will also determine the relationship of cognitive factors (intention to quit, beliefs about the consequences of smoking, and self-efficacy to cope with urges to smoke), social support (the smoking behaviors of co-workers, family, and friends and their attitudes towards the smoker's quitting), smoking history (frequency and duration of smoking, number and duration of quitting attempts), and demographic variables to smoking behavior over the 6-month follow-up period. Smoking behavior will be measured by self-report for respondents to the health promotion survey and, for program participants, levels of saliva thiocyanate (SCH) and, to confirm quitting, cotinine. The findings will demonstrate the effect of social facilitation on smoking behavior change and will increase our knowledge about the cognitive, behavioral, and social factors underlying the process of quitting smoking. In addition, application of the research will lead to more effective worksite smoking cessation programs.

PREVIOUS WORK

In this section the author describes recently completed research in two areas that are directly related to the proposed study. This demonstrates the long-term interest of the investigator and, by accentuating the fact that her work in the area already has been approved and funded, she lays claim to both success and competence. The proposed study is characterized as a replication of successful work already undertaken in a different environment. This serves to underscore continuity of interest and the programmatic nature of the author's research agenda.

Our research has two primary foci: (a) evaluation of the effects of a competition among program areas on recruitment into categories of a smoking cessation program and (b) analysis of the relationship between individual differences in cognitive structure, smoking history, and demographic variables and the likelihood of quitting smoking.

Our 1986-87 American Heart Association (AHA)-funded research compared the effects of a competition between two worksites in each of three regions of a large state human services agency on employee participation in the Great American Smoke Out (GASO) in three categories: number of nonsmoking supporters, number participating in a 20-day, self-help smoking cessation program, and number of smokers quitting for the GASO day only. The incentive was a cold turkey buffet for the total worksite on the day following the GASO for the worksite with the highest proportion of supporters and smokers joining the self-help program. Quitting for the day did not count in the competition. Significant differences ($p < .001$) between competition and noncompetition worksites were found for the proportion participating in each of the categories (69% versus 12% of nonsmokers were adopters; 24% versus 4% of smokers joined the self-help program; and 46% vs. 28% of smokers quit for the GASO day only). However, the total participation in the worksites was variable (ranging from 16% to 97% in the cooperation and 0% to 69% in the noncompetition worksites) and in half of the sites more smokers quit for the day than joined the cessation program. The results of the competition are promising, although the involvement is lower than that reported by Klesges and colleagues for banks (1). The low social facilitation condition is comparable to the participation we found for the Great American Smoke Out in an implementation of "Heart at Work" conducted at an insurance company (2). We propose to replicate this research (a) using competition among program areas, which seems to be a more natural line of competition in this agency than individual worksites, and (b) organizing the program around a Valentine's Day "Save a Sweetheart" theme in addition to GASO, which involves quitting during the holiday season. We also propose a more in-depth qualitative evaluation to examine the process of implementing the programs in the competition and noncompetition sites.

The next paragraph develops the theoretical base for the study. In the process, however, the author underscores several benefits to be achieved by funding the study. These include attractive outcomes at a number of different levels (levels likely to correspond to the differing interests of members of the review committee) such as improved design of cessation programs, improved worker health, and improved understanding of personality and behavioral characteristics of people who quit or persist in smoking.

The second focus of this research is individual differences in smoking cessation. The applicant's major research interest has been the social epidemiology of lifestyle health behaviors, with special emphasis on smoking. She has used local and national data to develop and specify a multi-level theoretical model of smoking, which includes cognitive, behavioral, and social structural variables (3,4). Using this model, she has shown gender differences in smoking to be related to gender-specific modeling effects of peer and parental smoking, group membership, and marriage. In addition, education, not attending church, life events, and belief in susceptibility to heart disease were directly associated with the likelihood of smoking for both men and women (3-9). Differences were also found by ethnicity in a national probability sample. Hispanic males and females were less likely to be current smokers than their Black and Anglo peers, while Anglo males and females had the highest proportion of quitters (10). In a probability sample of Texas residents, Gottlieb, Lloyd and Bernstein (11) found men more likely to smoke than women (34% vs. 27%) and recommended worksite-based programs as an especially effective way to reach adults younger than 65. Our current AHA-funded research involves testing the relative influence of social learning theory variables (including self-efficacy), behavioral variables, social facilitation, and demographic variables on smoking status immediately after and at six months following a self-help smoking cessation program. The 1986 GASO competition did not yield sufficient subjects in the self-help program to test these hypothesized relationships. Continued funding would allow recruitment of enough subjects for this aspect of the research.

Below, the author points out the specific ways in which this proposal is superior to previous studies: how it corrects errors in research design, and how its theoretical framework will allow the results of the study to be more than purely descriptive. The author makes clear that not only is she aware of the problems that attended previous research on the topic, but that she knows how to circumvent them as well.

Our AHA-funded research addresses several problems often found in smoking studies. Much of the research suffered from inadequate sample sizes to detect differences in quit rate, the use of self-report of smoking status as the sole dependent variable, and the use of cross-sectional surveys, which does not allow causal inferences to be made regarding the relationships of the independent variables and smoking behavior. At a level more fundamental than these methodological problems is the lack of an adequate theoretical model of smoking behavior to guide research. Such a model must move beyond the psychological level of explanation, to include social and cultural influences. In our current and proposed research, the two social facilitation groups are large enough to detect expected differences in quit rates, smoking self-report is confirmed using biochemical measures, and participants are followed through their participation in the self-help program and six months thereafter. Based on our theoretical approach, we include variables at the cognitive, behavioral, and social structural level in our analysis and manipulate social facilitation, using an organizational level intervention, in our controlled experiment.

Other investigators have examined the effect of competitions as an incentive to change health behavior. Brownell and colleagues have reported effective weight loss using competitions between organizations and divisions or teams within organizations (12). The cost/benefit ratio of this program was reported to be substantially better than other worksite-based weight reduction programs. Klesges and colleagues used a competition strategy to recruit smoking employees in three banks to participate in a self-help smoking cessation program (1). Almost all (88%) smokers in the organizations participated and the quit rate at 6 months following the treatment was 18%. The opposite result, however, was found in a competition among naturally occurring divisions of a nursing staff (13). No nurses volunteered for the self-help smoking cessation project. This was attributed to a boycott of the program by influential nurses. It appears that competition has great potential for increasing motivation and reinforcement for entering smoking cessation programs, adhering to them, and quitting smoking. However, the conditions must be carefully directed.

The importance of worksite culture is receiving increasing attention (14). Sorensen, Pechacek and Pallonen have recently reported different norms for co-worker discouragement of quitting attempts, perceived prevalence of smoking, and interest in quitting across worksites (15). We will examine these variables. We will also follow the advice of organizational theorists who have pointed out the necessity of examining organizational change from a process as well as a variance approach (16). While most of our proposed work on program outcome falls within a variance framework, we will carefully document the process of implementation using key informant interviews, observation, and other qualitative techniques.

> In the next paragraphs the author provides a rationale for selecting the intervention to be used in the study. Documenting the appropriateness of self-help programs, and combining this with a discussion of results from a recent pilot study, adds strength to the proposal.

The American Lung Association (ALA) self-help program we use has been evaluated and found to have a nonsmoking prevalence rate at 12 months of 18% and a continuous nonsmoking rate of 5% (17). These rates are comparable to those found for other self-help manuals (18). Windsor et al. obtained a quit rate of 6% and a quit/reduction rate of 20% using the ALA manual and a 10 minute health education skills counseling session in a study of pregnant women using a health department clinic (19). Preliminary results from a study of the effects of social support on quit rates using the ALA self-help manual show 20% quit rates with high social support and 6% with low social support (20).

Self-help programs for smoking cessation have several advantages over therapist-directed interventions. They can be made available to a large number of people, and those who quit using self-help can attribute quitting success to themselves rather than a therapist (21). Although these programs are not as effective as more intensive interventions, they may be more cost-effective than clinics and reach the large segment of the smoking population who wish to stop smoking without professional assistance (22).

The next paragraph is one of the few that might be deleted. It introduces a sharp change in the focus of the section, without contributing additional information that will help reviewers make a judgment about the present proposal.

Individual differences in cognitive structure, social reinforcement of smoking, social status, and smoking history have been shown by a number of investigators to be predictive of smoking, both independent of treatment type and, in some cases, in interaction with treatment type. DiClemente has studied the influence of self-efficacy expectation, a key variable from social learning theory, on the maintenance of smoking cessation (23). Ratings of one's ability to cope with various situations that provide cues to smoke, and the degree of temptation each situation presented, were predictive of recidivism following a cessation program. Horwitz, Hindi-Alexander and Wagner found that recidivists, in comparison to abstainers, had lower scores on internal locus of control, did not actively cope with others smoking, and had less support from spouse, other family, and friends. In that study, continuing smokers held the strongest beliefs that smoking causes heart disease and emphysema (24). Intention to stop smoking and normative beliefs about the expectations of significant others regarding one's smoking were found to predict smoking status in college women by Fishbein and colleagues (25).

CONTEMPLATED METHOD OF APPROACH TO THE PROBLEM

Research Questions

The author now provides a clear introduction to the two major research problems. She then goes on to establish directional hypotheses based on previous research findings. This is a good example of the strategy discussed in Chapter 1 of this guide using powerful directional hypotheses and listing them in a sequential order that parallels the logic of the research problem.

Our research questions fall in two categories, the findings regarding our controlled intervention and the specification of a general model for the process of smoking cessation. First, we will ascertain whether the competition/high social facilitation condition is more effective in the control of smoking at the worksite than the control/low social facilitation condition. We will test the following research hypotheses:

1. A higher proportion of smokers will volunteer for the smoking cessation program under the high social facilitation condition than the low social facilitation condition.
2. Of those smokers who volunteer for the program, a higher proportion will quit smoking at the end of the program in the high social facilitation group than in the low social facilitation group.
3. Of those smokers who volunteer for the program, a higher proportion will be abstinent six months following the program in the high social facilitation group than in the low social facilitation group.
4. The change from pre- to post-program saliva thiocyanate level will be greater for the high social facilitation group than for the low social facilitation group at the end of the program and at the six-month follow-up.

We will then specify models for the prediction of the process of smoking cessation and maintenance of cessation. The models will include the following independent variables: cognitive variables from social learning theory (self-efficacy, intentions, motivations for smoking), behavioral variables (smoking history, level of self-help program adherence), social facilitation (modeling of smoking by others, normative beliefs regarding others' expectations, assignment to competitive or control condition), and sociodemographic variables (ethnicity, age, pay level, education, gender). Their relative influence on (a) the probability of quitting after the 20-day self-help program, (b) the probability of abstinence at the 6-month follow up, and (c) the change in thiocyanate level at the 6-month follow up will be specified.

Here, a new idea with an extended purpose is introduced. If it is a truly important part of the study, it would have been better to have included it at an earlier point in the proposal. Given the late introduction and the small amount of detail provided, the idea runs the risk of being regarded as "filler," or as a last minute inspiration that has not been thoroughly thought through by the author.

Besides these variance-oriented research questions, we will conduct case studies of the process of implementation in each region. We will be particularly interested in documenting the sequence of events, explanations of decisions made during implementation, and program area leaders' and employees' perception of the recruitment and cessation processes.

Subjects

Potential subjects are 4781 Department of Human Services (DHS) employees from four regions: Houston, San Antonio, Beaumont and Austin. The numbers of employees by program area within regions are shown in Table 1. The two smallest programs will be collapsed to make approximately equal groups.

In an earlier section, the author proposed to analyze results by age, gender, salary level, and education. Thus, in addition to the information provided in Table 1, it would be appropriate to present a breakdown of the subject population by those factors (a footnote directing reviewers to an appendix containing that information would keep the main body of the proposal uncluttered, while sustaining the image of thorough attention to detail).

The employees are predominantly female, and ethnic breakdowns vary by region. In 1983, a needs assessment of the central office and Travis County region of the Department of Human Services, which was designed by the applicant, indicated that 22.4% smoked, that 36% of the smokers had tried to quit in the last 2 years, and that 70% of the smokers would be likely or very likely to use a stop smoking program at work. Most (81%) of the respondents agreed/strongly agreed that "Cigarette smoke is in the air I breathe at work."

PROPOSAL 4: TABLE 1 Description of Employees by Program Areas Within Regions

REGION	Administration	Protective Services	PROGRAM AREA Aged and Disability	Income Assistance	Family Self-Support	TOTAL
San Antonio	125	247	171	504	75	1122
Houston	180	594	220	998	95	2087
Austin	93	256	212	353	61	975
Beaumont	59	144	118	272	44	637

Study Design

This paragraph shows how data from previous work could supplement the data and interpretations from the proposed study. Again, this reminds reviewers that approval would provide funds for a sustained effort in an important area of health behavior.

The study employs a quasi-experimental control group design (26). Because our intervention is an organizational one, random assignment of individuals to treatment conditions is not possible. We have already conducted three replications of high/low social facilitation conditions using worksite based competitions. For the renewal of this grant, we will assign two social facilitation conditions (based on competition among program areas within a region) to two geographically defined regions of the Texas Department of Human Services in two replications. The first replication will be in conjunction with the Great American Smoke Out and the second with Valentine's Day. Although the groups are nonequivalent, we know that employees of TDHS are similar, and we will have additional comparisons on smoking characteristics and other relevant variables from the initial health promotion survey. Our research design will control adequately for such threats to internal validity as history, maturation, and testing.

The author provides here an exemplary demonstration of thoughtful planning for sample size. As indicated in Chapter 4 of this guide, the power analysis yields concise and credible support for the proposed decision concerning sample size. This also has the double advantage of adding credence to the funding requests that will come later in the proposal. The closing sentence of the paragraph, however, is unfortunate in that it alludes to a recruitment process (not mentioned elsewhere in the proposal) that already is under-way. Reviewers might well regard such action as premature. At the least, the reference will leave them puzzled.

The experimental regions employ 1612 persons, of whom 403 (25%) are expected to be smokers; 3209 are in the control worksites, of whom 802 are expected to be smokers. A smoker is defined as a person who had smoked at least one cigarette in the 7 days previous to the orientation assessment. From the work of Klesges (1), the 1983 TDHS needs assessment, and our 1986 self-help program recruitment figures (24% in competitive sites and 54% in noncompetitive sites), we estimate a 30% recruitment rate using competition and a 10% rate in the standard condition, yielding 121 and 80, respectively, in the smoking programs in the two conditions. A power analysis, using estimates from Klesges (1) and Lowe (20) for recruitment rates under low and high social facilitation, indicates that, with *alpha* = .05, power = .80, a 20% difference in program recruitment (p^1 = .30; p^2 = .10) can be detected using 71 subjects per group. Similarly, using treatment outcomes under low and high social support conditions from the literature (17,19,20), groups with 58 subjects are needed to detect a 20% difference in cessation rate (*alpha* = .05; power = .80; p^1 = .05; p^2 = .25) (27). We currently have 47 subjects in the high social facilitation and 9 in the low social facilitation cessation conditions.

An organization-wide health promotion survey to determine the number and characteristics of smokers will be administered to employees in each region in September, 1987. For three weeks prior to GASO or Valentine's Day, an intensive recruitment campaign for smokers to enlist in the minimal intervention cessation program will be conducted in each region. Sessions to introduce the self-help materials, along with recruitment and program awareness activities, will be held during this period. Contest awards will be made on either the Great American Smoke Out, an important time for antismoking awareness for the population at large, or Valentine's Day. Program participants will be pretested at their orientation session and will receive posttests at the end of the 20-day program and 6 months later.

Description of Interventions

The section that follows provides a detailed description of the intervention. As the incentive value of rewards is one of the driving forces behind the competitive aspect of the intervention, it would have been helpful to give reviewers an explicit example of how they would be determined—a point on which the opening paragraph is not entirely clear.

In the high social facilitation condition, social support to quit will be engendered through a competition among the four program areas in the competition condition regions to enroll the most smokers in the intervention and to enlist the most smoker supporters. The contest will be highly publicized, and progress will be visually presented in a region-wide newsletter distributed to all employees and in a lobby display at the regional headquarters. Besides this recognition of winning, participants from the program area that enrolls the highest proportion of smokers and smoker-supporters will have a chance to win a $100, $50, or $25 savings bond in a drawing on GASO or Valentine's Day.

In the standard (low social facilitation) condition, recruitment to the program will be through messages directed to smokers. The amount of publicity (number of memos, numbers and size of posters, etc.) will be the same in both groups. Also, visible signs of program participation ("I Quit" buttons, no smoking desk and wall signs, etc.) will be available for employees in both treatment conditions.

The marketing interventions will be coordinated by the research assistants, who will work closely with the DHS Regional Wellness Coordinators and designated DHS employees in each region. Smokers and smoker supporters will return program registration forms to the designated DHS employees. Smokers will be assigned to a group orientation at their convenience, and smoker supporters will receive a packet of materials to assist them in encouraging smokers to quit.

The self-help intervention to be received by all smoking cessation program participants will be *Freedom from Smoking in 20 Days*, a 64-page cessation manual (28). Subjects who report quitting at the completion of this program will receive *A Lifetime of Freedom from Smoking*, a 28-page maintenance manual (29). These materials, which use a cognitive/behavioral approach with emphasis on self-management, have been evaluated (17,19,20). We add an orientation session to this self-help treatment following the protocol developed and tested by Windsor and colleagues (19,30). In 1986, we produced and used a videotape introduction to the program. The tape included TDHS employees who served as coping and mastery models for smoking cessation, describing why and how they quit and remained abstinent. A clinical psychologist provided an overview of the self-help manual, discussed ambivalence about quitting, and attempted to raise viewers' self-efficacy about quitting. The orientation is aimed at enhancing commitment to cessation, social support, and skills in behavioral self-monitoring and deep-breathing used in smoking cessation. All subjects will be told that the biochemical tests at the orientation and 6-month follow-up will measure exposure to cigarette smoke.

Commitment to adherence and cessation will be enhanced by having participants pay $5.00 to join the program, which will be refunded if they turn in their self monitoring sheets and have quit smoking by the end of the program. Funds not returned will be pooled and divided among the smokers who have quit. This will be done within each program area in the noncompetition regions. In the competition regions, the funds will be pooled across program areas and divided among the quitters in the program area with the highest proportion of quitters.

Collection of Data

Data will be collected four times. A 25% sample in each region will be requested to complete the initial health promotion survey. The self-help program participants will be asked for information at the orientation session, at the completion of the program, and at the 6-month follow-up. The smoking supporters will be queried concerning their activities 1 month after they volunteer.

> Here the author creates an effective summary by listing all the variables in a single table. By grouping them within the sequential steps of the study, the reader gains a sense of the wider time frame for the investigation. In addition, examples of survey and measurement instruments are referenced to an appendix—where they are available for interested reviewers without intruding on the main presentation. It would have been helpful to note that the follow-up system also appears in an appendix.

The specific variables to be measured at each of the four time periods are outlined in Table 2. Description of measurement of the dependent and independent variables and copies of the 1986 questionnaires are included in the Appendix. The longest instrument (75 items) will be completed during the group orientation

PROPOSAL 4: TABLE 2 Overview of Data Collection: Variables by Testing Times

Initial Health Promotion Survey/All Employees (18 items)	Self-help Program Participant Pretest (75 items)	Self-help Program Participant Immediate Posttest (38 items)	Self-help Program Participant 6-Month and 1-Year Follow-up (33 items)
Age	Age	Smoking Status	Smoking Status
Sex	Sex	Self-efficacy for Coping with Urges	Self-efficacy for Coping with Urges
Ethnicity	Ethnicity	Program component Usefulness	Saliva Thiocyanate
Pay Group	Pay Group	Co-worker Support	Saliva Cotinine (quitters only)
Education	Education		
Family History of CHD	Family History of CHD		
Smoking History	Smoking History		
Intention to Quit	Intention to Quit		
	Perceived Consequences of Smoking		
	Smoking Topology		
	Smoking Models		
	Normative Beliefs about Smoking		
	Motivation to Quit		
	Self-efficacy for Quitting		
	Saliva Thiocyanate		

287

session. For the initial employee survey, we will use two follow-ups, with a post card system to ensure anonymity, for the initial survey. Program participants will be followed-up by mail and telephone to ensure completeness of the data for each case.

Data Analysis

Tests of proportion using Chi-Square (27) will be used to test differences in the proportion of smokers who volunteer under the two conditions, the proportion of volunteer smokers who quit (using self-report confirmed by SCN level) at program completion, and the proportion of smokers who are abstinent at 6 months following completion of the program. Regional differences in quit levels within treatments will also be tested. Participants will be compared to smokers at the worksite using the health promotion survey and pre-test data to see whether they differ in demographic, smoking history, or heart disease risk characteristics.

Analysis of covariance, using baseline SCN as covariate, will be used to examine the main effects of treatment group and region upon the dependent variable of SCN level at the 6-month follow-up. Significant regional differences may be a function of the ethnic or other demographic differences of employees within region, organizational variation in the way the marketing conditions were implemented or some other factor, such as smoking policies, unique to a region. A better understanding of such differences may be gained through the regression models of influences on reduction, quitting, and abstinence from smoking.

At the next stage of our analysis, we will examine the influences of individual difference variables that would be expected to influence changes in smoking behavior under both social facilitation conditions. Logistic regression, a multivariate technique for binary dependent variables analogous to least-squares regression, will be used for smoking status dependent variables. Logistic regression models will be used to study the selective effects of social support, health locus of control, self-efficacy expectations for quitting or coping with urges to smoke, smoking history, ethnicity, education, occupation, and level of program participation on the log-odds of quitting and abstention from smoking at 6 months. A similar analysis using SCN at the 6-month follow-up as the dependent variable and the psychosocial, behavioral, and social structural variables as independent variables will be carried out using multiple regression. Hierarchical models will be used to isolate the relative explanatory power of program adherence, smoking history, psychosocial correlates of smoking, and demographic variables consistent with our multilevel theoretical orientation.

EXPERIMENTAL PROBLEMS

This is a section of the proposal that is specified in the application format used by the funding agency. In the process of responding to the demand for comment on the experimental problems, the applicant takes the opportunity to point out the close and ongoing relationship she has with both the managements at the test sites where the study will be conducted, and the administrators of state and regional health agencies to be involved.

No experimental problems are expected in the course of this research. The proposed research is an extension of the TDHS smoking cessation programs begun in 1986 under AHA funding. The self-help smoking cessation intervention is widely used and has been evaluated. Likewise, the testing procedures have been used in many studies. The adequacy of the competition to generate high social facilitation is dependent on the cooperation and active support of management at each of the worksite offices. The investigator worked closely with the TDHS regional wellness coordinators and with the state wellness coordinator and personnel director (see letters of support). The research project is embedded within the regions' wellness programs, which have the full support of DHS management.

SIGNIFICANCE OF THE RESEARCH

In the following section the author relates potential findings to several areas of benefit: the participants, the worksites, the theoretical basis for the field of public health, and, of considerable interest to reviewers from the American Heart Association, the implementation of state legislation through agencies charged with responsibility for public health.

The 1987 Surgeon General's Report "The Health Consequences of Involuntary Smoking" calls for smoke-free worksites (31). This report will add impetus to the movement to establish worksite smoking policies and to reduce ambient tobacco smoke in the worksite. When such policies are established, it is important to offer smoking employees opportunities to quit smoking. Self-help smoking cessation programs offer great promise in the worksite setting because of their flexibility. Recruitment to programs and maintenance of cessation following a program are key concerns. Our research field tests in a worksite setting the impact of high social facilitation generated through a competition to increase the penetration and effectiveness of an already evaluated self-help smoking cessation program.

In addition, we will specify a multilevel model of smoking behavior, including the relative influence of self-efficacy, health locus of control, social support for smoking and quitting, smoking history, and demographic variables upon quitting, independent of the social facilitation condition. Programs may then be designed to augment levels of those variables shown to be important and individual treatment approaches based on these factors can be planned.

Our research findings are immediately useful for the implementation of the Texas State Employee Health Fitness Act. The Governor's Commission on Physical Fitness (GCPF), which is responsible for overseeing the development of health programs in state agencies, needs field-tested, turn-key risk reduction programs for the worksite. Based on our findings, the GCPF can recommend a smoking cessation program to the state agencies and provide guidelines and training for its implementation.

ETHICAL ASPECTS OF THE PROPOSED RESEARCH

The risks to the participants in this project are minimal and are far outweighed by the benefits of stopping smoking. Successful quitters may feel some discomfort during withdrawal from cigarettes and nonsuccessful quitters may feel some sense of failure and low self-esteem. These outcomes are common, but are not serious. They are experienced by all smokers who attempt to quit. The competition approach to recruitment may exert some social pressure on smokers to participate and thus carries some risk of coercion. The possibility of perceived coercion from the competition is real, although the competition emphasizes improvement of health and the importance of local support, and the stakes are low. These risks will be minimized by providing techniques for dealing with withdrawal symptoms and specific behavioral strategies for "What to do if you fall off the wagon." The potential for coercion in the competition will be reduced by using a positive supportive approach in the marketing, as has been done with the Great American Smoke Out. Nonsmoking supporters will be given specific instructions for being supportive to smokers attempting to quit. The health promotion hotline questionnaire is completely confidential, with no identifying number. Program participants' records are linked by a code available only to the principal investigator, which will be destroyed following completion of data collection. Informed consent will be obtained from all project participants (see letters).

> The budget for the proposed study is presented below. Notice both the level of detail provided and how the following justification section is used to rationalize individual items. Inclusion of experience from previous studies lends powerful support to these arguments.

OUTLINE OF PROPOSED BUDGET

ITEM

Personnel (itemize)

Graduate Research Assistant II (B.S.; 9 mo; 50%)	$6,470
Graduate Research Assistant II (B.S.; 9 mo; 50%)	6,470
Social Security and other benefits	3,105
Subtotal	16,045

Equipment (itemize)

30MB half-height hard disk and cable	560
Desktop publishing software and PC mouse	675
2 Tape recorders, microphones, and transcription equipment	350
Subtotal	1,585

Supplies (itemize major purchases)
Thiocyanate and cotinine analysis	3,100
Videotapes, computer tapes, diskettes	100
Postage (posttest questionnaires, correspondence)	400
Photocopying	100
Stationary supplies, paper for questionnaires and forms, posters and displays	350
Long distance telephone	150
Competition prizes and incentive for survey returns	450
Subtotal	4,650

Other expenses, including travel and printing
Travel of PI and Research Assistants to sites	1,620
Travel of PI to professional meetings	700
Publication costs	400
Subtotal	2,720
Overhead (10%)	2,500
TOTAL	$27,500

JUSTIFICATION OF BUDGET

Graduate Research Assistant (GRA) II: The two half-time (50%) Graduate Research Assistants II will assist the principal investigator in the administration of this project and will be responsible for the collection of qualitative and quantitative data in Houston and San Antonio in the fall and Austin and Beaumont in the spring. They will be responsible for the management of data collection, the organization of the recruitment campaigns, and will conduct focus groups, interviews, and observations at the regions. They also will conduct the behavioral skills sessions for the project participants. They will not receive university credit for this work. My experience in conducting the research program last year in these regions (one of which was Austin) with one GRA II has led to a request for two such positions. It is essential that one person maintain full attention on one region for the program to be implemented successfully. The expanded qualitative research makes this even more essential.

Equipment: The hard disk will be used for back up on the computer system funded in 1986, which has one half-height hard disk drive. The desktop publishing software and mouse will be used to prepare professional quality newsletters for publicity at the sites. The tape recorders are for use by the GRAs in the conduct of interviews and focus groups for the qualitative research.

GRA II and PI travel to sites: The organization and implementation of the program and conduct of the qualitative research will require extensive time on site. The budget item covers 4 trips to Beaumont (@ $50), and 6 trips to Houston (@ $120). This essential item was underbudgeted in the 1986 grant.

Note: Self-help smoking cessation materials are being donated by the American Lung Association of Texas. Data entry will be provided at no charge by the Texas Department of Human Services.

At this point the proposal included the list of references and four appendices: (a) letters of support, (b) questionnaires, (c) consent forms, and (d) information concerning measurement of the primary variables. We have reprinted here only selected portions of the last two appendices. The letter to employees and the attached post card are reproduced below because they represent a unique means of obtaining consent—one particularly appropriate to the conditions of the proposed study.

PROPOSAL 4: APPENDIX 1
CONSENT FORM FOR QUESTIONNAIRE

You have been selected in a random sample of employees from two regions of the Department of Human Services. You are invited to complete this questionnaire regarding your lifestyle health habits for a worksite health promotion research project funded by the American Heart Association and being conducted by the University of Texas at Austin. The questionnaire is completely anonymous. It will take approximately 10 minutes to complete. An interoffice postcard is attached to the questionnaire. Your signing and returning it will remove your name from the mailing list. If you agree to fill in the questionnaire, return it separately through interoffice mail. When we receive your postcard, we will eliminate your name from the follow-up list so you will not be contacted again regarding your completing the questionnaire.

Thank you for your assistance. It is very important that you respond so that we will have a complete picture of employee health behavior at your worksite before we begin the research program. Your decision whether or not to complete the questionnaire will not prejudice your future relations with the University of Texas at Austin or the Department of Human Services. Please call me at 512-555-1234 if you have any questions about the questionnaire or the research project.

Sincerely,

Nell H. Gottlieb, Ph.D.
Assistant Professor
Principal Investigator

The content of the attached post card is indicated below.

_____

Please return this post card through interoffice mail.
I have read the information at the beginning of the survey.
__I have agreed to fill in the health promotion questionnaire for the University of Texas at Austin and have returned the questionnaire separately through interoffice mail.
__I do not wish to complete the questionnaire.
Please remove my name from the follow-up list.

_____   _____
Signature   Date

(Please print first initial and last name
if your handwriting is difficult to read)

PROPOSAL 4: APPENDIX 2
MEASUREMENT OF DEPENDENT
AND INDEPENDENT VARIABLES

The original appendix contained detailed descriptions of how each variable would be measured, complete with references to information on reliability and validity. That material is reproduced here in abbreviated form.

Self-reported smoking will be measured using the Health Insurance Study Smoking Battery (32,33). These items include whether or not the respondent uses specific tobacco products and the frequency and duration of current or former cigarette smoking. In addition, the number of attempts to quit smoking, the types of approaches used, and the longest duration of abstinence will be obtained. Intention to quit smoking in 3 months will be measured on a 4-point Likert scale from "very unlikely" to "very likely." For the follow-ups, whether or not the respondent has been continuously abstinent since the program will be asked. At the orientation and follow-ups, respondents will be asked the number of hours per day they are exposed to second-hand cigarette smoke. This will be used to evaluate borderline thiocyanate measures for validation of cessation.

Saliva thiocyanate (SCN) and *cotinine* will be used as physiological indicators for smoking (34,35). Thiocyanate is a metabolite of the hydrogen cyanide in smoke, which has a half-life of 14 days. Although estimates vary, specificity (93%) and sensitivity (98%) using a cutoff point of 85 M/L to distinguish smokers from non-smokers have been reported. Limitations include dietary interference from passive smoking, marijuana smoking, and consumption of beer and certain other foods, and the inability to distinguish light smokers from nonsmokers. Cotinine, a metabolite of nicotine, is unique to tobacco, has a half life of 30 hours, and is able to distinguish light smokers from nonsmokers. Costing four times as much as SCN, it is too expensive to use for all subjects. However, it will be used to confirm quitting. Saliva samples will be taken at the orientation session and at 6-month follow-up. The biochemical assays will be carried out by the Division of Epidemiology, University of Minnesota, which does this as a nonprofit service.

Self-efficacy to cope with specific urges to smoke is measured using the 31 item Smoking Situations scale of DiClemente and Prochaska (23,32). Respondents are asked to rate on a 5-point Likert scale, "How tempted you would be to smoke in this situation?" and, "How confident are you that you would not smoke in this situation?" for such situations as "when alone and feeling depressed" and "when I am feeling accepted by someone." The *alpha* reliability scores for the temptation scale (.97) and confidence scale (.98) are very high. Inter-item correlations for the self-efficacy scale ranged from .44–.93 (mean = .69).

APPENDIX A:
ANNOTATED BIBLIOGRAPHY
OF SUPPLEMENTARY REFERENCES

Information that will be helpful in preparing a research proposal can be found in a variety of publications. Some valuable direction can be found in sources that focus primarily on other topics. In the first category of such references are the textbooks that deal with the conduct of research. Some of them do contain sections or chapters on the proposal, but as the central concern of the text is with the technical specification of design and method, the treatment of the proposal generally is brief and superficial. Standard references, such as Borg and Gall's *Educational Research* (1989) and Lincoln and Guba's *Naturalistic Inquiry* (1985) are available in most college bookstores and libraries. Colleagues, committee advisors, and research professors can help the novice locate a research text that will best serve his or her particular proposal.

A second category contains books designed to assist the reader in obtaining a grant—for support of research or (commonly) a development project. In many of these, the focus is on how to locate funding sources, how to match proposed projects with the agency agenda, and how the proposal evaluation process works. We have included several of these in the annotations below, but again, because the primary focus often is not on the development of a research proposal, readers will do well to examine library or bookstore copies before purchase.

A small third category consists of documents prepared by professional and scholarly organizations as guides in the area of research ethics, manuals for document preparation, or as general advice for novice investigators. An appropriate selection of these should be on the desk of everyone who does research, and the novice will soon find that the standard references among them, such as the *Publication Manual of the American Psychological Association* (1983), quickly becomes dog-eared with use. We have not attempted to include the publications for each disciplinary specialization, but some of the most helpful generic documents are listed below.

Finally, a small number of texts are now available that, like this one, are directed to the needs of people faced with the task of preparing a research proposal—whether for academic or grant solicitation purposes. Some of these presume investigation in certain areas (education, medicine, or social service, for example), but others are directed to a more general audience. Most are oriented toward empirical/quantitative studies, but some, like Marshall and Rossman's *Designing Qualitative Research* (1989), serve investigators who wish to employ other paradigms. The political and social circumstances that are unique to graduate study are central in some texts, while the mechanics of writing are given greater attention in others. We have tried to include a wide selection of the proposal books now on the market. The best choice for many novices would be to combine several of those that serve your particular needs—with the present text (of course).

American Psychological Association. *Ethical principles in the conduct of research with human participants.* (1982). Washington, DC: Author.

In the first few pages of this monograph, a committee of the American Psychological Association presents 11 ethical principles by which to guide the conduct of research with human subjects. The principles make worthwhile reading by themselves. The remaining sections of this booklet provide a detailed discussion of issues that were considered in the development of the principles. This is an essential reference for those conducting research involving human subjects.

American Psychological Association. *Publication manual of the American Psychological Association* (3rd ed.). (1983). Washington, DC: Author.

This paperbound manual contains a comprehensive set of standards for the technical process of scholarly writing. It is a standard reference that is consulted frequently by most graduate students and professors in the social and behavioral sciences. The major topics covered are: (a) content and organization of a manuscript, (b) expression of ideas, (c) editorial style, (d) typing instructions, and (e) submitting a manuscript and proofreading. The book includes thorough illustration of standards for punctuation, construction of tables, and use of citations in the text. The sections on headings, seriation, and nonsexist language will be particularly valuable to novice proposal writers. The suggested format and citation style are now accepted or required by a large number of universities and research journals.

Bauer, D. G. (1988). *The "how to" grants manual* (2nd ed.). New York: Macmillan.

Written by a specialist who has conducted seminars for thousands of grant seekers, the manual is aimed at making the grant seeking and proposal process efficient and cost effective. Although written for social service agency personnel who wish to receive programmatic funding, the book will be valuable for novice grant seekers in other areas. The sections on both federal and foundation/corporate funding sources provide excellent information on finding grants. The author presents the grant seeking and proposal process in a series of steps and provides advice for each of them. Inclusion of detail such as forms and checklists for maintaining a proposal-development notebook, questions to ask funding sources, and sample letters will make the text interesting even for the veteran grant seeker.

Becker, H. S. (1986). *Writing for social scientists*. Chicago: University of Chicago Press.

In the short interval since its 1986 publication, this slim paperback has become an underground classic among graduate students in the social sciences and education. At a few institutions it is recommended or required in research methods courses and dissertation seminars, but most of the dog-eared copies circulate through student support groups or are loaned from professorial shelves in an effort to jar loose a few pages from a hopeless case of "dissertation block."

Becker has not given us another form and style manual. The book is a collection of nine elegantly simple essays dealing with the problems of writing about research (a 10th chapter on confronting the psychological risks of writing is contributed by sociologist Pamela Richards). Becker attends to the day-to-day work demands of producing a document—whether a research proposal, dissertation, or journal article. These include the familiars of procrastination, writing successive drafts, editing your own work, getting help, using (or not using) the word processor, and how to write clear and attractive prose within the confines of academic conventions.

It takes a special kind of confidence to write a book about good writing, particularly if that book also has to give helpful advice to people who don't know how to do it. Becker does it with grace and gentle humor that will remind many readers of another slim volume—Strunk and White (1979). Easy for him, you say? Yes, Becker is a well-established scholar with a formidable reputation for his writing style. He succeeds, however, by remembering exactly why writing is not at all easy for most people. If you don't have a reputation, tenure, solid work habits, and lots of confidence in your prose voice, in fact, if you suspect your writing might reveal you as an inarticulate clod, or even as an academic fraud, Becker is the man for you.

Behling, J. H. (1984). *Guidelines for preparing the research proposal*. Lanham, MD: University Press of America.

University Press provides only limited capacity to market the books on its list. It therefore is testimony to the worth of this slim volume that it has survived for more than a decade and passed through at least one revision. Its virtues clearly are resident in two characteristics. First, this is one of the few manuals explicitly devoted to research grant proposals that does not take a "grantsmanship" approach. For this author, sound research, carefully and thoroughly explained, is the only way to sell a proposal—and the only reason it should be funded. Sound scholarship, not slick strategy, is the focus here.

The second virtue is the use of an outline procedure for proposal development that will have particular appeal for some researchers designing some studies. One evident limitation is that nearly all of the attention is given to experimental designs rather than to historical or qualitative studies. In addition, all of the recommendations for reference material are now out of date. With those limitations in mind, however, if the particular strengths of this text fit the needs of your proposal task or your personal values, this is an honest and inexpensive little book that may return your investment with interest.

Campbell, D. T., & Stanley, J. C. (1963). *Experimental and quasi-experimental designs for research.* Chicago: Rand McNally.

Although this is ordinarily thought of as a classic treatise on research design (certainly it is one of the most lucid treatments of design ever produced for a broad readership), the authors of this elegant monograph have so much to say about the broad standards of systematic inquiry that it should be consumed by every graduate student early in his or her research preparation. Building on the format provided by a theoretical model of validity for inquiry, the authors examine 16 different quantitative designs for research and a host of vital issues that touch on the preparation of sound proposals.

Committee on the Conduct of Science. (1989). *On being a scientist.* Washington, DC: National Academy Press.

This small 22-page booklet was a project of the National Academy of Science's Committee on the Conduct of Science. It provides an overview of the scientific process and is interesting reading both for those beginning their research careers and experienced researchers. With two major sections on the nature of scientific research and social mechanisms in science, a wide variety of topics are covered—for example: values in science, treatment of data, human error, fraud, and apportioning credit. Easy to read with sidebars to supplement the text, this booklet is well worth the modest price ($5.00 at the time this was written) and the investment of reading time.

Day, R. A. (1988). *How to write and publish a scientific paper* (3rd ed.). Phoenix: Oryx.

Although the author did not set out to address issues related to the proposal process, he provides an excellent overview of the writing process for young scholars. In a logical sequence, he examines each aspect of writing a paper for publication. Topics in the book include how to prepare a title, list the authors, design a table and submit or present a paper. Chapters in the second half of the book give attention to the mechanics of writing and provide an overview of important concepts in scholarly exposition. While the book is written from the perspective of a scholar in the natural sciences, it requires no specific knowledge of that area. The liberal and effective use of humor throughout the book makes easy reading for both novices and experienced writers.

Krathwohl, D. R. (1988). *How to prepare a research proposal* (3rd ed.). Syracuse, NY: Syracuse University Press.

The 1965 edition of this venerable text consisted of 50 pages. The latest version runs to over 300, nearly all of that expansion being devoted to the preparation of proposals by postdoctoral researchers seeking support from granting agencies. Only 48 pages are devoted to dissertation and thesis proposals, and much of that deals with executing the study and writing the final report. Although those pages contain much practical advice about negotiating life as a graduate student (selecting an advisor, forming a committee, and using the dissertation or thesis as a self-development project), there is not much directed to the specifics of preparing the proposal document itself.

Within the much larger sections of the book devoted to writing grant proposals, Krathwohl's strength continues to be his ability to describe the process of conceptualizing and defining the research problem in logical progressions and common sense terms. For that, the book is unexcelled by anything on the market. The rest seems more like a collection which has grown through three editions like an unruly child, without the discipline of orderly sequence or the shaping force of strong thematic content. You may find something valuable in the 14 chapters and 24 figures—or you may not. Unless you are preparing your first research grant proposal, this is a book to be thumbed through in the library, or borrowed from a colleague, before investing.

Lauffer, A. (1983). *Grantsmanship.* Beverly Hills, CA: Sage.

In this easy-to-read book, a master of grantsmanship and resource development describes in step-by-step detail how to write successful proposals for grants to support social service programs. The author makes clear the distinctions among government, foundation, and business/professional sources of funding. This book does not describe the specific process of developing research proposals, but the imaginative reader will find that many of the suggested procedures travel well from social service to scholarship.

Strategies to use in working with different kinds of funding sources are described in detail. This includes a discussion of how various review processes work and differences in the review criteria used by various grantors. Also included are excellent exercises designed to develop the analytical skills described in the chapters. Sections on what to do after the proposal has been submitted, how to deal with rejection, and how to swing into action if the proposal is funded make this text a particularly useful guide for the beginner.

Long, T. J., Convey, J. J., & Chwalek, A. R. (1991). *Completing dissertations in the behavioral sciences and education.* San Francisco: Jossey-Bass.

The title here is accurate. The book is about completing dissertations. The authors have written a survival guide designed to help students finish the degrees for which they enrolled in college. To that extent, then, it is reasonable that this book pays far more attention to navigating through graduate programs, and life as a graduate student, than most texts that deal with dissertations. It does systematically what many research training programs do only unsystematically. It shows how to lay out a timetable, develop a topic for inquiry, craft good research questions within that area, execute pilot studies, and prepare a proposal. The book also confronts a host of problems for which most graduate programs make little accommodation and provide no advice: the stress of study on family life, financial difficulties, lack of continuity in program structure, and the recruitment and use of technical consultation and secretarial assistance.

The 43 pages devoted to the proposal itself are sound, if rather traditional (with most of the emphasis on quantitative studies), and general rather than specific. Though extensive, the list of references now is a decade old and thereby less helpful than it should be. There are no specimen proposals included, and the utility of the proposal section suffers accordingly. The small chapter on the proposal defense and subsequent revisions, however, is an unusual and valuable feature.

Lucy, B. (1990). *Handbook for academic authors* (revised ed.). Cambridge, UK: Cambridge University Press.

Although it provides little direct information about the proposal writing process, this book offers practical advice on publishing for the beginning scholar. Written by a university professor who has been an editor, author, and owner of a publishing company, the book provides instructions for writing journal articles and extensive information about preparing a manuscript for publication in book form. It also contains many examples and a detailed reference list. The book's nontechnical language, will be especially valuable to those wanting to turn a dissertation into a book or to prepare a research report for submission to a journal.

Madsen, D. (1992). *Successful dissertations and theses* (2nd ed.). San Francisco: Jossey-Bass.

With the addition of new material on the use of computers, this new edition largely mirrors the 1983 volume, and with good reason. That text was explicitly devoted to the needs of graduate students writing dissertations and theses. With logical organization, nontechnical, straightforward prose, and excellent use of examples drawn from actual proposals, it fully deserved its reputation as a sound introductory handbook.

Unlike many other dissertation guides, this one focuses primarily on the proposal rather than on performing the research or writing up the results. Within the broad rubric of educational research, it is more eclectic than many texts, including proposals for both experimental and historical studies in the appendix. The book does not, however, make any explicit provision for the development of proposals using the qualitative paradigm—and given the presumed audience, that is a considerable limitation.

The three chapters covering use of reference sources, library retrieval, and the transition from notes to document, when taken together, represent a fine introduction to that phase of proposal preparation. Altogether, this is a thoughtfully prepared guide directly aimed at the needs of the first-time investigator.

Marshall, C., & Rossman, G. B. (1989). *Designing qualitative research.* Newbury Park, CA: Sage.

In the present market, this is the only book devoted exclusively to designing qualitative research. It does not put primary emphasis on preparing the proposal itself (this is not a how-to-do-it guidebook for writing). What it does focus on are: (a) framing the research question within the traditions of the paradigm, the existing body of theory and research, and the conventions of methodology; (b) designing the study through selection of data collection strategy and analysis procedures; and (c) managing time and resources so that the study can be completed.

Graduate students will find the final chapter on defending the value and logic of qualitative research particularly helpful. Many professors who teach graduate research courses in qualitative research find such argument uncomfortable, often feeling that the time is past when there is any need to defend the paradigm. The authors understand full well, however, that graduate students still must face those questions. They provide a firmly positive and pragmatic commentary on the matter which nicely avoids sounding defensive. It is impossible for us to imagine a qualitative thesis or dissertation proposal which would not profit from a reading of this volume—as early in the process as possible. Teamed with our own text, the two would offer a solid basis for launching the design of a qualitative study.

Martin, M. D., & Landrum, J. W. (1990). *Proposal power.* Bloomington, IN: Phi Delta Kappa.

For unalloyed optimism, this book takes the prize. "If you have never written a proposal before, we hope this handbook will make the task easy, even fun." One suspects at the outset that they can't be talking about dissertations or, perhaps, even about research. Such proves to be the case, as the target is the grant proposal, the audience is educators (taken broadly to include school teachers and administrators as well as service agency personnel), and the proposed activity is not research, but service projects and program development. Nevertheless, if you need help with the sections of a research grant proposal dealing with such things as budget, staffing, activities, management, and facilities, this text would be an excellent place to start.

Complete with check lists and tear-out work sheets, reading the book and working through the training examples is much like taking a proposal-writing workshop (for beginners), and that is precisely how the authors use the present document in their Phi Delta Kappa-sponsored two-day, regional workshops. Knowing a great deal about preparing grant proposals in education, and having expertise in preparing instructional materials, proves to be a happy combination in this handy workbook.

Ogden, E. H. (1991). *Completing your doctoral dissertation or masters thesis*. Lancaster, PA: Technomic.

The author is irreverent and blunt. She defines the task of writing a dissertation as a contest between the graduate student and the university. There is no heady talk here about acquiring the sacred skills of scholarship, or having a transformative experience through inquiry. This is about getting the job done, period! With an outrageous subtitle ("In two semesters or less") and a chapter on selecting the research topic that begins with, "Forget interesting, go for tolerably non-boring," the text clearly is designed to inflame academics like us.

We have read the book, however, as have some of our graduate students. Although it does neatly skewer a number of sacred cows grazing on the lawns of the graduate school, it contains little that is actively subversive to writing a good proposal, doing a good study, and learning all you can in the process. The author simply believes that the whole thing could be done with a good deal more attention to economy of time and effort. There is nothing inherently wrong with that. By ignoring such factors, many programs do encourage some students to drift along without acquiring any additional benefit from the extra time and cost involved.

Ogden has lots of advice and a number of process aids designed to get you moving and maintain momentum once under-way. There is little substantial help offered for doing the work of designing and writing the proposal, but dozens of small things that can make it all go faster (and cheaper) are given close attention. Some of you don't need that advice, and others would consider it irrelevant (if not improper). For those who want some help in pulling everything together and pushing on with the job, this may be what you need.

We want to enter one serious caveat. The emphasis on time inevitably has the effect of making some studies (particularly those using qualitative or quantitative designs that require fieldwork) sound less than desirable. If Ogden were to persuade you not to try your hand at something because it might take a bit longer to collect and analyze the data, we would think that an unhappy result. Thoughtful attention to how you use your time and money is one thing, letting the calendar run your life is quite another. The final arbiter has to be doing good work and learning what you need to learn, not simply getting a degree. Anything that serves to undercut that goal is indeed subversive to your best interest.

Panel on Scientific Responsibility and the Conduct of Research. (1992). *Responsible science: Ensuring the integrity of the research process* (vol. 1). Washington, DC: National Academy Press.

Published as a cooperative effort by the National Academy of Sciences, the National Academy of Engineering, and the Institute of Medicine, this volume contains a comprehensive and critical examination of the factors that influence scientific integrity. With details about how the panel developed its recommendations, an executive summary provides 12 standards intended to strengthen the research enterprise in all contexts. Topics addressed in the book include factors influencing integrity, the research environment, misconduct in science, handling allegations of misconduct, and guidelines for encouraging responsible research. This book will be of interest to those starting their research careers, as well as senior scholars with an interest in research ethics. For those experiencing ethical dilemmas, the book will be a valuable source of advice that is both pragmatic about the trade-offs that attend alternative decisions and clear about what constitutes ethical behavior.

Pyrczak, F., & Bruce, R.R. (1992). *Writing empirical research reports: A basic guide for students of the social and behavioral sciences.* Los Angeles: Pyrczak Publishing.

At first glance, this 8 x 11-inch book appears to be just another how-to-do-it cookbook. First impressions, however, are not always accurate. It provides excellent advice for writers of empirical research. Each chapter addresses a section of the research report (e.g., hypotheses, title, introduction, method, etc.) with principles to be followed in writing that particular section. The principles are supported by examples and "improved versions" emphasizing their correct use. The appendices include a checklist of all the principles (probably itself worth the modest price of this paperbound book), a reprint of an article addressing what reviewers look for in research manuscripts, and a list of suggested readings, software, and videotapes. Even though the authors concentrate on research reports, most of the principles also apply to writing proposals.

Rudestam, K. E., & Newton, R. R. (1992). *Surviving your dissertation: A comprehensive guide to content and process.* Newbury Park, CA: Sage.

This text styles itself as a comprehensive "how to" compendium. It falls short of that ambitious goal, but it does contain some good advice that will be useful to students embarking on preparation of a proposal. The authors do consider proposal building as a major step in the research process, devoting three chapters to that task. Those include attention to selecting a research problem, reviewing the literature, and describing the methods. Other chapters provide support for the proposal writer through attention to such considerations as use of a personal computer, overcoming emotional barriers, confronting ethical problems, and dealing with the task of writing.

Reflecting their own background and research interests, the authors draw most of their examples from the behavioral sciences, particularly from studies in the areas of mental health and social services. It is not surprising, therefore, that the text does introduce the possibility of qualitative research. Brief attention is given to this option in both a general chapter on approaches to inquiry, and in the section on explaining the research plan. While it may not be the promised comprehensive "how to" resource, some elements will be valuable to the graduate student writing his or her first proposal.

Schumacher, D. (1992). *Get funded!* Newbury Park, CA: Sage.

This small book is advertised as "a practical guide for scholars seeking research support from business." It begins with an explanation of the corporate environment, gives suggestions on how the researcher can discover the needs and interests of corporations, how the researcher can convince corporate managers that the research project is important to the corporation's success, and how such research programs, once developed, can be organized. The author emphasizes that only by thinking in terms of developing a partnership with business, rather than attempting to acquire a grant with no strings attached, will the researcher be successful.

The book is written in very simple, straightforward language, explaining the criteria to be used to select a company, the differences in the research climate of business and academia, the realities of corporate politics and how they affect research partnerships, and how to develop and write the contract that will be signed by the corporation and the university. The author adds a particularly thoughtful discussion of the dangers posed by such partnerships to the university's cherished role as a reservoir and incubator of free thought, unbiased observations, and unrestrained publication of research findings. Declining support for research by both state and federal governments dictates that most investigators will have to widen their search for funding. As the author suggests, developing research partnerships with business may very well be the wave of the future. Those who wish to test the corporate waters will find this text to be extremely helpful.

Smith, R. V. (1990). *Graduate research: A guide for students in the sciences* (2nd ed.). New York: Plenum.

Although intended for students in the natural and biomedical sciences, this book will be valuable for novice researchers in all fields. The author provides an overview of the graduate student experience in research-oriented departments and universities. The book begins with a review of department and university organization, information that may be particularly helpful to graduate students attempting to understand the obscurities of graduate education in large institutions. The chapters on "Ethics and the Scientist" and "Research with Human Subjects, Animals, and Biohazards" and an appendix containing advice on preparing consent forms for human subjects will be especially valuable to readers who have not previously dealt with such matters.

Sternberg, D. (1981). *How to complete and survive a doctoral dissertation*. New York: St. Martin's.

In terms of the beliefs expressed concerning scholarship, research, graduate education, writing, and the nature and purpose of proposals, this text is the closest match to *Proposals that Work* now in print. The difference between the two lies in the distribution of attention to those topics. In that respect, the books are mirror images of each other. Sternberg provides two large sections, one dealing with the complex psychological process of preparing to undertake a dissertation, the other with the complexities of executing that task—and in the middle is a third, much smaller, section devoted to the proposal.

Written by a professor who has had long experience in the dissertation-advising business, the approach throughout is thoughtful and deeply sensitive to the difficulties that most doctoral candidates encounter. The section on proposal writing shares our own definition of the document as a contract with the university, as a plan for action, as the first chapters of the dissertation, and as a basis for interaction with advisors. The document itself, however, is given only general treatment, and no specimens are provided. The two larger supporting sections on preparation (including detailed instructions for developing a unique filing system), and pushing on through the study, the writing, and final defense—to the first publications—is honest, well informed and an easy read.

To have at your disposal both sympathetic advice about being a graduate student faced with the need to write a thesis or dissertation, and utilitarian instruction about completing the pivotal step of writing the proposal is comforting. We believe that adding Sternberg's fine paperbound volume to our own guide will form a well-matched set.

APPENDIX B:
STANDARDS FOR THE USE
OF HUMAN SUBJECTS
AND SPECIMEN FORMS
FOR INFORMED CONSENT

Most colleges and universities have an Institutional Review Board (IRB) responsible for overseeing and approving research involving human subjects. At some larger universities, departments may have human subject review committees that first act on the proposed research and then report to the IRB. Whether the study proposal is associated with a graduate degree or with a grant application, investigators should obtain the guidelines for human subject review at their institution, and do so early in the preparation process.

An almost universal step in conducting research with human subjects is obtaining the informed consent of each participant. Subjects must have the opportunity to be informed about the study (particularly what they will be required to do, and the risks and benefits of their participation), ask any questions they might have, make a decision as to whether they wish to participate, and sign a letter of informed consent. Chapter 2 contains a detailed discussion of informed consent accompanied by a listing of the primary requirements in that process.

Figure B.1 presents a consent form checklist that will be useful when preparing consent letters. It contains all information that might be included on a consent form. All items are not appropriate for every consent form—for example, if subjects are not receiving compensation, it does not need to be included.

The three informed consent letters presented in this appendix are edited examples from successfully completed research projects. An additional example is found in the appendix of Specimen Proposal 2 in Part 2 of this guide. The individual documents reflect the specific demands for informed consent in each research context. The first example is from a laboratory study. The second and third examples are from a field study conducted in a school setting where both teacher and parental consent were required. By changing the details, these letters can be adapted for use in other research settings.

308

ITEMS	YES	NO	COMMENTS
1. Does the title of the study appear at the top?			
2. Is the general purpose of the study stated—what the researcher expects to learn?			
3. If for student research, is how the study relates to the student's program of study specifically stated (project, thesis, dissertation)?			
4. Is a statement included indicating to the subject his or her right to choose to participate?			
5. Is a statement included indicating why and how the subject was selected as a possible participant? Are the population and sample clearly identified?			
6. Is the procedure to be followed in implementing the project explained (time, frequency, nature of information, questions asked)?			
7. Is a statement included that addresses possible discomforts and inconveniences that the participant might expect?			
8. Are any participant risks that are involved in the project described? If pregnancy presents a risk, have specific precautions been taken?			
9. Are benefits, if any, to the subject identified?			
10. If the project requires that any standard treatment is withheld, is this clearly designated? If alternative treatments are available are they described?			
11. Is subject confidentiality explained? Is the use of any tapes and other materials (e.g., audio or video tapes, photos, use of data for other purposes) explained and the disposition of materials clear?			
12. Are compensation and costs included in the project and are they specifically identified for the subject?			
13. Is the location where the subject can contact the investigator to have questions answered indicated? If a student is the investigator is the supervising professor also identified and a phone number given?			
14. Is it specifically stated that he or she can withdraw at any time from the project? Are procedures indicated for orderly withdrawal from a complex study? Are procedures described for terminating a subject's participation?			
15. Does it state that the subject is entitled to a written copy of the consent form?			
16. Does a statement exist expressing that the subject's signature indicates a willingness to participate?			
17. Is a place for the subject's signature, investigator's signature, parent's signature (if required), and dates available?			
18. Is provision for child assent (generally for children 7-18 years old) made?			

Figure B.1. Consent Form Checklist

NOTE: This checklist was adapted (with permission) from: Office of Sponsored Projects, The University of Texas at Austin (1987). *Policies and procedures governing research with human subjects.* Austin: Author.

SAMPLE A: LABORATORY STUDY
letterhead of the institution/agency

The Effects of Age, Modality and Complexity of Response, and Practice on Reaction Time

You are invited to participate in a study in which the response speed of young and older adults is examined. You are being asked to participate in the study because you fall into one of the age classifications and responded to a request to participate. If you choose to participate in the study it will be necessary for you to be tested on three occasions. You will be asked to do the following tasks: (1) react as rapidly as possible to a light stimulus by saying the consonants "ss" and "zz" into a microphone, and (2) react as rapidly as possible to a light stimulus by pressing one or two fingers against microswitches. All trials on each occasion should take less than one hour.

Data compiled from your performance will be kept in strict confidence at all times. Only the investigator and supervising professor will have access to the information. Following the collection of data your individual identity will be removed from all records. In this manner, information regarding your participation will be kept confidential.

Possible risk factors from your participation are no greater than normal daily activity. However, you cannot expect to be compensated for any discomforts or injury as a result of your participation in the experiment described here.

The investigator in this study is L. L. Student and the research is being completed to fulfill the thesis requirement for a master's degree. The supervising professor is Dr. X. Bert Supervisor. If you have any questions that we have not answered in person you may contact either of us at 555-1234.

Your signature below indicates that you have decided to participate in this study and that you have read and understood the information in this consent form. Your decision to participate in this study will not prejudice your present or future association with this university. If you decide to participate, you are free to withdraw consent and discontinue participation at any time without prejudice. If you desire a copy of this consent form, one will be provided for you.

Thank you.

Participant's signature _____ Date _____
Investigator's signature _____ Date _____
Witness' signature _____ Date _____

SAMPLE B: FIELD STUDY

letterhead of the institution/agency

A Comprehensive Investigation of the Correlates of Instructional Effectiveness

I would like to request your cooperation in the conduct of a study of instruction in classes you are teaching this year. You were selected to participate in this study because you teach third grade students in a school in the Innovative School District. We hope to learn more about how teacher and student behaviors are important for learning. This information will contribute to research in education, and may be beneficial to future teachers.

If you should decide to participate, you will be asked to teach a two week unit of instruction for approximately 30 minutes per day wearing a miniature microphone. The class will be videotaped for future coding of teacher and student behaviors. Students will be pretested and posttested. Your students will be asked to maintain their normal seating patterns throughout the course of instruction. Should you decide to participate, one thirty minute orientation session will be required prior to beginning the study. Except for normal preparation time, no other time outside of class will be required. Possible risk factors from your participation are no greater than your normal school activity.

Any information obtained in connection with this study that can be identified with you will remain confidential and will be disclosed only with your permission. Only averages and other descriptive statistics will be reported in any publication. In addition, only three trained coders associated with the university will view the tapes and none will be able to identify you by name. Your decision as to whether or not to participate will not prejudice your relations with the Department of Education or the University. If you decide to participate, you are completely free to withdraw consent and discontinue participation at any time.

If you have any additional questions, please contact me (A. Professor) at 555-1234. Thank you.

You may keep a copy of this form.

I have decided to participate in a study of learning, to wear a miniature microphone while teaching the unit of instruction, and to allow my class to be pretested, posttested, and videotaped. My signature indicates that I have read the information above and have decided to participate. I realize that I may withdraw without prejudice at any time after signing this form should I decide to do so.

Teacher's Signature	Date
Investigator's Signature	Date

SAMPLE C: PARENTAL INFORMED CONSENT

letterhead of the institution/agency

Date

Dear Parent:

I am presently involved in the preparation of future teachers at State University. I am interested in the aspects of schooling that relate to how students learn to read. This information is valuable in preparing teachers and can contribute to our knowledge of how to help students improve their reading skills.

I would like permission for your child to participate in a study that will be conducted as a part of his or her regularly scheduled class. The study is titled "A Comprehensive Investigation of the Correlates of Instructional Effectiveness." Your child was chosen to participate in this study because he or she is in a class in which the teacher has agreed to participate. The only changes from the normal class will be an initial test of student reading ability and that each class, for a two week period, will be videotaped. Possible risk factors from your child's participation are no greater than his or her normal school activity.

Your son or daughter will be identified on the videotape, but at no time will his or her scores on the tests or their videotapes be available to anyone but researchers involved in this study. Students will not be identified by name at anytime in any reports of this research. If you decide to allow your child to participate, you or your child are completely free to withdraw consent and discontinue your child's participation at any time.

As the results of this study are completed, I will provide the principal of your school with a summary, which will be available to you upon request. If you have any questions, please contact me at 555-1234.

Please sign and return this form as soon as possible. Thank you very much.

Sincerely,

A. Professor
Assistant Professor

Please check here if you would like a copy of this form for your records___

I have decided to allow my child to participate in a study of learning that will be conducted in his or her regularly scheduled class. My signature indicates that I have read the information above and have given permission for my child to participate. My child's signature indicates that he or she understands that a study will be conducted in class and agrees to participate. I realize that I may withdraw my child (or my child may withdraw) without prejudice at any time after signing this form should either of us decide to do so.

Child's Name _____
Parent's signature_____ Date _____
Child's signature _____ Date _____

References

Adler, T. (1991, December). Outright fraud rare, but not poor science. *The APA Monitor, 22*(12), 11.

American Psychological Association. (1982). *Ethical principles in the conduct of research with human participants.* Washington, DC: Author.

American Pschologucal Association. (1983). *Publication manual of the American Psychological Association* (3rd. ed.) Washington, DC: Author.

American Psychological Association. (1990). Ethical principles of psychologists. *American Psychologist, 45,* 390-395.

American Educational Research Association. (1992). Ethical standards of the American Educational Research Association. *Educational Researcher, 21*(7), 23-26.

Atkinson, P. (1992). *Understanding ethnographic texts.* Newbury Park, CA: Sage.

Atkinson, P., Delamont, S., & Hammersley, M. (1988). Qualitative research traditions: A British response to Jacob. *Review of Educational Research, 58,* 231-250.

Bauer, D. G. (1988). *The "how to" grants manual* (2nd ed.). New York: Macmillan.

Bogdan, R., & Biklen, S. (1982). *Qualitative study for education: An introduction to theory and methods.* Boston: Allyn & Bacon.

Borg, W. R., & Gall, M. D. (1989). *Educational research: An introduction* (5th ed.). New York: Longman.

Brownowski, J. (1965). *Science and human values.* New York: Harper & Row.

Buchmann, M., & Floden, R. E. (1989). Research traditions, diversity, and progress. *Review of Educational Research, 59,* 241-248.

Burgess, R. G. (Ed.). (1985). *Field methods in the study of education.* London: Falmer.

Burgess, R. G. (1989). *The ethics of educational research.* London: Falmer.

Cantrell, K., & Wallen, D. (Eds.). (1986). *Funding for anthropological research.* Phoenix, AZ: Oryx.

Carr, W., & Kemmis, S. (1986). *Becoming critical: Education, knowledge and action research*. London: Falmer.

Chandler, S. (Ed.). (1992). Qualitative issues in educational research. *Theory Into Practice. 31*, 87-186.

Chilcott, J. H. (1987). Where are you coming from and where are you going? The reporting of ethnographic research. *American Educational Research Journal, 24*, 199-218.

Coley, S. M., & Scheinberg, C. A. (1990). *Proposal writing*. Newbury Park, CA: Sage.

Committee on the Conduct of Science, National Academy of Science. (1989). *On being a scientist*. Washington, DC: National Academy Press.

Delamont, S. (1992). *Fieldwork in educational settings*. London: Falmer.

Directory of grants in the humanities: 1992/1993 (6th ed.). (1992). Phoenix, AZ: Oryx.

Directory of research grants. (Yearly). Phoenix, AZ: Oryx.

Dobbert, M. L. (1982). *Ethnographic research: Theory and application for modern schools*. New York: Praeger.

Douglas, J. D. (1985). *Creative interviewing*. Beverly Hills, CA: Sage.

Eisner, E.W., & Peshkin, A. (Eds.). (1990). *Qualitative inquiry in education: The continuing debate*. New York: Teachers College Press.

Erickson, F. (1986). Qualitative methods in research on teaching. In M. C. Wittrock (Ed.), *Handbook of research on teaching* (3rd ed.) (pp. 119-161). New York: Macmillan.

Fanger, D. (1985, May). The dissertation, from conception to delivery. *On Teaching and Learning: The Journal of the Harvard-Danforth Center, 1*, 26-33.

Fetterman, D. M. (1987a). A rainbow of qualitative approaches and concerns. *Education and Urban Society, 20*, 4-8.

Fetterman, D. M. (Ed.). (1987b). Perennial issues in qualitative research [Special issue]. *Education and Urban Society, 20*, 3-122.

Fetterman, D. M. (1989). *Ethnography step by step*. Newbury Park, CA: Sage.

Fielding, N. G., & Lee, R. M. (Eds.). (1991). *Using computers in qualitative research*. Newbury Park, CA: Sage.

Flinders, D. J. (1992). In search of ethical guidance: Constructing a basis for dialogue. *International Journal of Qualitative Studies in Education, 5*, 101-115.

The foundation directory. (Yearly). New York: The Foundation Center.

The foundation grants index. (Yearly). New York: The Foundation Center.

Foundation News. (Periodically). Washington, DC: Council on Foundations, Inc.

Gage, N. L. (1989). The paradigm wars and their aftermath. *Educational Researcher, 18*(7), 4-10.

Glesne, C. (1989). Rapport and friendship in ethnographic research. *International Journal of Qualitative Studies in Education, 2*, 45-54.

Glesne, C., & Peshkin, A. (1992). *Becoming qualitative researchers: An introduction*. White Plains, NY: Longman.

Grants and fellowships of interest to historians.(1981/82). Washington, DC: American Historical Association.

Grants Magazine. (Quarterly). New York: Plenum Publishing.

The Grantsmanship Center News. (Bimonthly). Los Angeles: The Grantsmanship Center.

References 315

Grove, R. (1988). An analysis of the constant comparative method. *International Journal of Qualitative Studies in Education, 1*, 273-279.

Guba, E. G. (1981). Criteria for assessing the trustworthiness of naturalistic inquiries. *Educational Communication and Technology, 29*, 75-81.

Hammersley, M. (1992). *What's wrong with ethnography?* London: Routledge.

Harding, S. (1987). *Feminism and methodology.* Bloomington: Indiana University Press.

Howe, K. R. (1988). Against the quantitative-qualitative incompatibility thesis: Or dogmas die hard. *Educational Researcher, 17*(8), 10-18.

Howe, K., & Eisenhart, M. (1990). Standards for qualitative (and quantitative) research: A prolegomenon. *Educational Researcher, 19*(4), 2-9.

Jacob, E. (1987). Qualitative research traditions: A review. *Review of Educational Research, 57*, 1-50.

Jacob, E. (1988). Clarifying qualitative research: A focus on traditions. *Educational Researcher, 17*(1), 16-19, 22-24.

Jacob, E. (1989). Qualitative research: A defense of traditions. *Review of Educational Research, 59*, 229-235.

Kelly, D. E., & Shipp, A. (1991). Odds of being funded by NIH. *The Physiologist, 1*, 28-29.

Kimmel, A. J. (1988). *Ethics and values in applied social research.* Newbury Park, CA: Sage.

Kraemer, H. C., & Thiemann, S. (1987). *How many subjects? Statistical power analysis in research.* Newbury Park, CA: Sage.

Kroll, W. (1993). Ethical issues in human research. *Quest, 45*, 32-44.

Krueger, R. (1988). *Focus groups: A practical guide for applied research.* Newbury Park, CA: Sage.

Kuhn, T. S. (1970). *The structure of scientific revolutions* (2nd ed.). Chicago: University of Chicago Press.

Lather, P. (1986). Issues of validity in openly ideological research: Between a rock and a soft place. *Interchange, 17*(4), 63-84.

Lather, P. (1988). Feminist perspectives on empowering research methodologies. *Women's Studies International Forum, 11*, 569-581.

Lauffer, A. (1983). *Grantsmanship.* Beverly Hills, CA: Sage.

LeCompte, M., & Goetz, J. (1982). Problems of reliability and validity in ethnographic research. *Review of Educational Research, 52*, 31-60.

LeCompte, M. D., Millroy, W. L., & Preissle, J. (Eds.). (1992). *The handbook of qualitative research in education.* San Diego: Academic Press.

Lerner, C. A., & Turner, R. (Eds.) (Biennial). *The grants register.* London: Macmillan.

Leskes, A. (Ed.). (1986). *Grants for graduate students 1986-88.* Princeton, NJ: Peterson's Guides.

Lincoln, Y. S. (1989). Qualitative research: A response to Atkinson, Delamont, and Hammersley. *Review of Educational Research, 59*, 237-239.

Lincoln, Y. S., & Guba E. G. (1985). *Naturalistic inquiry.* Beverly Hills, CA: Sage.

Lincoln, Y. S., & Guba, E. G. (1990). Judging the quality of case study reports. *International Journal of Qualitative Studies in Education, 3*, 53-59.

Locke, L. F. (1989). Qualitative research as a form of scientific inquiry in sport and physical education. *Research Quarterly for Exercise and Sport, 60*, 1-20.

316   PROPOSALS THAT WORK

Lofland, J., & Lofland, L. H. (1984). *Analyzing social settings: A guide to qualitative observation and analysis*. Belmont, CA: Wadsworth.

Maguire, P. (1987). *Doing participatory research*. Amherst, MA: Center for International Education, University of Massachusetts.

Marshall, C., & Rossman, G. B. (1989). *Designing qualitative research*. Newbury Park, CA: Sage.

McCracken, G. (1988). *The long interview*. Newbury Park, CA: Sage.

Merriam, S. D. (1988). *Case study research in education*. San Francisco: Jossey-Bass.

Miles, M. D., & Huberman, A. M. (1984). *Qualitative data analysis: A sourcebook of new methods*. Newbury Park, CA: Sage.

Millsaps, D. (1983). *The national directory of grants and aid to individuals in the arts, international*. Washington, DC: Washington International Arts Letter.

Morgan, D. L. (1988). *Focus groups as qualitative research*. Newbury Park, CA: Sage.

NSF Bulletin. (Monthly). Washington, DC: National Science Foundation.

Panel on Scientific Responsibility and the Conduct of Research (1992). Responsible science: Ensuring the integrity of the research process. (Vol. 1). Washington, DC: National Academy Press.

Patton, M. C. (1990). *Qualitative evaluation and research methods* (2nd ed.). Newbury Park, CA: Sage.

Peshkin, A. (1988a). In search of subjectivity—one's own. *Educational Researcher, 17*(7), 17-22.

Peshkin, A. (1988b). Understanding complexity: A gift of qualitative research. *Anthropology and Education Quarterly, 19*, 416-424.

Phelan, P. (1987). Compatibility of qualitative and quantitative methods: Studying child sexual abuse in America. *Education and Urban Society, 20*, 35-41.

Phillips, D. C. (1987). Validity in qualitative research: Why the worry about warrant will not wane. *Education and Urban Society, 20*, 9-24.

Reason, P., & Rowan, J. (Eds.). (1981). *Human inquiry: A sourcebook of new paradigm research*. New York: John Wiley.

Reece, R. D., & Siegel, H. A. (1986). *Studying people: A primer in the ethics of social research*. Macon, GA: Mercer University Press.

Richardson, L. (1990). *Writing strategies*. Newbury Park, CA: Sage.

Rizo, F. M. (1991). The controversy about quantification in social research: An extension of Gage's "Historical Sketch". *Educational Researcher, 20*(9), 9-12.

Roberts, G. C. (1993). Ethics in professional advising and academic counseling of graduate students. *Quest, 45*, 78-87.

Roberts, H. (Ed.). (1981). *Doing feminist research*. London: Routledge.

Rogers, V. R. (1984). Qualitative research: Another way of knowing. In P. L. Hosford (Ed.), *Using what we know about teaching* (pp. 85-108). Alexandria, VA: Association for Supervision and Curriculum Development.

R. R. Bowker's Data Publishing Group. (Yearly). *Annual register of grant support*. New Providence, NJ: R. R. Bowker.

Safrit, M. J. (1993). Oh what a tangled web we weave. *Quest, 45*, 52-61.

Salomon, G. (1991). Transcending the qualitative-quantitative debate: The analytic and systemic approaches to educational research. *Educational Researcher, 20*(6), 10-18.

Schumacher, D. (1992). *Get funded!* Newbury Park, CA: Sage.

Seidman, I. E. (1991). *Interviewing as qualitative research*. New York: Teachers College Press.

Shaffir, W. B., Stebbins, R. A., & Turowetz, A. (Eds.). (1980). *Fieldwork experience: Qualitative approaches to social research*. New York: St. Martin's Press.

Shulman, J. H. (1990). Now you see them, now you don't: Anonymity versus visibility in case studies of teachers. *Educational Researcher, 19*(6), 11-15.

Shulman, L. S. (1981). Disciplines of inquiry in education: An overview. *Educational Researcher, 10*(6), 5-12, 23.

Sieber, J. E. (1982). (Ed.). *The ethics of social research: Fieldwork, regulation, and publication*. New York: Springer-Verlag.

Sieber, J. E. (1992). *Planning ethically responsible research*. Newbury Park, CA: Sage.

Smith, M. L. (1987). Publishing qualitative research. *American Educational Research Journal, 24*, 173-183.

Smith, J. K., & Heshusius, L. (1986). Closing down the conversation: The end of the quantitative-qualitative debate among educational inquirers. *Educational Researcher, 15*(1), 4-12.

Soltis, J. F. (1989). The ethics of qualitative research. *International Journal of Qualitative Studies in Education, 2*, 123-130.

Source book profiles. (Revised quarterly). New York: The Foundation Center.

Spindler, G. (1982). *Doing the ethnography of schooling*. New York: Holt, Rinehart & Winston.

Spradley, J. (1979). *The ethnographic interview*. New York: Holt, Rinehart & Winston.

Spradley, J. (1980). *Participant observation*. New York: Holt, Rinehart & Winston.

Stacey, J. (1988). Can there be a feminist ethnography? *Women's Studies International Forum, 11*, 21-27.

Stanley, L., & Wise, S. (1983). *Breaking out: Feminist consciousness and feminist research*. London: Routledge.

Stewart, D. W., & Shamdasani, P. N. (1990). *Focus groups: Theory and practice*. Newbury Park, CA: Sage.

Strunk, W., Jr., & White, E. B. (1979). *The elements of style* (3rd ed.). New York: Macmillan.

Tesch, R. (1990). *Qualitative research: Analysis types and software tools*. New York: Falmer.

Tesch, R. (Ed.). (1991a). Computers and qualitative data [Special Issue, Part 1]. *Qualitative Sociology, 14*, 225-288.

Tesch, R. (Ed.). (1991b). Computers and qualitative data [Special Issue, Part 2]. *Qualitative Sociology, 14*, 289-385.

Thomas, J. (1992). *Doing critical ethnography*. Newbury Park, CA: Sage.

Thornton, S. J. (1987). Artistic and scientific qualitative approaches: Influence on aims, conduct, and outcome. *Education and Urban Society, 20*, 25-34.

Tuthill, D., & Ashton, P. (1983). Improving educational research through development of educational paradigms. *Educational Researcher, 12*(10), 6-14.

United States Department of Health and Human Services. (Periodically). *NIH guide for grants and contracts*. Washington, DC: Government Printing Office.

United States Department of Health and Human Services. (Semiyearly). *NIH public advisory groups: Authority, structure, functions, members*. Washington, DC: Government Printing Office.

United States Office of Federal Register. (Periodically). *Federal Register*. Washington, DC: Government Printing Office.

United States Office of Management and Budget. (Annually). *Catalog of federal domestic assistance*. Washington, DC: Government Printing Office.

Walker, D. F. (1992). Methodological issues in curriculum research. In P. W. Jackson, (Ed.), *Handbook of research on curriculum* (pp. 98-118). New York: Macmillan.

Weber, S. J. (1986). The nature of interviewing. *Phenomenology and Pedagogy, 4*(2), 65-72.

Werner, O., & Schoepfle, G. M. (1987a). *Systematic fieldwork: Volume 1. Foundations of ethnography and interviewing*. Newbury Park, CA: Sage.

Werner, O., & Schoepfle, G. M. (1987b). *Systematic fieldwork: Volume 2. Ethnographic analysis and data management*. Newbury Park, CA: Sage.

Whyte, W. F. (1990). *Participatory action research*. Newbury Park, CA: Sage.

Williams, L. (Ed.). (1992). *The grants register: 1993-1995*. New York: St. Martin's.

Willoughby, T. L., & Bixby, A. R. (1991). Cross-validation of the Quarterly Profile Examination. *Educational and Psychological Measurement, 51*, 691-697.

Wilson, S. (1977). The use of ethnographic techniques in educational research. *Review of Educational Research, 47*, 245-265.

Wolcott, H. F. (1990). *Writing up qualitative research*. Newbury Park, CA: Sage.

Index

About the Authors

LAWRENCE F. LOCKE is Professor of Education and Physical Education, and Chairperson of the Department of Professional Preparation at the University of Massachusetts at Amherst. A native of Connecticut, he received bachelor's and master's degrees from Springfield College and a Ph.D. from Stanford University. He has written extensively on the production and utilization of research on teaching and teacher education. As a teacher, graduate advisor, and consultant he has supervised the preparation of many research proposals. Much of his present work focuses on the use of the qualitative research paradigm in the study of teachers, teaching, and teacher development.

WANEEN WYRICK SPIRDUSO is Ashbel Smith Professor in the Department of Kinesiology and Health Education and Professor in the College of Pharmacy at The University of Texas at Austin. She is a native of Austin and holds bachelor's and doctoral degrees from The University of Texas and a master's degree from the University of North Carolina at Greensboro. Her research focuses on the effects of aging on the mechanisms of motor control. She has directed students in the proposal process for nearly three decades and has received numerous research grants from the federal government.

STEPHEN J. SILVERMAN is Associate Professor in the Department of Kinesiology and the Department of Curriculum and Instruction at the University of Illinois at Urbana-Champaign. He is a native of Philadelphia and holds a bachelor's degree from Temple University, a master's degree from Washington State University, and a doctoral degree from the University of Massachusetts at Amherst. His research focuses on teaching and learning in physical education. He is an experienced research consultant, has directed graduate research, and has, for many years, taught classes in research methods, statistics, and measurement.